The story of Jeep

Jeep®

Patrick R. Foster

© 1998 by
Patrick R. Foster

Published by

700 E. State Street • Iola, WI 54990-0001
Telephone: 715/445-2214

Please call or write for our free catalog.
Our toll-free number to place an order or obtain a free catalog is 800-258-0929
or please use our regular business telephone 715-445-2214
for editorial comment and further information.

Library of Congress Catalog Number: 97-80609
ISBN: 0-87341-564-7

Printed in the United States of America

DEDICATION

This book is dedicated to Roy D. Chapin Jr., former Chairman of American Motors Corporation, who enabled Jeep to have a new birth of creativity, and made it possible for the company to enjoy some of the best years it ever had. Thanks, Roy, for a job well done!

CONTENTS

FOREWORD

Exactly what is a legend? What qualities, and precisely what quantities of them, make up the mysterious blend from which springs forth a fabled thing? There must be heritage, certainly, as well as a history that is reasonably long and amply heroic.

But at its essence, its core, there must be something which cannot be synthesized nor copied or purchased, and that thing is greatness itself. No matter how humble, obscure or misunderstood are its roots, a true legend is built on inherent excellence, regardless of whether it's directed at achieving a modest task or some noble undertaking.

The Jeep is just such a legend, and its enduring greatness continues.

What I have attempted to do within the pages of this book is to recount as much as any person can the circumstances, the happenstances and incidents that define the history of Jeep, and from which grows its legend. Every American can be proud of the heritage of Jeep, for it is by any measure the most American of all vehicles, a symbol of America itself, and by virtue of its multi-nation distribution system has long served as a goodwill ambassador throughout the world. And every person who today breathes the sweet air of freedom should, now and then, remember to say a silent thank you to the men and women responsible for creating the Jeeps that helped make a free world possible. It is my hope that as you read about Jeep and the many companies that make up its story you'll come away with a deeper understanding of the automotive industry, its challenges and rewards.

I believe you will also recognize the forces of destiny.

A book is usually the end result of the work of many hands, and that certainly is true in this case. I would like to thank the following people who kindly lent their time, talent and knowledge to this project: former Chairman of American Motors, Roy D. Chapin Jr.; former American Motors stylist and product planner, Jim Alexander; Jeep historian, Ron Szymanski; Ron Kowalke and Pat Klug of Krause Publications; John Wimble; John Ziemer; Bill Wilson; the Society of Automotive Historians; Paul Barry of Willys America; the wonderful photographer Denise Barton; Art Ponder; Dave Grondin of Milford Jeep; Richard Lech of *The Chrysler Times* newspaper; my good friend and colleague Kit Foster; Chrysler's terrific VP of Public Relations, Steve Harris and his able associates Dawn Shoskes and Sjoerd Dijkstra; Chrysler's Design Director-Truck and Jeep, Trevor Creed; Chrysler Executive VP, Tom Gale; Leslie Peters of the Brooks Stevens Automobile Collection; Dr. Bob; the good folks at Milford Photo; Bill McCarthy of SVE Performance, Milford, CT; plus a hearty thank you to the legendary Jack Teahen of the *Automotive News* for providing us with Jeep sales figures. Special thanks to Pat McAllen of the Milford Public Library.

I have been very blessed in my life; besides being allowed to do the work I've always wanted to do, I've enjoyed the love and support of a beautiful wife, Diane, and a wonderful daughter, Caitlin, and they mean more to me than words could ever express. For them I give my greatest thanks of all.

This, then, ends our foreword. The pages that follow will recount the story of the Jeep vehicle and the companies it served under. Enjoy it, and if you should come away with a sense of wonderment, do not harbor doubts as to why—for the story of Jeep is an amazing and wonderful tale.

Patrick R. Foster

Milford, Connecticut

May 25, 1998

A NOTE ABOUT NUMBERS

Within the text of this book you will see quoted many sales and/or production numbers. These numbers are expressed several different ways, and it is important to understand the differences between them.

Retail sales

These sales represent vehicles sold to retail customers, and are usually expressed as calendar year sales. These sales usually include more than one model year since new vehicles are introduced in the Fall of any given year—not on January 1, and thus model years overlap. In the case of Jeep, retail sales figures are far less than production, since in early years a large percentage of Jeep production was for military and government fleets—and these would not appear with the retail figures. In virtually all years, Jeep sold many vehicles overseas, and these too, would not appear with the retail sales numbers.

Wholesale sales (or sales to dealers)

These numbers usually appear in company annual reports, and represent total sales by the factory to its dealers, and also usually include military and government deliveries, since those are on a non-retail, or wholesale basis.

In addition, to better understand sales figures it is necessary to pay attention to whether the numbers refer to calendar year, model year, or fiscal year periods—and whether they include U.S., North America, or worldwide sales. In most cases, the differences should be noted in the text.

To date there are no exact figures for Jeep production since 1941. Although various sources offer numbers, the truth is that many old Jeep production records were scrapped years ago, and thus all Jeep production and sales figures should be considered estimates. For sales figures we relied on several published sources, primarily the trade paper *Automotive News*.

Chapter One

JEEPS AROUND THE WORLD

An American in Paris? Photo from the late 1980s when Renault was the distributor for Jeep in France and certain other markets.

They are everywhere—it is a fact, not an illusion. Here in America one can find Jeep vehicles in every town, city, and hamlet. They are found parked in long rows at suburban shopping malls, idling in frantic little clusters outside of day care centers, or pulling into parking lots at the trendy restaurants favored by upscale suburban owners. More traditional owners can be found jumping from rock to rock in the Badlands of the Old West, exploring ghost towns, breaking trails that others seldom (if ever) travel. They all have one thing in common; generally they are having a great time doing it.

Meanwhile, in other parts of the world, other Jeep owners are driving their machines down the grand boulevards of Paris, across the rugged terrain of Malaysia, up the rocky volcanic slopes of Hawaii and on the frenzied streets of downtown Tokyo.

Today's modern Jeeps, descendants of the mighty Jeep MB of World War Two, still travel some of the same paths their military forebears trekked in the Philippines, along the victory routes of wartime Europe and the bitter tracks of Vietnam and Korea.

They are sold just about everywhere, too: over 140 countries as of this writing and the list is likely to continue to grow. Over the years Jeeps have been sold in pretty much every country in the free world, and in several countries in the not-so-free world. In many instances, small assembly or manufacturing plants were put into operation in these far-off places, producing small quantities of Jeeps for local markets. Some of these operations lasted

秋から冬の休日を、おおらかに愉しむ。特別な魅力を装備した、アスペン登場！

Jeep Grand Cherokee Laredo
ASPEN

A special Grand Cherokee, produced for the Japanese market, featured right-hand-drive and special "Aspen" trim.

MORE スポーティ＆アクティブ── 魅力の装備がうれしい、スペシャルバージョン登場！

Jeep Cherokee Sport
Special Version

Another Jeep for Japan, this one a right-hand drive Cherokee Sport "Special Version."

As reported in the *Chrysler Times* newspaper, President Clinton visits a Tokyo Jeep showroom.

only a few years, some a few decades, and others endure even to the present.

Many of today's Jeeps are manufactured right where they have always been built—the massive Jeep plant in Toledo, Ohio. That's where Wranglers and Cherokees come from. Grand Cherokees are built in the Jefferson North plant in Detroit—one of the most modern auto making facilities in the world. A brand new plant is now under construction in Toledo that will modernize Jeep assembly operations there while adding additional needed production.

But these facilities alone cannot build enough product to satisfy the whole world, so additional plants are located in Europe (assembling Grand Cherokees in Graz, Austria), Thailand (Cherokees), Indonesia (Cherokees and Wranglers) Malaysia (Cherokees), Egypt (Cherokees), China (Cherokees), Venezuela (Cherokees and Grand Cherokees), as well as a plant in Argentina that builds Grand Cherokees for Argentina, Brazil, Paraguay and Uruguay, and which is adding Cherokees to its product line-up.

To make them completely at home anywhere in the world, Jeeps are offered with right-hand-drive in Japan, Thailand, the United Kingdom, Australia and South Africa and other right-hand-drive markets. Even diesel-powered versions are available in non-U.S. markets.

There is a story behind this worldwide trend to Jeeps. Throughout its long history, from its early roller coaster corporate existence, through good times and bad, the company has always had an eye to export sales. It began, really, before the Army had even settled on exactly what the Jeep was going to be, in the days just prior to World War II. It continued after the war, when Willys-Overland, the first producer of the civilian Jeep, settled on a post-war business plan that included a strong reliance on overseas sales. Kaiser Industries, which owned Jeep for many years after buying it from Willys, continued this trend with its own philosophy of emphasis on sales in Latin America and the Pacific Rim. American Motors, caretaker of the Jeep name and heritage for 18 years, strengthened its overseas business and expanded Jeep production into Cana-

The new Jeep CJ-Diesel.

Et harumd dereud facilis est er expedit. Distnct nam liber tempor cum soluta nobis eligend. Opro congue nihil impedit, doming id quod maxim placeat facer. Possim omnis voluptas assumenda est, omnis dolor repellend. Temporibud autum quinusd et aur office debit aut tum rerum necessit atib saepe event etut er repudiand seint et molestia. Non recusand itaque earud hic tenetury sapiente delectus au aut prefer endis. Dolorib asperior repellat hanc ego cum tene sententiam.

Quid est cur verear ne ad eam non possing accommodare: nost ros quos u paulo aen cum memorite tum etia ergat. Nos amice et nebevol, olestias access potest fier ap augenndas cum conscient to factor tum. Nos amice et nebevol, olestias access potest fier ap augendas cum conscient to factor tum peon legum odioque civiuda. Et tamen in busdam, neque pecum modut est neque nonor imper ned libiding gen epular religuard cupiditat, quas nulla praid om undant. Impro minuit, potius inflammad ut co and et dodecendesse vid igitur vera ratio bene sano itated ifdem.

Et harumd dereud Distnct nam liber tempor eligend. Opro congue ni id quod maxim placeat fac voluptas assumenda est, lend. Temporibud au

enndas cum conscient to factor tum. Nos amice et nebevol, olestias access potest fier ap augendas cum conscient to factor tum peon legum odioque civiuda.

Et tamen in busdam, neque pecum modut est neque nonor imper ned libiding gen epular religuard cupiditat, quas nulla praid om undant. Improb pary minuit, potius inflammad ut coercend magist and et dodecendes videantur. Invitate igitur vera ratio bene sanos ad iustitiam, aequitated ifdem.

Quid est cur verear ne ad eam non possing accommodare: nost ros quos u paulo aen cum memorite tum etia ergat. Nos amice et nebevol, olestias access potest fier ap augenndas cum conscient to factor tum. Nos amice et nebevol, olestias access potest fier ap augendas cum conscient to factor tum peon legum odioque civiuda.

Jeep

Diesel Jeep for export market, as shown in a 1977 Jeep press photo.

Jeep pickup was a popular offering from Willys-Brazil in the 1960s, and was based on the U.S. Willys Jeep design but had a unique body.

This Jeep, pictured at a European auto show circa 1968, shows French-market Hotchkiss Jeep. Note nameplate above the grille bars.

Unique look at the Hotchkiss Jeep assembly plant shows unfinished bodies, boxes of parts and 24 completed units.

Also built in the 1960s was this "Rural Willys" built by Willys-Overland Brazil.

RURAL Jeep ®

— A CAMIONETA BRASILEIRA
COM TRAÇÃO NAS 4 RODAS (OU 2)

CONSAGRADA COMO IDEAL PARA TRABALHO E PASSEIO — NOVA CONCEPÇÃO
DE EFICIÊNCIA E BOM GÔSTO, NO VEÍCULO MAIS COMPLETO QUE EXISTE

Willys-Overland Brazil's "Rural" also came in a two-door model.

ÚNICO EM SUA CLASSE DE PREÇO COM 4 PORTAS E CAPACIDADE PARA 6 PESSOAS

TRAÇÃO EM 2
OU NAS 4 RODAS

UTILITÁRIO **Jeep** modêlo **101**
UNIVERSAL

4 PORTAS

UM VEÍCULO VERSÁTIL, FORTE, EFICIENTE

Nova versão do utilitário "Jeep" Universal. Tem a distância entre eixos aumentada para 101 polegadas, banco dianteiro inteiriço e regulável e maior capacidade de carga. É de grande mobilidade e oferece estabilidade incomparável em qualquer tipo de estrada. A tração nas 4 rodas e a fôrça extra da reduzida garantem excepcional desempenho até mesmo em atoleiros e barro.

Famoso motor Willys de 6 cilindros e 90 H. P. Confere ao utilitário "Jeep" Universal modêlo 101 — 4 portas extraordinária reserva de potência, máximo rendimento com o mínimo consumo de combustível. Sua manutenção é facílima e econômica.

WILLYS-OVERLAND DO BRASIL S.A. WILLYS
SÃO BERNARDO DO CAMPO — ESTADO DE SÃO PAULO

Willys-Overland Brazil's Jeep '101' was unique to the Brazilian market—note the illustrations of other Willys Brazil models at the bottom of the brochure.

NUEVO FURGON

"UTILITARIO"

Willys

DIMENSIONES
DE LA CAJA:

Altura .... *1.245 mm.*
Largo .... *1.740 "*
Ancho .... *1.480 "*

con tracción en 2 y 4 ruedas!

INDUSTRIAS KAISER ARGENTINA

IKA — INDUSTRIAS KAISER ARGENTINA

The 1960 "Utilitario" Willys was produced by Industrias Kaiser Argentina (IKA).

da, China, and Egypt, among other locales. Chrysler Corporation, now Jeep's parent company, has made Jeep a big player in Japan and Europe, strengthened its position in Latin America and is expanding further in Asia. Jeep is truly a world car.

As one can see by the photographs shown in this chapter, Jeep has been a successful product in many countries, under many names, in many styles and under various owners. The French-made Hotchkiss Jeep, built under license from Willys beginning after World War II, had many unique body panels, yet is unmistakably a Jeep vehicle. Or look at the "Utilitario Willys" wagon produced years ago by a company known as Industrias Kaiser Argentina (IKA), a joint venture partly owned by the Kaiser company. Another Latin American firm, Willys-Overland Do Brazil S.A. produced many Jeep models including the "Rural Jeep" family sta-

tion wagon, the uniquely styled "Pick-up Jeep," and the popular "Utilitario Jeep Universal." The Brazilian Jeep works grew so large that at one point their production level nearly rivaled the main Jeep plant in America! Willys Motors Australia, now defunct, built many Jeep models, including panel trucks, station wagons and pickups. During the same time in Japan, Mitsubishi Motors began manufacturing a version of the old CJ-3B under license from the 1950s and continued right up to modern times, even as Chrysler was offering unique right-hand-drive Jeep Cherokee Aspens in that country.

Travel to Egypt, and the Jeeps you will see there appear quite familiar, although they are built locally in a plant at Heliopolis. Go to the Philippines and you'll likely wonder at the greatly lengthened "Jeepney" taxis, made even more striking because they carry an astonishing amount of

3 MODELOS À SUA ESCOLHA... UM PARA CADA TIPO DE TRABALHO

Willys-Overland Brazil had an extensive model range in the 1960s—note the three models here, including a four-door CJ-type.

Unique Jeep van was available in Spain during the 1960s.

From the 1968 Annual Report: top picture shows an Asia-market Jeep while bottom photo shows headquarters for Willys-Motors Australia.

glittery ornamentation added by their owners. In Mexico, many Jeep CJs produced in the 1980s by a company known as VAM (Vehiculos Automores Mexicanos) proudly wear stripes that proclaim them to be "Renegados."

If by chance you find yourself on the high plateaus of Venezuela, you may spot something that looks like a Jeep, but has a handsome mini-wagon body and carries the name Llanero on its hood—rest assured, it's still a genuine Jeep. In downtown Beijing or by the Great Wall of China you're likely to see a lot of what look to be Jeep Cherokees with nameplates written in Chinese characters. You're looking at a fellow American, although one that has adapted more readily to the locale than you have. In other parts of Asia you might spot some heavy duty pickup trucks with the nameplate Jeep CJ-10, and you'll walk away wondering why we don't have those neat vehicles here in the States.

In 1980, Vehiculos Automotores Mexicanos (VAM) produced AMC passenger cars and Jeep vehicles, including this Jeep "Renegado" for the Mexican market.

Jeep CJ-10 pickup was developed by American Motors for world markets.

The truth is that most Jeeps sold throughout the world are, with some exceptions, nearly identical to the U.S. product. There's a good reason for that. Stated simply, the Jeep is superior to other utility vehicles. It is so technologically advanced that it is salable anywhere in the world. And, as any Jeep salesman will tell you, there are only two types of people in the world—those who own a Jeep and those who *wish* they owned a Jeep!

Yet originally, the Jeep was developed only for war, to be a tool for the soldier, a sturdy machine to scout the advance, haul the weapons, and carry orders and messages. And despite its starkly basic appearance and all its rugged strength and utility,

A Successful Venture. The Launch of Cherokee in China.

In 1985, overseas vehicle sales were at their highest levels in four years. They were fueled by improvements in our Latin American markets, especially Venezuela, and the success of the Jeep Cherokee in Europe and China.

The Company has major joint ventures in Venezuela, Egypt and China and, together with Renault, produces Jeep vehicles in Mexico. As an integral part of the corporation's strategic plan, American Motors is developing a unique distribution system in conjunction with Renault in Europe.

In the fall of 1985, Jeep Cherokee was launched in China. This marks the first time that a state-of-the-art vehicle has been produced in that country and the first time the Jeep Cherokee has been assembled outside the United States.

Jeep Cherokee is fast becoming an "in" vehicle in Europe. As it has done in the United States and Canada, Cherokee has begun to earn awards. It was named *"4x4 of the Year for 1985"* by the French magazine *4x4*.

Beijing Jeep builds Cherokees for the China market. This photo originally appeared in the 1985 American Motors annual report.

Mitsubishi Jeeps came in several models, some with bodies unique to Japan.

Mitsubishi was still building a version of the old CJ-3B for Japanese market in the 1990s.

Jeep Wrangler can't be mistaken for any other vehicle.

when the Jeep was first developed it was considered one of the most audacious and technologically advanced machines of all time, a true state-of-the-art design. The army, bless 'em, tried to design the thing by dictate, and because of its rigid requirements it almost killed the whole project. However, the Jeep endured the army's unusual procurement procedure, survived its initial testing and was eventually approved for production.

Perhaps it was destiny. Or perhaps providence decided to lend a hand, to make certain the armies of democracy would have the Jeep to aid their struggle. After all, it certainly was needed. The fate of the free world hung in the balance.

Chapter Two

THE BIRTH OF A LEGEND

1940-1945

Unique photo shows four military Jeeps: (left to right) the Willys Quad prototype, Jeep MB, Jeep M38 and Jeep M38A1.

To say that any one individual should wear the mantle of Jeep creator wouldn't be exactly correct. A great man named Karl Probst is generally, and correctly, recognized as the person who designed the original Jeep. Yet as great as his contribution was, even he can't be said to have been its sole architect. There were several companies and individuals that contributed, in greater or lesser degrees, to the job of bringing forth the Jeep. However, the legacy of the Jeep began in Washington, D.C.

War was raging in Europe and thus far it had all gone badly for Britain and France. America was not yet in the fray, but the nation's leaders could see where things were heading. The Nazi war machine had trampled over country after country. Great Britain was barely holding on by her fingernails. The English needed huge numbers of warplanes to hold back the German Luftwaffe. In desperation Britain turned to America for help, and America turned to its auto industry. The president of General Motors, William Knudsen, was asked to head an effort to produce more planes than had ever been built before. A Danish immigrant who had ris-

en to the head of America's biggest company, Knudsen was respected as a production genius and leader of men. Big Bill Knudsen soon had the nation's car builders busy producing aircraft parts and subassemblies. He was soon asked to oversee other military procurements.

Washington's military planners, eyeing the German's highly-mechanized Blitzkrieg tactics, realized that the conflict would be a war of machines. It was plain that the army mule of World War One was obsolete. Yet there was nothing available that could replace it for carrying light loads. The slow, heavy military trucks then available were fine for cargo and troop hauling, but little else. What was needed was a lightweight, high-speed machine that could carry men and weapons, especially heavy machine guns, both on and off-road. They directed that a new military vehicle be designed, one that could carry weapons and ammunition, travel difficult terrain like the mule, and additionally serve as a scout car.

The armed forces had earlier tried to develop an off-road military car, but had enjoyed scant success. Several lightweight, so-called "cross-country vehicles" were tested at the military's Aberdeen Proving Grounds in Maryland in 1921. In addition, a motorized road cart which could also float on water (though, lacking a prop, it couldn't actually power its way *through* the water) was tested in 1923. The cart could carry a decent load, but the design required the operator to walk behind it, lawnmower style, thus limiting its usefulness.

Many of the early designs emphasized lightweight, including several adaptations of the Ford Model T chassis, and some utilized caterpillar tracks for the necessary traction off-road. Motorcycles were also tested, but to quote an officer who recalled the experiment the "motorcycles were tried out and had to be hauled back in a truck when they got stuck in the sand or mud." Too, the motorcycles were unable to carry a heavy machine gun up to the line of battle, a task considered essential for the coming new era of warfare.

One hopeful effort was a Ford Model T stripped down to its bare essentials, weighing only about 1200 lbs. With oversized tires installed, its off-road performance was superior to the belt-track types tested up to that time. However, the machine quickly grew in weight as various military officials suggested additional features and equipment. As one man involved later recalled, the military men, "...kept putting on standard equipment until they got it back up to a standard commercial touring car with cushion seats. This ruined the whole idea." Back to the drawing board.

A vehicle that had certainly proved its worth in World War One, was the Jeffrey/Nash Quad four-wheel-drive truck. A heavy-duty carrier, it had slogged through the mud of France better than any other vehicle. Although it showed the value of four-wheel-drive, the Quad was both heavy and slow. What the military had in mind for the coming conflict was something much quicker and more agile, a lightweight military scout car/weapons carrier. Some promise was seen in a much later group of military vehicles, Ford pickups converted to four-wheel-drive by the Marmon-Herrington Company. These too had also helped to demonstrate the value of four-wheel-drive. There was yet another device, a hand-built light machine, dubbed the "Belly Flopper," which had been cobbled together by two army men, Captain Robert Howie and Sergeant Melvin Wiley. It was a low-slung platform chassis whose rear-mounted engine drove the front wheels,

with a machine gun mounted at the front. It got its name from the manner in which it was operated, with both the driver and the gunner riding lying down on their bellies offering only a very low silhouette to stymie enemy gunners. Interestingly, the engine used was a four-cylinder Austin. The Belly Flopper showed the value of a lightweight fighting machine, but testing also proved it was not the best way to go. For one thing, it had poor ground clearance and for another, it wasn't sturdy enough for rugged, long-distance use. Because of its springless chassis and lack of seats, it had to be carried to battle sites on a flatbed truck. Its small size restricted its load capacity as well.

But whether the army knew it or not, by 1940 it had on hand or had tested almost all the essentials it needed for an ideal military scout car: a lightweight chassis, four-cylinder power, and four-wheel-drive. All it needed to do was draw all these elements together into one vehicle. To design such a thing would take the hand of a very skilled engineer. But the army came up with an idea. It would write out a list of specifications for an ideal vehicle and then put it out to bid, even though the vehicle on paper had yet to be seen on the road. A committee of Army officers from the Infantry, Cavalry, Ordnance and Quartermaster was established to develop the specifications for a new type of military vehicle. They road-tested some designs, including several specially modified American Bantam cars produced in Butler, Pennsylvania. These last were tested both on and off-road by a small contingent of Army personnel just weeks before the contract was to be solicited. The Bantams seemed to show great promise. Army engineers, under the committee's direction, at last drew up the specifications of what they had in mind. First and foremost, the new car had to have four-wheel-drive; this was essential for off-road duty. Next, wheelbase, weight, width and height were settled on, and finally, minimum performance, carrying capacity, horsepower, grade-climbing capability and ground clearance. The details were quite specific.

On June 27, 1940, the final recommendations for the new vehicle were approved at a meeting of the Ordnance Technical Committee in Washington. Bidding invitations on the contract for building the new machine were sent out to 135 manufacturers, a number that represented, according to published sources, "...the largest number of manufacturers ever contacted on any one single motor vehicle." One can imagine the great excitement with which the military awaited the return of the bids.

As it ended up, there was scant reason for anyone to get excited. Only two companies bothered to submit proposals. The rest didn't even fake an attempt. There were many reasons why the job was found unappealing by the companies. Probably many, or even most, were not motor vehicle builders, and therefore, the contract called for expertise they didn't possess. Some were already busy with war work and didn't want to take on any additional projects. But most likely the primary reason for the lukewarm response was that the contract the army offered was just too unattractive. It required a company to design an all-new scout car weighing just 1300 lbs., yet also capable of carrying a 600-lb. payload. A company would be allowed only a very short time in which to design the vehicle and deliver the blueprints, plans and their lowest bid. After that, the winning bidder would have just 49 days to deliver a complete running vehicle for testing, after which, they would be allowed a mere 26 additional days to build and deliver 70 pilot models. These models would additionally need to incorporate any design changes indicated by the army's initial testing.

That was reason enough for the tepid response to the bid request. Simply put, what the army wanted was impossible to many minds. First of all, no one could build a four-wheel-drive vehicle of only 1300 lbs. out of existing components, which would also be sturdy enough for combat use. Possibly with enough time and research, all-new components could have been designed. However, the time allotted meant that only existing engines, transmissions and axles could be used. The additional requirement of being able to haul a 600-lb. payload, or nearly half its own weight, was likewise a completely unrealistic expectation. Lastly, few believed it could be done in the limited time available. After all, there were few engineers with experience in designing four-wheel-drive machines—it was still a fairly unusual technology. A lightweight scout car that incorporated so many disparate requirements had yet to be developed. There simply was no template to use, no vehicle in the world that met the specifications. Only a truly desperate company, one's whose corporate existence depended on securing a military contract in order to avoid bankruptcy, would even attempt such a thing. Luckily for the army, there was just such a company out in Butler, Pennsylvania.

American Bantam was on the ropes, and had been for some time. Formed in 1937 to build an improved version of the old American Austin minicar, the company had enjoyed a short, somewhat successful run with its minuscule Bantam auto. Yet Americans had little enthusiasm for tiny cars in those days and American Bantam soon found itself in financial trouble. By 1940, production was shut down, and the company was barely in business selling spare parts to its dealers. The firm was clearly heading towards bankruptcy; it was only a matter of time. Then came the news that the military would be offering companies a chance to bid on a military vehicle contract.

It seemed like the answer to a prayer to the folks at Bantam. The military wanted a lightweight car, and all of Bantams experience was in the light car field. It had to have a four-cylinder engine, and Bantam was one of the few U.S. automakers still building fours. Besides, the military had already tested some Bantam experimental 'reconnaissance cars' in May of that year and expressed quite an interest in them.

In fact, the military men had used their favorable impressions of the Bantam reconnaissance cars when they drew up the preliminary plans and specifications of what they wanted. They had even left the preliminary specifications with the Bantam people for perusal, after first inspecting Bantam's plant to determine if the company had sufficient capacity to produce vehicles in the quantities expected. Bantam's president, Frank

The first Jeep, the Bantam prototype, pictured the moment it was first rolled out of the plant. Legendary engineer Karl Probst, in shirtsleeves, is leaning against the spare tire at the rear of the vehicle.

Fenn, was understandably hopeful, believing that the contract would call for a car much like the experimental Bantam's that had so impressed the military. Such a contract would be easy for his firm to win. It seemed like a sure thing.

Speed was of the essence. War production boss Bill Knudsen let it be known that he wanted the scout car as soon as possible. Bantam, lacking engineers with the specialized expertise, felt that Karl Probst, an experienced engineer who had his own firm in Detroit, was the right man to hire for the job. But the company could offer Probst only a contingency fee arrangement. In other words, the engineer would be paid only if Bantam won the contract. If no contract was won, Probst would go home with nothing. As Probst later recalled, "Nineteen Forty was a time to work and pay your bills, not consider jobs with no guaranteed salary. But July 1940 was also a time you could hear the nervous joke: "Hitler has ordered 10,000 tanks from GM." Hitler said, "Never mind shipping them–we'll pick them up on our way through Detroit." Probst agreed to think it over.

Bantam's Frank Fenn called Probst on Monday July 15, 1940, saying he expected to receive the army's final specifications within a few days. Fenn was still confident the contract would call for a vehicle much like his experimental Bantams (although, of course, incorporating four wheel drive). For his part, Probst was still uncommitted. However, the very next day he received a phone call from Art Brandt, a member of Knudsen's National Defense Advisory Committee. Brandt relayed a message to Probst that Bill Knudsen was asking him to forget about salary, forget about his own concerns.

Brandt told Probst, "We think you can do this job faster than the big companies. Financing will be available if you produce a vehicle to specs." Probst knew what was being asked of him; he could put a great deal of work into the project and still not get paid. But he was a man of deep, old-fashioned patriotism. That very day, he later recalled, he had read of Winston Churchill's determined declaration to the people of Great Britain, "We shall fight on the beaches, we shall fight in the fields and in the streets. We will never surrender." Probst's reply to Art Brandt's request was simple, "Well," he said, "if you put it like that, I can't refuse Mr. Knudsen."

Wednesday, July 17, brought the bid specs and the first major problem. The army had changed several of the key preliminary specifications, ones that were particularly crucial to Bantam. Whereas Bantam's expectation had been that the new scout car would be a fairly easy adaptation of the Bantam chassis and running gear, the bid specs killed that idea. An excited and extremely upset Frank Fenn called Probst, shouting into the phone, "We have the formal bids. Somebody made just one "little" change. They raised the minimum horsepower from the Bantam's twenty to forty! Karl, you know what this means. Our transmission won't take it, our axles won't take it, frame, suspension–we'll have to jack up the horn button so you can design a new car under it!"

The army specifications also included the requirement for a 1300-lb. maximum weight and a delivery time of 49 days for the prototype. Fenn was frantic but Probst calmed him down. Probst told Fenn, "...we can produce drawings faster than our competitors. Of course, we can't make that weight but neither can anyone else."

Probst left Detroit that day, driving his 1938 Buick Special coupe. He stopped at the Spicer company in Toledo to discuss axles with one of their representatives. It was obvious the Bantam axle would be too weak to hold up under the strain of the specified horsepower, but Spicer had another axle, one which was used on the Studebaker Champion, that should work fine. The Studebaker's engine was 65-hp, so the axle should provide plenty of reserve strength in the 40-hp scout car. Probst then headed his Buick east towards Butler, Pennsylvania, mentally putting pieces together as he drove. He reached town around midnight.

Reporting in at Bantam on the morning of Thursday, July 18, Probst looked over the bid specs. They called for a one-quarter ton 4x4 and included a general outline shape, with maximum length and width dimensions. In fact, as Probst later wrote, the outline, "...even looked something like the car that I subsequently designed–but outlines are not design." Probst sat down before a drafting table about 1 PM to work on what he couldn't know would end up being one of the most important contributions ever to the cause of freedom. He probably could guess from the project's urgency just how important the military felt the vehicle was for the coming conflict. He was stouthearted and ready for the task of coming up with a competitive design proposal, including layouts and prices, all of which the army wanted by the morning of Monday July 22.

The army wasn't the only entity desperate for the scout car. Winning the contract would mean the difference between life and death for Bantam. The plant was shut down and all workers laid off, save for a skeleton crew of managers. Bantam was broke and had absolutely no prospects for recovery outside of this one vital military contract. Probst had a great responsibility resting on his shoulders—the hopes and dreams of out-of-work Bantam employees.

He worked on the design that first day straight through to 11 PM, then returned to work at seven the following morning. He worked all that Friday, finally finishing up in the evening. It had taken him a total of only 18 hours to lay out the complete design. Tired but exhilarated, Probst knocked off work and went to town to catch a movie starring Hedy Lamar. Saturday was spent on preparing cost and weight estimates. Probst concluded the thing would weigh about 1850-lb. On Sunday, he and a

handful of Bantam people filled out the formal bid forms and prepared the blueprints, then drove to Baltimore for a late night meeting with Bantam's Washington representative, a retired Navy Commander named Charles Payne. It was Payne's job to submit the bids to the proper authorities at Camp Holabird. Payne reviewed the bids, abruptly stopping at Probst's weight estimate. The problem was that Bantam's bid would be automatically rejected for not meeting the military's weight specification. Payne realized the weight target was unachievable but told Probst, "...you've got to bid it at 1300 lbs. We'll get it revised after we get the contract."

Unfortunately, the bid forms were already filled in and they had no extra copies—but Payne was undaunted. Even though it was midnight by now, he contacted a friend at the army base and had him send over some blank forms. He then told the hotel manager to get a stenographer over on the double (she arrived about 3:30 AM), and by daybreak the revised bids were typed up and ready. The new weight figure was 1273 lbs. By 8:30 that morning (July 22nd),

A later Bantam Jeep is shown here. Note its square front fenders. This is likely one of the early production models, since final Bantams built have a squarer hood.

Early Bantam Jeeps being tested in convoy.

Payne, Probst and Fenn arrived at Camp Holabird. Although representatives from Ford, Crosley and Willys were present, only Willys had a competing bid, and it paled in comparison with the Bantam presentation. Willys gave only a time and cost bid—no plans, weights or prints. Thirty minutes after the bids were received, the army called in the representatives to give their verdict. Probst was sweating. He originally believed it was caused by the tense situation, but later heard that the temperature that day was 101 degrees.

The officer in charge of purchasing and contracts, Major Lawes, stunned the Bantam people when he announced that Willys had submitted the low bid. Probst's heart fell. But Lawes went on to explain that Willys couldn't meet the requirement of having a complete running prototype (which he referred to as a 'pilot car') in 49 days. (According to Wade Wells' book *Hail to the Jeep*, Willys had offered to deliver their car in 75 days; the army assessed a $5 per day penalty for each day past 49 days and that made the Bantam quote lower. That's possible, of course, but one tends to think that in awarding the contract, the army, in this case, placed speed above cost).

Bantam thus won the contract. Probst, Payne, Fenn et-al were delighted of course, but what they had won was simply another challenge. The contract they had struggled for called for the delivery of a fully-operational pilot model of the all-new design in just 49 days. The army would levy a penalty for failure to meet the deadline. There was a bit of good news, though. It would take somewhere between 10 to 18 days for the army to process the contract and the 49 days wouldn't officially begin until it was typed and ready for signatures. As a result, Bantam got some extra time in which to get started, and as far as the penalty for late delivery, Probst later recalled saying to Fenn. "...what difference can that make to a company that is, in effect, bankrupt?"

So the battered Bantam company was saved at the eleventh-hour by the new contract. Probst and Bantam went to work on building the new design. In this regard, Bantam had some advantage. Probst had designed the vehicle with standard automotive components in mind, had already spoken with several of the suppliers, and had of course a complete design package to work from. Against those advantages was the unbelievably tight 49-day deadline. The men went to work. The contract came days later, and was dated August 5.

The time constraint forced the men to work round the clock. Luckily, the basic design was so

Ford GP front end design was judged most useful, and became the standard 'look.'

good that Bantam didn't have to make any major alterations to Probst plans. The Bantam's Austin-derived four-cylinder, a small engine of just 20-hp, couldn't be used since it couldn't produce the requisite 40-hp. Probst settled on a Continental four, a sturdy if unremarkable engine. A serious problem popped up: Spicer encountered trouble adapting the Studebaker axles to four-wheel-drive. Probst kept the National Defense Advisory Commission advised of Bantam's progress, but later recalled that three weeks before the September 23 deadline, he felt they would not be ready in time. Incredibly though, the difficulties were overcome. So tight was the timing, however, that Probst notified his major suppliers that they would each be able to spend only one hour test-driving the prototype prior to its delivery to the army, and the test day had to be Sunday, September 22, 1940—one day before the deadline.

That day soon arrived, and the little machine stood ready for inspection by the engineers from the various suppliers. It was a machine unlike anything that had ever been seen before. Small, low slung, with a rounded hood, round, almost cycle-style front fenders, a scooped out door opening, a tall windshield and a square, flat-sided body of stark simplicity. It was a unique, purposeful looking design. Someone filled the gas tank and Karl Probst stepped in and took it for a spin. Running up to a 45% grade he engaged the four-wheel-drive and powered up the steep incline with muscle to spare. He told his passenger, "Whatever it is, it's a performer." Adjustments were made and by night time everything was ready for the crucial day.

Monday, September 23, 1940, was a big day for Bantam, Probst and America. The experimental vehicle was to be delivered to Camp Holabird, Maryland. People of today might have a hard time believing this, but the Bantam prototype, the one and only one in existence, the object of so much toil and sweat, was *driven* to its delivery point. No delivery van or heavily guarded haul-away was used. Probst and Bantam's factory manager, Harold Crist, simply climbed into the little machine, started it up, and headed off for the Maryland line. Because it was brand new, Probst initially kept the speed down, so the engine could be properly broken in. However, as the day wore on and the little

Willys Quad was heavier than Ford or Bantam prototypes, but much more powerful.

Bantam wound its way through Pennsylvania, Probst and Crist grew increasingly concerned with making certain they would reach Maryland before the 5 PM deadline specified. Probst gradually upped his speed until finally he and Crist were pushing the little vehicle to the limit. Good thing he did it too, because the two men rolled into Camp Holabird at 4:30 PM! The seven-week deadline was beaten by just 30 minutes. As Probst remembered later, newspaper headlines read "Japanese Invade Indo-China."

Engineering philosophy of that era placed a high degree of respect on proving-ground testing, the more rugged, the better. The Bantam experimental was not going to be tested in an indoor laboratory by white suited inspectors. Rather, as soon as it had been given a quick once-over by curious soldiers, Major Lawes himself took the wheel and sped out to the proving grounds. As Probst recalled, Lawes gave the little machine a short rough run through the punishing off-road course. Upon his return Major Lawes rendered his judgment to Probst and the assembled onlookers. "I have driven every unit the services have purchased for the last twenty years," pronounced Lawes, *"I can judge them in fifteen minutes. This vehicle is going to be absolutely outstanding. I believe this unit will make history."*

The army, however, had another question it had to have answered satisfactorily before it would okay production of the 70 pilot models. One general, rubbing his chin, asked, "What does it weigh?" Probst was on the spot. He knew that the vehicle was way over the contract specification of 1300 lbs. The army's decision hung on how Probst would answer the question. He could tell them either what they wanted to hear or the truth. Probst decided to take the high road. "Less oil, fuel and water," he answered, "This vehicle weighs 1840 lbs. We'll probably have to add thirty to fifty lbs. to strengthen weaknesses that will

Willys leaves the ground during severe testing.

show up in your tests." There was a moment of silence while those words sunk in. The vehicles weight was clearly way over the specifications and furthermore, here was the chief engineer of Bantam telling them the weight would likely *increase*, not decrease, on production models. Just then, a cavalry general stepped in to offer a creative interpretation of the rules, "If two men can take it out of a ditch," he said, "we need it." The officer was a big man, six-foot-three-inches tall, 250 lbs. and he immediately strode over to the Bantam. Grunting with exertion, he single-handedly lifted the back end of the vehicle off the ground. Looking at the others, he nodded his approval. With that single, noble act he clinched the deal for Bantam.

The little machine would go on to make history, just as Major Lawes had predicted. But history was still in the making, and it would turn out much different than the Bantam people believed at that moment. In the crowd of onlookers were representatives from Ford, Chrysler, and General Motors

Willys Engineering boss Barney Roos with the Willys Quad.

Willys Quad evolved into the Willys MA. Note squarer hood and fenders and Willys name stamped on hood front.

This Bantam production model has flat hood and square fenders.

Jeep was known as a powerful machine, able to power its way through practically anything.

plus worst of all for Bantam's hopes and dreams, the Washington representative for Willys-Overland. The Big Three automakers were there because they had other, larger military vehicles undergoing tests. But the Willys' rep was there solely to investigate the competition for the scout car. He phoned the Willy's plant in Toledo, Ohio, and told the engineering department to speed up work on their unit.

While Willys worked on perfecting their vehicle, the little Bantam would be undergoing additional testing even as the company struggled to build the 70 pilot models. Changes were incorporated as testing showed up flaws. Of these there were many, such as broken frame rails, shifting problems, tail lights that fell off, worn gears and broken shock absorbers—but then, the army test track was known as an extremely tough course, and

the military men were under orders to try their hardest to break things. Despite the problems, however, the soldiers pronounced themselves very pleased with the Bantam's performance.

The 70 Bantam pilot cars were built within the time allotted, and even included eight models equipped with four-wheel steering, in accordance with the army contract. The idea behind the four-wheel steering, according to Probst, was that a second driver would occupy a rear-facing seat, with a second steering wheel to grip. In the event of an ambush, the regular driver was to shift into reverse and take his hands off the wheel. The rear-facing driver would then floor the gas pedal and drive the vehicle out of danger! The feature wasn't adopted because tests proved the maneuver didn't work very well, and the four-wheel steering made the vehicle squirrelly to drive. A contract for an additional 1500 Ban-

President Franklin D. Roosevelt, seated in Jeep, doffs his hat for the flag.

Jeep shown next to larger military truck.

tams was under discussion, when the decision was made that additional vehicles be built and tested. Some of the military people wanted to obtain bids from larger companies, which could potentially offer certain advantages.

While Willys continued developing its model, Ford was also invited to bid on the contract for production models. Knudsen and others were beginning to feel that a dual source of supply was needed for these new vehicles. In addition, some officers within the military felt that Bantam's small factory wouldn't be able to produce enough vehicles to meet expected demand. They felt contracting with Ford would ensure, by virtue of its vastly larger facilities, that sufficient production would be available when needed. Here, Willys also had an edge over Bantam. Willys had once been the second largest auto maker in America (behind Ford, as a matter of fact), and it still owned an extremely large plant in Toledo that was vastly under-utilized building the slow-selling Willys' "Americar" economy cars.

Ford had long since abandoned four-cylinder engines for its passenger cars, switching over to its renowned V-8 as well as an inline-six. Since its scout car, dubbed the Pygmy, had to have a four-cylinder engine (the minimum allowed by the army contract), Ford chose to use one from its farm tractor line—certainly not an ideal choice. The Ford engine, rugged enough but lacking refinement, was rated at about 40-hp. Both the Ford Pygmy and the Willys Quad basically copied the overall 'look' of the Bantam car. To do so was well within their rights, since the army let all prospective bidders check out the Bantam as well as take any number of measurements and anyhow, the low-profile 'look' was what the army had specified and provided sketches of. Although similar in appearance, each of the three manufacturer's designs had distinguishing style features as well as important advantages and disadvantages in comparison with each other.

Willys had one big advantage besides the large size of its production plant. The Willys passenger car, which had been aimed at economy buyers, was one of the few remaining cars on the market that still used a four-cylinder engine. The Willys' mill was an especially good engine. In years past, it had earned a reputation for poor service life. In response to customer complaints, Willys' chief engineer, Delmar Roos (nicknamed Barney) had gone

through the Willys' four-cylinder a couple years previous with an eye to greatly improving the engine's durability and output. He beefed-up bearings and valve springs and improved the manifolds and carburetor, producing a four-cylinder engine of great power and smoothness. Willys' four-cylinder engine would prove to be its ace in the hole.

Testing of the first Willys' pilot model began on November 13, 1940. It was run on a 5000-mile test and it greatly impressed the soldiers who drove it. Its performance was outstanding. The Ford prototype arrived about ten days after the Willys. Whereas the Willys' vehicle resembled the Bantam, with a rounded hood and rounded front fenders, the Ford wore a flat, square hood and fenders. In comparison with the Bantam, the Willys and the Ford were both heavier. The Willys' car proved to be the most powerful. Its engine was Willys' strongest feature but it was also the source of its greatest trouble. Because of the large size and stout construction of its four, (which Willys called the 'Go-Devil') the Willys' pilot car, dubbed the Quad, was much heavier, at 2423 lbs., than either the Bantam or the Ford offerings.

All of the vehicles were deemed acceptable so far as performance was concerned, so each company received an order for 1500 additional units of their vehicles. To Bantam and Ford, this was the best news possible. Their vehicles already met all the specifications listed by the army. For Willys-Overland, however, there was still another hurdle to jump. The new standard weight limit was set at 2160 lbs., and the army let Willys know they were unhappy with the Quad's 2450-lb. weight. Willys would simply have to reduce the weight of their car to meet that standard. In fact, the army would refuse to approve production of any additional Willys' vehicles, beyond the 1500 initial models, until its weight could be brought down to an acceptable level.

The solution seemed easy. All Willys had to do to eliminate a substantial part of the Quad's excess weight was to replace the Willys' four-cylinder with something lighter, like the Continental used in the Bantam. But as Roos learned, the most important advantage the Willys had over its competitors was its robust engine. To switch to a lighter unit would likely ruin Willys chance at winning the contract. Roos decided to look for other ways to trim weight from his design, a difficult task in a vehicle that was stark and stripped down to begin

"Plane" on Car Is Machine-Gun Target

TRAVELING at a lively pace around an oval track, an Army car, carrying a scaled-down plane fuselage above its roof, affords realistic training for machine gunners of the bomber command at Moody Field, Fla. Lest a novice prove more enthusiastic than accurate, a thick earthen wall leaving only the "airplane" exposed keeps him from winging the driver. Track and target are built to a scale permitting a student to fire at equivalent ranges from point-blank to 1,000 yards. Guns swing and tilt like aircraft weapons, and can be brought to bear upon the "enemy" with equal rapidity. The arrangement is suited both for testing aptitude and for mass training. A few trials show whether an aspirant is a "natural-born" gunner, whether he has the qualities that will enable him to learn, or whether he is hopeless.

This Army car takes a scaled-down fuselage around a track to give target practice to the machine gunner below. A dirt wall, at right, shields driver and car

From *Popular Science* magazine, September 1942: A Jeep set up to train machine gunners techniques for shooting down aircraft.

with. Roos, however, was an engineer of immense talent. He and his staff tore into their vehicle with an eye for trimming an ounce here, a pound there, until the machine would meet the weight specified. Roos team checked each part on the vehicle, cutting the length of bolts, reducing the size of cotter pins, studs, screws and washers, switching to lighter weight, higher strength steel where possible, including the frame and some body panels. Finally, Roos had his men weigh the paint used in finishing the vehicle, which resulted in the decision to restrict painting to just one coat. According to legend, a second coat of paint would have put it over the limit. It all worked; the Willys' model now came in under the weight parameters. The first "production" units would be known as the Willys' MA and were notable for their flatter hood design (though still somewhat rounder than the Ford design), which featured the Willys' name stamped into the front edge, square grill and with body sides that more closely mimicked the Bantam.

So each competitor built 1500 units of their design. These vehicles were sent to various military units for some 'real world' testing. In addition, in May 1941, the Adjutant General ordered the Quartermaster General to have one of each type sent to the Infantry Board for more formal testing. The Infantry soon had a clearer picture of the comparative strengths and weaknesses of each product and some of the results are surprising. The Infantry liked all three, though they felt that the only real difference between the Ford and Bantam entries were the different engines and the Ford's squared-off hood. The Willys' MA was more unique, partly as a result of its more powerful engine. The Willys also required a heavier duty transmission to match up with the engine output and that had necessitated trimming weight in other areas to compensate.

In the Infantry tests, the Willys proved superior in most of the performance trials while, surprisingly, the much lighter Bantam was rated second. The Ford model, known as the GP, came in last in most areas. The highest top speed on a level road was found to be 74-mph for the Willys, 64-mph for the Bantam and 59-mph for the Ford. In grade-climbing ability the Willys' MA was again first, followed by the Bantam and with the Ford again bringing up the rear. In one such test, the Ford failed to reach the top of a slope; the Bantam barely made it, finishing with no reserve of power; the Willys topped the slope with power to spare. Bantam came in first in fuel economy, not surprisingly, while the powerful Willys came in last. Bantam came in first in braking too. In summary, however, the Willys design was rated the best, and the Infantry's report stated that, "the standard vehicle should be based upon the Willys chassis ...." albeit to include the best features of the other two vehicles.

By July 1941, the Quartermaster General was calling for production of 16,000 units of a standardized design. In what marked another change in procurement policy, this was to be an all-or-nothing deal—the entire contract would be awarded to only one company. The QM proposed buying the vehicles on a 'single source' negotiated contract basis rather than opening the contract up to bids. Surprisingly, the QM's preferred contractor was Ford! The reason for wanting to use the contractor whose vehicle had come in last in testing was the oft-mentioned desire to work with a manufacturer whose ability to produce large numbers of vehicles was unquestioned. This idea was rejected and the contract was opened to competitive bidding.

An interesting wrinkle arose when the Checker Cab Company of Kalamazoo, Michigan, became interested in the contract and submitted what turned out to be the lowest bid. However, Checker's offer was not accepted because the company required an excessive amount of time before they could commence delivery of the vehicles. What was also surprising was that of the three remaining bidders, the Willys-Overland company was the lowest cost. Willys' bid was $748.74 per vehicle, while Ford's was $782.59 and Bantam came at $788.32. Despite that low bid, however, the army's recommendation came through to accept the Ford offer. Again, this was done to ensure that the vehicles would be available in a timely manner. It was argued that the Willys company was financially shaky and might not be able to build the vehicles in a timely manner. At this point Bill Knudsen stepped in, refusing to approve the Ford deal. Knudsen stated that in his judgment the Willys concern was a competent source of supply for the number of motor vehicles in question. Since Knudsen was the most knowledgeable man in the world regarding the mass production of motor vehicles, there was scant room for further discussion. By August 1941, Camp Holabird was notified of the decision to go with Willys for the new military car, with deliveries to begin in November 1941.

The thing had to have a name, of course, and the army came up with one of its typical dry, official sounding tags that no layperson was likely to understand or remember. They called it the "truck, 1/4 ton, 4X4." It was also referred to as the General Purpose 1/4 ton. Soldiers, however, called it a jeep, a nickname they had already bestowed upon several other military vehicles, including a tractor used to haul heavy guns, some heavy duty trucks and, reportedly, a military plane. Exactly where that name originally came from is a matter of opinion. Some credit it to a character with magical powers that appeared in the Popeye comic strip. According to another legend the initials of the Jeeps official designation of General Purpose, or GP, were slurred together to create the jeep name. In any case, none of the other vehicles that had worn the jeep nickname captured the public's imagination the way the little Willys did. In a short time, newspaper reporters took to referring to the little scout car, in print, as a jeep. The public picked up on the name, liked it and it stuck. The term 'jeep,' previously a generic name for any handy military vehicle, now became the term that was understood to describe the Willys Jeep. Thereafter, all other military vehicles had to get new nicknames, because there would be one, and only one, Jeep.

The selection of Willys standardized the design on the Willys' chassis, though the final product incorporated the Ford's square hood design and grille made up of heavy bars, as well as flat fenders. The Willys' name was no longer stamped on the front edge of the hood and the head lamps were now set into the grille area. The final, standard version was dubbed the Willys MB. After a run of nearly 26,000 units the grille design was revised yet again to the slotted grille stamping that is most familiar today.

Bantam and Ford were frozen out of the action for the moment, though events would soon alter that. On December 7, 1941, Japan launched a murderous sneak attack on the American naval base at Pearl Harbor, Hawaii, sinking or disabling several of the Navy's largest ships and killing hundreds of young American boys in uniform. Despite American efforts to remain on the sidelines, we were at war. The need for the new military car was now going to be greater than even the most optimistic had envisioned. Besides the U.S. Army's needs, thousands of the new scout cars would eventually be supplied to Allied armies in virtually every theater of the war.

Events picked up speed. The previous Jeep orders, which had seemed so lucrative, now seemed insignificant. Even the 16,000 unit order that went to Willys paled in comparison to what the military was now calling for. Along the way, and actually before the attack on Pearl Harbor, Ford won the right to also produce Jeeps for the military. The Quartermaster still wanted a second source of supply. A compromise was reached by having Ford agree to produce the Willys design under license. Willys would turn over copies of all the designs so that the Ford could build the now standardized Jeep. The Ford product would be designated the GPW (for General Purpose Willys, indicating it was a Ford GP built to the Willys standard design). Willys received no fees or remuneration for this, however.

Bantam, however, was now out of consideration for Jeep production. The army reported that Ford offered to expend the large amounts of money necessary to set up production of critically needed Jeep components, particularly the constant velocity joints needed for its front-end drive, items which had created a bottleneck in the production lines. Bantam was financially unable to do the same, although it did submit a plant to have additional suppliers put the components into production. Again, Bantam's small size and precarious financial condition served to deny the company its rightful role in Jeep production. As the army saw things, with two large production sources, Willys and Ford, building Jeeps, there was no need for a third supplier. There is a hint in all the official papers that some military officers were just plain determined to see that Ford be a part of the project, despite Bantam's role as the designer of the original prototype. Looking back, it seems blatantly unfair that Bantam didn't get to share in the abundant Jeep contracts after working so hard to see the thing through its birthing, but back then the people involved were consumed by the urgency of the times. Bantam was given contracts to build trailers for the Jeep. This work kept it in business for the time being, but did nothing to help keep it in the auto business in the postwar market.

The Jeep did go on to make history, just as Major Lawes had so predicted. It was the soldier's mascot, manservant, burden-carrier, weapon's mount, supply delivery truck, mail van and more. Army chap-

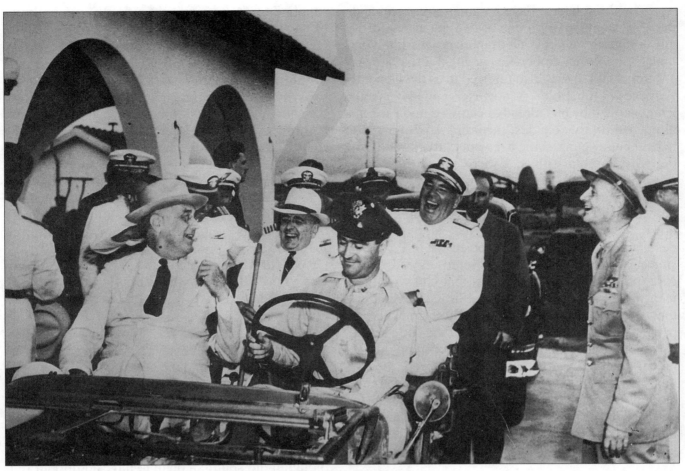

FDR, again seated in Jeep, enjoys a light-hearted moment with officers.

lains used its hood as an altar for serving Mass in the field, officers used them as command cars, Air Corps men used them to tow planes around air fields, and to serve as mobile Control Towers. Soldiers fixed farm plows to Jeeps and used them to lay telephone lines, put on snow plows for clearing parking lots, and welded vertical bars to the front bumpers to cut any booby trap wires that the Nazis were known to string across roads to snap the neck of any unsuspecting motorist.

In areas where the locomotive stock had been captured or destroyed ingenious soldiers fixed special steel wheels to Jeeps and used the vehicles to haul train cars along the tracks. In desert areas the Jeep was rigged to work water pumps at wells, and in virtually every theater of war GI's soon learned that a warm running Jeeps' radiator was a good source of hot water for a comfortable shave. Jeeps brought ammunition and supplies to the men at the front, and if a soldier was wounded he could be brought back on a stretcher strapped to a Jeep. All

of America's allies wanted Jeeps, and in most cases they got them. Many of the Bantam production models, the BRC-40, ended-up serving in Russia as part of our Lend-Lease program, along with hundreds of Willys and Ford models.

As a mobile machine-gun carrier, there was nothing that could out-run or out-maneuver a Jeep. Raiding parties of daring soldiers would drive all night in the dark, appearing miles behind enemy lines to swoop down on search and destroy missions. It was more than a new weapon, and much more than a new style of military vehicle. It revolutionized mechanized warfare and forever changed the way the military would use light vehicles.

A water-going version was built, complete with hull and propeller, allowing it to motor across rivers and streams. Nicknamed the 'Seep' (for sea-going jeep, apparently) it never won the level of admiration that its land-based brother enjoyed. Another version had removable skis on the front wheels for traveling in Arctic conditions.

Wartime advertisement for Willys touted Jeep, but asked civilians to "... make your first postwar car a Willys, the Jeep in Civvies."

Tribute for the Jeep was lavish and came from levels high and low. As beloved war correspondent Ernie Pyle, reporting from Africa, put it "...Good Lord, I don't think we could continue without the Jeep." General George C. Marshall, U.S. Army Chief of Staff at the time called it, "America's greatest contribution to modern warfare." Soldiers developed strong attachments to their vehicles and their praise was both deep and heartfelt. There are hundreds of stories that demonstrate this, but we'll relate only one as a good representative example. A corporal was found weeping beside his Jeep which was bombed-blasted beyond repair. A sympathetic onlooker attempted to cheer the soldier by assuring him that things weren't as black as they looked—certainly he would soon be given a new Jeep to replace the wrecked one. The young man was not consoled, however, explaining through his tears that, *"you see, I loved this one."*

Willys' Chief Engineer, Barney Roos, was less emotional about his baby, saying "It is purely a combat vehicle, designed with simplicity, to do a specific job. It makes no concessions to art, and damn little to comfort." But the army itself loved the Jeep, and it awarded one Willys' model two Purple Hearts for "wounds" (shrapnel holes in the windshield) received during the battle for Guadalcanal. Retired from service, it was sent to the Marine Museum at Quantico, Virginia. Another Jeep, one of the early Bantams, was donated to the Smithsonian Institute.

It seemed altogether fitting, then, that when officers representing the military forces of Imperial Japan set out to sign the articles of surrender in September 1945, they were driven part of the way in a Jeep. The war in Europe had already ended, and the stubborn Japanese military had determined to fight on to the last ditch, until the bombing of Hiroshima and Nagasaki finally convinced them that further struggle was senseless. At that point, the war was over.

Later on, there would be arguments about exactly who invented the Jeep. Senate hearings were

Many Jeeps were shipped partially disassembled, with soldiers and civilians providing final assembly wherever it was possible—such as this outdoor assembly area.

even held to look into the claims made by the parties involved, as well as to investigate the military contracts that were awarded for its production. During one day of testifying before a Senate committee, Bantam's Frank Fenn spoke of how his vehicle was looked over by other manufacturers, saying, "...I personally saw Ford Motor Company representatives in under our car in a grease pit at Holabird with a clipboard making freehand drawings of the lay-out." A prominent Infantry officer wrote, "The Ford and Willys-Overland models are copies of the original Bantam design." As Frank Fenn would later testify to a Senate committee investigating war contracts, his company hadn't realized that the army wasn't going to split the order up among the three companies. The realization came, he later recalled, "...as an extreme shock."

One army representative felt strongly that the Jeep was a collaborative effort, stating in a magazine article, "Credit for the original design of the Army's truck 1/4 ton, 4x4, may not be claimed by any single individual or any single manufacturer. This vehicle is the result of much research and many tests. Army engineers, both military and civilian, at the Holabird Quartermaster Depot did the bulk of the work in designing it." Another military man noted, rightly, "Not a single unit of the original Bantam is in the present vehicle, nor is a single major unit of the present vehicle produced by the Bantam Company itself." However, he was ignoring the obvious; Bantam never claimed that the Jeep was made of Bantam car parts, nor did they claim to be the manufacturer of its major components. Bantam's claim simply was that it had designed the original Jeep, and it certainly had done so. When the first Jeep was driven at Holabird, it was the Bantam vehicle. When Willys and Ford went looking for a design to copy, it was the Ban-

40

tam vehicle they crawled underneath. Karl Probst would later write, "There was no way I could have visualized the succession of events which would see Willys and others get credit for the Jeep's development, as well as production contracts, while we at Bantam would get little of either."

During the war, Willys' then-president Joseph W. Frazer shrewdly had the Jeep name registered as a Willys' brand and that copyright settled who would be selling Jeeps after the war. For Willys it was the coup of the century. They would never again have to worry about sweating out a profit on economy car sales. With the Jeep as their main postwar product, they could at last conduct their business in an end of the market that had no real competition, and in which they would be selling a well-known and beloved machine. Ford never really had a chance anyway, since the Ford GPW was a copy of the Willys. Poor little Bantam never re-entered the automobile market and eventually faded away.

So Willys looked at the postwar American market with great hope. The war years had been good to them; the profits allowed Willys to greatly improve its factory and equipment, and there was money in the bank to fund new products. Meanwhile, a fundamental change that occurred in the automobile business would prevent Willys from going back to passenger car production for some time. As things worked out, Willys was going to have to sell Jeeps to civilians whether it wanted to or not. As it happened, a great new leader would force through a new product line that would shape Willys' fortunes for years to come. Ex-Ford production boss "Cast Iron" Charlie Sorensen was beginning his term at the helm of Willys, and he would make history during his short time in command.

Chapter Three

THE JEEP TURNS CIVILIAN

1946-1952

Willys plant in Toledo was a beehive of activity in the postwar era.

The war's termination didn't catch Willys unprepared. During the midst of the conflict, even as the company was turning out thousands of military Jeeps, Willys' planners were readying new products for the postwar market. Since it had mostly been, historically speaking, an automobile manufacturer, Willys planned to re-enter the automobile business with an all-new, greatly improved full-sized economy car similar in concept to its prewar American. In addition, a line of civilian Jeeps would be marketed mainly for farm and industrial use.

Aside from its universally respected Jeep, the greatest asset Willys possessed in 1945 was a management team of crack professionals. This team was overseen by an unusually sharp man who was both autocratic and firmly entrenched in command of Willys-Overland. In the previous decade, the company had weathered a crisis that saw the business nearly go under, and also witnessed several changes of leadership. At the time of his death in 1935, company founder and namesake John Willys had been involved in a mighty struggle in bankruptcy court, trying to revive his moribund firm. During the proceedings the court installed David Wilson, head of the company that cast engine blocks for Willys, in charge of day to day operations, while plans were devised to make the business solvent once again.

Willys Administration Building was large and ornate. Unfortunately, it no longer exists.

Ward M. Canaday was the real power behind Willys-Overland.

Through a complex and shrewd stock transfer, control of the company fell into the hands of a man by the name of Ward Canaday. Canaday was aided in this effort by a small group of investors that included John Willys' first wife (there was a second Mrs.Willys, John Willys having divorced the first wife some years previously). A former Willys' employee who had left years earlier to found his own advertising firm, Ward Canaday had retained the Willys' advertising account and was familiar with a plan John Willys and attorney George Ritter were readying in an attempt to wrest the company out of bankruptcy. After Willys' untimely death, Canaday, Ritter, Mrs. Willys, and several associates put the plan into effect. They formed a new company called Empire Securities, which bought out the majority of Willys' bonds from its creditors, as well as outstanding claims against Willys, at a considerable discount—the group spent under $2.5 million. Willys-Overland was split into two separate companies—Willys-Overland Motors, Inc. and the

'Cast-Iron' Charles E. Sorensen became president, later vice-chairman of Willys.

Delmar G. Roos, nicknamed Barney, was the brilliant head of Willys Engineering.

Willys Real Estate Realization Corp. The later firm was meant to be a sort of holding company for the vast Willys' real estate holdings.

Empire Securities exchanged its Willys' bonds and claims for 1,400,000 shares of Willys stock, gaining control of the motor company as well as the majority of stock in the real estate company. With its debts wiped out W-O Motors was able to obtain the money needed to once again produce cars on a volume basis. Willys wrote up the value of its plant and equipment from its appraised value of $1.29 million (as a 'distressed' company) to a 'going-concern' value of just under $10 million dollars. Between the new appraised value of the plant and equipment, plus some $3.5 million dollars raised in a stock sale, Willys was now a $15 million company—or more than 10-times its value as a troubled, near-bankrupt company.

Meanwhile, Willys Real Estate Realization Corporation retained ownership of the fancy Willys Administration building, which it rented out to various firms—including Willys-Overland Motors, which leased two floors for its headquarters—and about a third of the huge Willys plant, space which wasn't needed for the level of car production at that time. The Real Estate company sold off some of its unneeded properties and eventually was able to retire most of its preferred stock, paying off its debt to Empire Securities. Canaday and his associates retained control of Empire Securities and through it, a rejuvenated Willys-Overland.

For 1937, Willys-Overland managed to produce about 75,000 cars and netted a profit of some $800,000. The complex takeover plan seemed to work out well. But evidently there was trouble in the boardroom. Chairman Canaday was viewed by some as having an overbearing personality. He sometimes rubbed people the wrong way. According to one magazine, during a board meeting in 1939, an agitated David Wilson had, "emphasized a point with such vigor that the Board Chairman was reportedly precipitated into a nearby wastebasket."

Canaday soon hired Joseph W. Frazer, a top notch Chrysler sales executive, as the new president of Willys. Frazer pushed through some inexpensive changes to the basic car, christened the revamped model the 'Americar' and soon had sales on an upswing. World War II interrupted that effort, but winning the Jeep contract finally put Willys' finances in solid shape, at the same time earning it an enviable reputation as builder of the toughest and most admired vehicle of the decade. Willys lost money in 1940, but earned about $800,000 for 1941. In 1942, profits rose to $1,265,000, and then rose again to about $3 million in 1943. In 1944, Willys earned $4 million, and the company's assets were valued at $73 million!

Yet well before then, Frazer and Canaday had begun to disagree and in 1943, Frazer resigned. Although it's not certain what disagreements stood between the two men, Frazer evidently had soured on Canaday. A close associate recalled Frazer one

The Universal 'Jeep' Will Work and Save

Willys touted many uses and worldwide appeal of Jeep.

day gazing out of his office window at Willys' factory workers entering the plant. Frazer said to his companion, "You see all those people out there? Canaday doesn't give a damn about them or the cars. All he wants to see is the stock going up." For a time, Canaday occupied both the chairman and president's roles at Willys. However, in June 1944, Charles Sorensen, formerly Henry Ford's chief of production and right hand man, signed on as Willys' new president. He was to have an immense influence on the shape of Willys' postwar products, though as it turned out, he wouldn't be around to take the credit.

'Cast Iron' Charlie Sorensen was one of the greatest production managers in the world. A self-made man, he had worked his way up the old-fashioned way. Starting as a pattern maker in the Ford factory, he eventually rose to become head of all Ford production. There was little Sorensen didn't know about making automobiles, and what he saw at the Willys' plant concerned him a great deal. The problem was that like many small auto companies, Willys did not manufacture their own automobile bodies.

Before the war, they had bought bodies from an independent body maker, in this case Briggs. That arrangement had served them well in the recent past, keeping tooling costs and fixed expenses low. But as Sorensen knew, the old ways of doing business wouldn't work in the postwar world. The

The 4-in-1 vehicle the whole world wanted—The Universal "Jeep" by Willys-Overland. It has power, stamina and reliability equal to that of the wartime "Jeep," plus features that fit it for a thousand varied peace-time jobs.

The Universal "Jeep" has added convenience and comfort for driver and passengers—improved springs and shock absorbers, cushioned spring seats, etc. Removable front top with curtained doors and rear curtains is optional accessory.

Ready for Winter—"Jeep" with front and rear top, and door curtains. Side and rear curtains are removable, as shown above.

The Universal
'Jeep'
for the
Peacetime World

THE "JEEP" WILL TAKE YOU WHERE YOU WANT TO GO IN ANY KIND OF WEATHER

WHEN THE "JEEP" ISN'T WORKING, IT WILL HELP YOUR FAMILY ENJOY LIFE IN THE OPEN

Willys *Builds the Universal* 'Jeep'

Willys claimed dozens of peacetime uses for its Jeep. Note that in this early postwar catalog it's referred to as the "Universal Jeep." Later, it would be turned around to "Jeep Universal."

Willys pinned its postwar hopes on the Jeep.

ranks of the independent body makers had thinned out, and there would likely be a major shortage of production capacity in the years just after the war's end. A big company wouldn't be hurt much, but a marginal firm like Willys was likely to get frozen out of the action when the industry went back to building cars again. Sorensen pondered the obstacles he was likely to face at war's end.

Obviously, it was a huge problem; Willys couldn't make cars without bodies, and it was unlikely that any body maker would allocate any of its production to Willys at the risk of losing the business of a large company. The obvious solution of simply purchasing the tooling to make their own bodies, like some other companies had done before the war, was not a practicable option. In the capacity-constrained postwar market there wouldn't be any tooling to buy for several years, because of the tremendous pent-up demand in the industry. The original plan of building a low-priced postwar

economy car simply wouldn't work. Well then, Sorensen pondered, what sort of products can Willys build? It could build the little Jeeps obviously, but these alone wouldn't generate enough sales to stay in business. Other products were needed if Willys was to have any chance at prosperity.

During the war, a brash young freelance automobile designer by the name of Brooks Stevens proposed, in a magazine article, that a line of passenger cars based on the Jeep be developed for the postwar era. Barney Roos, head of Willys Engineering, was impressed by the article and signed-up Stevens to design Willys' products. By 1943, Stevens was at work on his idea for the all-new postwar Willys' car, the one that Frazer and Roos had hoped for. First called the Victory, then the 6/66, the name was later changed to the Willys 6/70 and a running prototype was built.

It was a good enough car, a basic automobile certainly, but with a dash of style. Work on it continued until the hiring of Charlie Sorensen. As Stevens later recalled, in an article he wrote for Car Classics magazine, within days of arriving at Toledo, Sorensen called Stevens into his office. Stevens assumed he was going to be fired, replaced perhaps by a designer brought over from Ford. He was therefore greatly relieved and astounded to learn that not only was he not being canned, Sorensen was praising his work and even decided to double his salary! Then, according to Stevens' account, Sorensen said, "Sit down, let's talk a bit. You know I've been over this thing quite thoroughly; I haven't accepted this position on the spur of the moment. I am quite intrigued with the passenger car program, but there are some real problems of which I'll explain to you. First of all, Willys has no acceptance with any body builder anywhere anymore. Murray, Briggs, Budd, they won't even talk to us. It is ridiculous for me to even go there because they have no interest in our program whatever. They are too busy working on cars for the big automobile builders. So we have to think of something else."

What Sorensen had in mind was to utilize the metal stamping capacity from another industry, one that had a stamping plant available. He had checked out various industrial concerns, finally settling on a factory that supplied sheet metal stampings for home appliances. The plant could supply Willys' needs, though with certain limita-

Willys-Overland Presents
THE 'Jeep' STATION WAGON

New vehicles to meet new needs — this guide-star of Willys-Overland engineering brings to business, large and small, a long-needed dual-purpose vehicle—the "Jeep" Station Wagon.

In its roomy body are full-size seats for seven adults, with plenty of head, leg and shoulder space. All seats except the driver's are removable, providing 56 usable cubic feet of load space, easily accessible through the rear doors.

Body and top are *all-steel*, which means less weight, more safety and a lasting finish—no wood-body squeaks and peeling.

It is powered by the Willys-Overland "Jeep" Engine, world-famous for performance, long mileage and low upkeep. The "Jeep" Station Wagon is quality-built for years of efficient service.

There's a place in your business for this newest "Jeep." See it now.

The "Jeep" Station Wagon is quickly adaptable to changing needs—seats for 7 adults, as shown in diagram at left, or load space of large capacity.

Willys - Overland Motors Inc. TOLEDO 1, OHIO

TIME, AUGUST 19, 1946

99

Willys station wagon was one of the first all-steel station wagons produced, and was a handsome and useful machine.

tions to size of the bends and curves it could stamp. As Sorensen explained:

"I like what you have created, but I have to develop some vehicles that we can build in a washing machine plant. I'll give you a depth draw of six inches. That's it. There is no further press capacity. We can't go to deep drawing shapes and fenders and doors and that sort of thing. What can you develop in this vein? We need something that will rub off on our prowess as the builder of Jeeps."

Sorensen's decision to use an appliance factory to stamp-out his sheet metal had a profound and lasting effect on Willys. It saved the company from having to rely strictly on the little Jeep for sales, a move that in all likelihood would have eventually sunk the firm. More significantly, it changed Willys' whole product philosophy. The limitations of its tooling were going to force the design of vehicles that would be far different from anything else on the market. It was no longer possible for Willys to build conventional automobiles. The company had long competed directly against other automobile makers but now, for better or worse, it was going to take an entirely different direction with its products.

Stevens was fired up by Sorensen's words. The Willys' president evidently hadn't mapped out his ideas for a new product, but he wanted some design sketches as soon as possible to show his board of directors. Stevens considered the design parameters dictated by the depth draw of the presses— shallow fenders, flat sides, no complex bulges or curves, as well as Sorensen's directive that the vehicles have a visual family tie to the wartime Jeep.

Rolling up his shirtsleeves, the young designer went to work, sketching out an entirely new product line, vehicles that Willys would be selling for the next twenty years. The front-end styling would be similar in appearance to the little Jeep, though because the new products would be larger and wider, none of the sheet metal was interchangeable with the military cars. Stevens designed a steel-bodied two-door station wagon, disguising its utilitarian plainness by painting the body sides in such a way as to imitate the wooden side panels used on station wagons of the day. Stevens then drew the same wagon with its rear side windows filled in with sheet metal panels, creating a delivery wagon in the process. By chopping the back of the wagon off and sketching a short cargo box in its place, he created a light pickup truck. As a gesture to the en-

thusiast market, Stevens also drew a low-slung two-door sport convertible based on that same chassis. When the young designer finished he showed his work to Sorensen who, recognizing a winner, immediately authorized Stevens to begin developing the designs for production.

At war's end, the new vehicles weren't quite ready for introduction. Thus the first postwar Jeep offered to the public was, naturally enough, a modestly refined version of the military MB. Some of the improvements were slightly larger headlamps fitted up front, the spare tire was bolted to the vehicle's side, a tailgate was cut into the back end, and softer-riding springs were installed. In addition, more comfortable seats were added and gearing was changed to better suit civilian usage. The biggest change was the new array of colors offered— a startling appearance of bright, fresh hues after years of what the soldiers had dubbed "OD," or olive drab. Introduced in the summer of 1945, the new Jeep model was officially christened the CJ-2A. Legend has it that CJ stood for "Civilian Jeep." But early Willys' advertisements usually didn't refer to the new Jeep by its model number. Since it was felt that the Jeep's appeal was universal, Willys decided to call it the Universal Jeep, which later was reversed to Jeep Universal.

It was very easy for Willys to get the new Jeep-in-Mufti into production, since for the most part, it was the same as the military model. Charlie Sorensen even hosted a vehicle introduction/demonstration for the press at his farm in Michigan where several Jeeps displayed their ability to plow, seed, pull a harrow, and perform many other farm tasks. As Willys pointed out, in the Jeep, the same rugged, dependable machine that worked on the farm all day could also carry the farmer and his family into town for shopping or out for a pleasure drive. Initial demand for the civilian Jeep was high, due to the vehicles fabulous reputation and the fact that no such vehicle had ever before been offered to the public. After a run of 1,824 CJ-2As for 1945, 71,554 were built for 1946.

Of the three original producers of wartime Jeeps—Ford, Willys and Bantam—only Willys continued building Jeeps after the war. Ford at one time had been interested, but when its own Jeep design had been rejected by the military, forcing Ford to utilize the Willys' engineering plans instead, that pretty much killed any chance of Ford offering a peacetime Jeep. After all, it was unlikely that Willys would al-

Postwar Jeep trucks were rugged and handsome.

low Ford to produce a machine that Ford had almost no design input on. Even if Ford could prevail in a court battle, they still would have had to go begging hat in hand to Willys for the engines needed. In all likelihood, Ford knew it would have its hands full just trying to catch up with the postwar demand for cars. To them, the Jeep just wasn't important enough to worry about. The third party of original Jeep builders, poor little Bantam, never returned to the automobile market after the war, and was eventually absorbed by another company.

The name "Jeep" had been, as we know, a nickname, slang, an affectionate slurring of the GP initials; take your pick. As such, when it appeared in print it had usually been typed in lower case letters like this—jeep. Willys realized the magic, and economic value, inherent in the jeep name and boldly registered it as a trademark of Willys-Overland.

Henceforth jeep would be capitalized as Jeep, and Willys or its successors would own the name forever, so that even if anyone else should choose to build a similar vehicle they would not be able to refer to it as a Jeep. In all this, being sole builder of the postwar Jeep, and registered owner of the Jeep name, Willys was fortunate. From now on Jeep would be everything to Willys-Overland, even its very future.

Sorensen had realized that Willys couldn't survive on one model. Overhead at Willys' plant would have required a production level of at least 54,000 Jeeps per year—a level that Willys could attain in good years, like 1946—but one it might perhaps fall short of in lean years. Sorensen knew that rather than put all its eggs into one basket Willys must offer a complete line of vehicles in order to assure adequate production volume.

His instructions to Stevens and the Willys' engineering group to develop other Jeep vehicles came to fruition in July 1946, with the introduction of the revolutionary new Willys' "Jeep" Station Wagon. It was especially innovative in two ways: 1) because it was the first all-steel station wagon produced in America, and 2) it was one of the first all-new postwar autos introduced. It was a handsome machine, clean-lined, durable and wearing a definite "utility" look. The new vehicles 104" chassis revealed its Americar roots, as did the Willys' Go-Devil four-cylinder engine, basically the same engine as used in the wartime Jeeps.

Although four-cylinder cars were out of vogue, the 63-hp Jeep four, with its reputation for power and rugged construction, was considered acceptable. The station wagon was also highly useful; its interior was fitted with seating for seven, with all seats but the drivers easily removable for times when maximum carrying space was needed. One magazine writer of the day remarked how clever it was of Willys to position its station wagon, a car type previously thought of as a luxury item, as a smart, low-cost family car.

Charles Sorensen, however sound his business plan may have been, found himself replaced as president of Willys in January 1946. The new president was a former General Motors executive named James Mooney, to whom Ward Canaday granted the additional title of board chairman. Sorensen, whose employment contract guaranteed him $1,000 per week for ten years, whether he lived or died, was given the title of Vice Chairman, but left with little power in the corporation.

The problem may have been that Canaday and Sorensen were simply too far apart temperamentally to get along together with the stress of running the company. But a more plausible explanation may be that Canaday came to disagree with Sorensen over the decision to abandon the passenger car business, and decided to replace him with someone who wouldn't argue against cars. After all, in 1946-1948, passenger cars were a veritable gold mine. An indication of the soundness of this theory is found in the public statements made by incoming Willys president Mooney concerning his ideas about Willys' postwar line-up, "Our program is in line with the Willys tradition. Before the war, Willys always produced a lighter-weight smaller-capacity automobile. During the war—in a short period—we established the tradition of the Jeep.

By keeping both…we'll have a sound and successful program." Thus stated, he was refuting the plan of concentrating on Jeep vehicles only, and was committing Willys return to the passenger car market. Mooney even had some idea of what sort of car the new Willys was going to be, "We'll not get out a trick or miracle car. It will be stylish without pretending to be fashionable. We think a car is too expensive an item to follow ever-changing fashions."According to a 1946 story in *Fortune* magazine, the new Willys would be a small standard size car on a 104-inch wheelbase, weighing under 2500 lbs., but engineered with four-wheel independent suspension to provide excellent riding qualities. It would be equipped with a small, economical six-cylinder engine, and would be available only in two-door models. As described, it sounded very much like a modern Willys' Americar, improved and updated for the new decade. It was predicted the car would be introduced perhaps as early as 1947.

America's economy in the immediate postwar years was pretty much as the experts had predicted it would be. People had a lot of money saved up from good paying jobs in war production plants that for over three years had offered all the overtime anyone could want. There was an incredible pent-up demand for new cars and trucks. None had been built during the war, and most of the existing cars had been driven many more miles than owners would ordinarily have gone before trading for something new. What the war had created, then, was a gigantic demand for new vehicles. In such an atmosphere, Willys couldn't help but prosper, so Jeep sales were excellent and profits were splendid.

Brooks Stevens' clever Jeep designs, combined with Willys' sturdy yet economical chassis, meant that the Willys' product line was well suited for overseas distribution. Whereas most American cars of the time were large six- or eight-cylinder vehicles, the tall, narrow Willys' body and thrifty four-cylinder engine were ideal for sale in just about any country in the world. The rugged four-wheel-drive models were especially well suited for South American countries. Of course in Europe, the Jeep name needed no introduction; aside from long-established Ford, it was the best known American vehicle. Besides, the Willys' brand was already well known overseas. During the lean years after it got out of bankruptcy court the company had set a goal of doing 17% of its business overseas. Now, with

Jeepster was for the young-at-heart, a delightful, sporty car.

James Mooney took a turn at the helm of Willys-Overland.

the Jeep product line so well suited to emerging nations everywhere, the men who ran Willys-Overland set a new quota of 25% for overseas sales. Selling overseas became a tradition with Jeep, one it would never abandon. It was believed the new hoped-for Willys' car that Jim Mooney had spoken of would also be sold overseas, where its compact size and thrifty six-cylinder engine were sure to appeal to buyers.

There were soon other new products developed from the station wagon chassis. In the spring of 1947, came the new Jeep pickup truck. From the front it looked just like the station wagon-flat grille, angular, flat topped fenders, simple hood (which Brooks Stevens once described as "a simple piece of flat steel curved at the edges"). The wheelbase was longer than the wagon, and the chassis was wider in the rear. The cab was upright and tall, and modern-looking for the era. The trucks were available in both two- and four-wheel-drive models—unlike the station wagon,

52

SEE HOW MUCH MORE YOU GET
When You Get a Universal 'Jeep'

4-WHEEL-DRIVE TRACTOR

HAULING ON OR OFF THE ROAD

With the power of its 60-hp "Jeep" Engine and steady-pulling traction of 4-wheel-drive, the Universal "Jeep" operates plows, harrows, discs and other implements at tractor speeds of 2½ to 7 miles per hour. The efficiency of the Universal "Jeep" for tractor work has been proved by use on thousands of farms in every section of the country.

You get more than a tractor when you get a Universal "Jeep". Its selective 2- and 4-wheel drive gives you traction in the field and on bad roads, with normal road speeds for hauling and towing on the highway. With power take-off, the "Jeep" will operate all types of belt and shaft-driven equipment. The "Jeep" does more jobs.

COMPARE THE UNIVERSAL 'JEEP' FOR COMFORT AND CONVENIENCE FEATURES

DRIVER'S SEAT of spring and cushion construction, with full back, means more comfort with less fatigue from field work. Fenders help protect the driver from dust and mud.

FOR COLD DAYS, the "Jeep" can be equipped with half or full metal cab, as shown, or with canvas top and curtains, and car-type heater. Tops and heater optional at extra cost.

FOR NIGHT FIELD WORK and highway driving, the "Jeep" has powerful 7-inch sealed-beam headlights — same size lights as used on passenger cars — plus parking lights and tail light.

EASY TO DRIVE as a car. Full instrument panel, self-starter, conventional pedals and accelerator. Change from 2 to 4 wheel drive is made by merely shifting transfer-case lever.

The 4-Wheel-Drive UNIVERSAL 'Jeep'

WILLYS-OVERLAND MOTORS, TOLEDO, OHIO, MAKERS OF AMERICA'S MOST USEFUL VEHICLES

Willys advertised in *Country Gentlemen* magazine, highlighting many uses for Jeeps.

The 'Jeep' Works the Year 'Round

The Universal 'Jeep' is busy every season of the year—helping you get work done on time —spreading its cost over more kinds of jobs.

LEFT— The sure-footed 4-wheel-drive 'Jeep' gets you to any part of your place in a hurry—climbs steep grades, pulls its load through deep mud and sand, over ice and snow.

ABOVE— The Universal 'Jeep' is a 4-wheel-drive tractor for all kinds of field work, operating pull-type implements or, with hydraulic lift, standard lift-type farm equipment.

ABOVE— The 'Jeep' easily pulls loads like this 2100-lb. baler and loaded wagon. With its wide speed range, the 'Jeep' will tow your trailer to town in a hurry at normal road speed.

RIGHT— With power take-off, the 'Jeep' delivers up to 30 hp through pulley or shaft drive for operating hammer mills, buzz saws, silo blowers, sprayers and power mowers.

ONLY THE 'JEEP' HAS ALL THESE FEATURES:

Selective 2- or 4-wheel drive 6 speeds forward, 2 rev. Operating range from 2 mph in the field to 60 on the road.

More driver comfort—full-back, upholstered seat, shock absorbers, folding windshield.

Car-size 7-in. headlights for night field work.

Power take-off points at rear, center and front, for belt or shaft drive.

Steel bed for hauling.

Optional metal top for winter.

Optional hydraulic lift.

4-Wheel-Drive UNIVERSAL 'Jeep'

WILLYS-OVERLAND MOTORS • TOLEDO • MAKERS OF AMERICA'S MOST USEFUL VEHICLES

Jeeps were good for plowing, towing trailers, and off-road farm work.

The 1948 Willys advertising stresses advantages of four-wheel drive.

which could be had only in a two-wheel-drive model. With the new pickup truck, Willys could boast of a highly desirable line-up of vehicles—the Universal Jeeps, the wagons and now the pickups, all sharing the rugged Jeep reputation. Willys also introduced the panel delivery truck that Stevens had proposed back in 1944, based on the station wagon body. All in all, 1947 was a great year for Willys-sales totaled $138.1 million, which was the best since the heyday of 1928. Top model was the CJ-2A , with just over 65,000 units built. The company even reopened its West Coast plant in Los Angeles.

The year 1947 came and went without an introduction of the so-recently touted Willys' passenger car. In all likelihood Willys' president Mooney ran into the very problems that Sorensen had predicted—difficulty obtaining tooling, as well as greatly inflated prices for same. It was no matter, since Willys could sell all the CJ-2As, Jeep station wagons, panel and pickup trucks it could build. The auto market in America was still very much a "seller's market," and the public was snapping up just about anything on wheels. But according to at least one source, Ward Canaday was unhappy about staying out of what he perceived as a lucrative passenger car market. His dissatisfaction was likely to prove unfortunate for the current president of Willys-Overland, because Ward Canaday was not the sort of man one wanted to make unhappy.

At the beginning of the1948 model year, the Willys' line looked very much the same as the prior model year. One new model was the Station Sedan. Despite the name, the new vehicle was a variation of the wagon body, although with basket-weave outside body trim and a six-cylinder engine under the hood.

An additional new model was on the way but didn't actually arrive until April 3, 1948, with the introduction of the newest product based on the 104" Willys chassis. The new vehicle was called the Willys' Jeepster, and it was a sporty, open-bodied car; a vehicle that was in fact the last true phaeton introduced by a major automaker. It was an evolution of the roadster design Stevens had originally sketched for Charlie Sorensen. The need for volume products had pushed the wagons and pickups onto the market first, but now it was time for the open car to debut. The Jeepster was handsome, no doubt about it. It shared the basic front-end styling of the wagon and pickup, but looked fancier because of a stainless steel "T" bar that Stevens added to the grille area.

The body itself was unique, slab-sided like the rest of the Willys' line (had to keep the tooling simple, remember), but with details that made it look quite sporty and very distinctive. Although the cowl was rather high, the belt line dropped down at the doors, then kicked up again on the quarter panels just aft of the doors. To achieve a lower, sportier look a chrome trim strip ran along the body sides a few inches below the belt line, sweeping up over the cowl. In most cases, this "outlined" area and the windshield frame were painted black. Rear fenders were modified units borrowed from the pickups. Jeepsters had a more comprehensive list of standard equipment than the wagons, and came with richer-looking upholstery, wide whitewall tires, wheel trim rings, dual sun visors, front bumper guards and a top boot.

It was meant to be something of a sports car, or a sporty car at the very least, and came only in a two-wheel-drive model. Willys didn't want the public to think of it as a commercial vehicle, so four-wheel-drive was never offered, even as an option. The Jeepster was certainly a unique machine. It was a true phaeton; the doors didn't have rolldown windows, relying instead on side curtains for weather protection.

In one sense, the Jeepster was the fulfillment of Willys' dream of a postwar automobile; certainly, at least it was the first one that someone could purchase. Despite Jim Mooney's confident pronouncements regarding Willys' postwar economy car, no such machine, at least as he described it, ever appeared from Willys-Overland. His unnamed, never-built postwar Americar-type vehicle marked the first of several attempts by Willys and its successors to regain a spot in the American passenger car market.

All of them proved unsuccessful, the first attempt being the least successful, since the car envisioned was never even produced. In that sense, then, the Jeepster should be thought of as the second attempt by Willys to find a place in the passenger car market, especially since when it first debuted, the company talked as if it would be a volume product. Why a couple of smart businessmen might think a car with such limited appeal could ever sell in volume is worth pondering.

Willys 1948 wagon still looks good today.

"THAT'S THE SIGN TO LOOK FOR!"

Drive in with confidence wherever you see this sign. It identifies Willys-Overland Dealers from coast to coast and tells where to get Factory-Authorized Willys-Overland Service, using factory-approved methods and genuine Willys-Overland replacement parts. It's the one way to protect your investment and be sure of the highest performance at the lowest operating cost.

Willys new Jeepster for 1948 was a stylish, fun phaeton.

Jeepster looked the same for 1949, but offered detail changes.

After all, Ward Canaday and James Mooney were no naive young things wandering into uncharted waters. They were hard-boiled and sharp-eyed, and the car market should have held few surprises for them. The first question that comes to mind is why they introduced a phaeton-type automobile? After all, the reason it was the lone such entry on the market was because the popularity of that body type peaked in the 1920s, and then declined. Phaetons, with their poor weather sealing abilities, hearkened back to the days when an automobile was primarily a pleasure machine, a device for taking long drives out to the country on sunny summer days.

In the years since that golden past, automobiles had become a part of life—necessary for getting to work, school and to market. Buyers were interested in comfort and convenience features, and it was in precisely those areas that phaetons were at their worse. In addition, the Jeepster wasn't especially fast despite its sporty looks—the only engine offered the first year was the Willys' four, sturdy enough but by no means a high performance engine.

An additional strike against the Jeepster was its price. At $1765, it was roughly equal in cost to a Ford Super Deluxe Club Convertible ($1740), which had fancier styling, roll down windows, and a V-8 engine. Predictably, Jeepster sales were only modest, with some 10,326 built (it's not certain how many of that number were actually sold that first year, but indications are that many were not retailed until the following year, after being re-titled as 1949s) in the first year despite it being an excellent year for the industry in general. As things turned out, some Willys' executives would later view the sparse sales of the 1948 Jeepster as 'the good old days.'

There was another new product introduced into production at the tail-end of 1948. This was a revised small Jeep christened the CJ-3A. Changes included a one-piece windshield, wipers located at the base of the windshield, rather than at the top, and better ventilation. Although the CJ-2A remained in production for awhile, it was gradually supplanted by the CJ-3A.

For the year, Willys produced 136,648 vehicles, and in the fiscal year earned over $7 million,

Four-wheel drive Willys wagon was the first Sport Utility Vehicle (SUV).

both of which were excellent numbers. However, the postwar buying boom, with nearly every auto maker selling every vehicle it could build, and all of them scrambling to build more and more new vehicles, was coming to an end. From the end of the war in 1945, to the end of 1948, it had been a wonderful time for the American auto industry, prices high and rarely discounted, sales easy to come by, and a huge pent-up demand that seemed insatiable. However, 1949 was going to be the beginning of a change in the auto industry.

For 1949, Willys fielded basically the same product line as before, with the CJ-3A growing in production, as CJ-2A output was winding down. The Jeepster's prior year sales had been disappointing, and steps were taken to correct the weaknesses that dealers had complained about. First and foremost was the price—it was lowered to $1495, moving it into lower price classes. It wasn't a simple price cut, however. Willys decontented the Jeepster, by making whitewall tires, wheel discs, overdrive, and the fancy T-shaped grille bar, as well as other items, optional instead of standard equipment. A 72-hp flathead-six-cylinder engine called the "Lightning," from the station sedan/and six-cylinder wagon series, was added to the option list to address concerns about a lack of power.

Also new for 1949, was a four-wheel-drive version of the Willys' station wagon. This was a natural evolution of the expanding Willys' product line and utilized Willys engineering's talent for cost-effective product development—creating a "new" product by combining the existing station wagon body with the existing four-wheel-drive power train as used on the pickup. Since product development funds were always chronically short at Willys, they had become expert at creating new models on a shoestring by utilizing existing production tooling whenever possible.

With the undeniable advantage of hindsight, we can see the station wagon's greatest significance was for a reason that couldn't quite be seen back in 1949, and that is simply this: today's drivers of Grand Cherokees, Explorers, Pathfinders, Blazers and all other "Sport Utility Vehicles" (SUVs) can thank the Willys' Jeep four-wheel-drive station wagon for pioneering this new segment of the market. Prior to this historic machine, there had been four-wheel-drive vehicles and there had been utility station wagons, but the 1949 Jeep 4X4 wagon combined those two ideas into a machine that was the first true sport utility wagon, despite what the producer of the Japanese Subaru has sometimes claimed in its advertising. The 1949 Jeep four-wheel-drive station wagon started

Military M-38 Jeep was an improvement of World War II era design. It was produced in 1950 and 1951.

a trend that would grow slowly over the years, coming to full bloom during the 1980s, and continuing to this day. In every sense of the term, the new 4X4 Jeep station wagon was a landmark vehicle.

Even with the availability of two Universal Jeeps, the CJ2-A and the CJ-3A, plus the two-wheel-drive and four-wheel-drive Jeep pickups and station wagons, and also the sporty Jeepster, Willys-Overland sales in 1949 took an extremely sharp drop. For the calendar year production fell to 83,250 units. Part of the problem had to do with parts shortages caused by strikes at some of its suppliers, which in turn, caused temporary halts in Willys production. But the greatest problem was a shortage of buyers. With vehicle supply finally caught up with demand, the world seemingly had changed almost overnight, and the "sellers market" of the early postwar years was ended. From here on in, America's independent auto makers, Willys-

Overland included, would have to slug it out in the sales arena with the heavyweight champs—General Motors, Ford and Chrysler, the so-called "Big Three" of auto manufacturing. Looking back, it appears that Willys was affected the most by the evolving marketplace, most likely because the truck market was significantly smaller than it is today. The other independents, all of whom relied mainly on passenger car sales, enjoyed decent sales for the year, partly because they had already recently introduced new styling and/or exciting innovations. In comparison, Willys' new model introductions didn't seem all that spectacular.

There's a saying as old as the auto business itself, and it goes something like this: when sales go down, heads will roll. The person who gets the axe is seldom the president of the company, since in most firms, especially during the 1940s and 1950s, the president was the most powerful man in the company, unlike today, where the chairman of the

For 1951, Willys offered three special color variations of family wagon: the Grand Canyon, the Caribbean and the Jamaica, of which this is the latter. Jamaica had two-tone green paint, coordinated trim.

board of directors, or even the Chief Financial Officer (CFO) often holds the ultimate power. Willys-Overland wasn't like most companies, however, because one man, Ward Canaday held control of much of the company stock. Canaday must have been concerned about the abrupt drop in vehicle sales, as well as the downturn in profits, and he was not a shy man about letting his feelings be known. In April 1949, W-O president James Mooney announced he was resigning from the company. Ward Canaday stepped into Mooney's place at the head of Willys-Overland.

Regardless of what anyone might think to the contrary, it is certainly reasonable to believe that the twists and turns the Willys company made in the years 1949-1953, were the work of Ward Canaday. He had long been the power behind the throne, and he was that still, only now he was also in charge of the companies day-to-day operations. From here on, it seems plain that whatever road the great old Willys-Overland company took, it would do so because Ward Canaday himself had willed it.

One task Canaday did was to get back in touch with an independent automobile engineer he had first spoken with in 1948. Clyde Paton was a man who possessed sterling credentials; former chief engineer at that most prestigious of automobile firms, The Packard Motor Car Company. Mr. Paton had designed a sturdy compact car and pitched the idea to Willys (as well as Nash and Packard). In early August of 1949, only some three months after

Mooney was let go, Paton once again spoke with Willys engineering chief Barney Roos about a possible Willys small car.

From there events progressed slowly—on January 18, 1950, Paton had a luncheon meeting with both Canaday and Willys vice chairman George Ritter to discuss automobiles. However, it wasn't until June 1950, that Canaday told Paton he was being hired to bring the new car to market as a Willys' product. Paton's engineering would be combined with styling by associate Phil Wright to create a modern, low-cost compact automobile. The idea was that it would be a "modern Model A," in other words, a basic but well-built car for families on a budget. It was to debut in 1952, at which point Canaday would at last be able to offer both cars and Jeeps to the public and earn, we'll assume he believed, lush profits from doing so. Getting back to 1949, Willys cut some prices midyear, had the plant working on a reduced schedule and generally did everything it could to stem the losses caused by the reduction in sales. It thus managed to end the year with a profit of over $3 million.

The Jeepster returned for 1950, with significant improvements and alterations designed to increase its appeal. Gone was the flat-faced grille, replaced by one that was V-shaped and decorated with five chrome trim strips. The Jeepsters front fenders were even somewhat elegant, more rounded and forming a handsome peak at the front edge. The old

These men are testing a seating buck of a proposed new Jeep vehicle. This photo was taken in the Willys Engineering shop.

Extreme width marks this Jeep as an engineering prototype, though styling is similar to later CJ-5.

Popular Science **magazine ran an article on new M-38A1 military Jeep in its July 1952 issue.**

Go-Devil four-cylinder engine was replaced by a new four dubbed the "Hurricane." The Hurricane was simply an update of the old mill, converted to an F-head design (in which the L-head's intake ports are blocked off, replaced by larger intake ports in a newly designed cylinder head), which gave it an increase in power to 72-hp versus the old fours' 63-hp. Of course, that meant that the four was now rated for the same horsepower as the previous year's six-cylinder, so that engine was increased in displacement to 161.1 cubic inches and a rating of 75-hp. Jeepster production in 1950 totaled 5,845 units, of which 4,066 were four-cylinder models and 1,779 were six-cylinder.

Alcoa, the Aluminum Company of America, pitched an idea to Willys for a sporty coupe version of the Jeepster built with, as one might guess, a high percentage of aluminum. Alcoa had at least

two of the vehicles built (not one as is usually reported) and handsome machines they were. The coupe roof line gave the Jeepsters a low, very sporty look. The two known prototypes wore different front end styling, with one carrying the new 1950 production-style grille, while the other carried a more highly-styled look. Nothing came of the proposal, however, other than two exciting "Jeeps That Might Have Been," for historians of future years to ponder over. It wouldn't be the last time someone tried to make something more out of the Jeepster program.

The old CJ-2A was gone, leaving the CJ-3A now the standard Jeep vehicle. In June 1950, a war broke out between North and South Korea, and United Nations' troops, consisting mainly of American GI's, were soon in the thick of the fighting. There was a new military Jeep for 1950 which carried, as usually was the case with military vehicles, two designations—MC or M-38, the latter of which we'll use for this narrative. The M-38 was basically a military version of the CJ-3A, had larger head lamps like the earlier CJ's, and also a one-piece windshield like the CJ-3A. It was, however, equipped with a heavy-duty 24-volt electrical system. Its addition to the line-up of government vehicles was important for Willys, because, although it would be produced for only a short time, quite a number would be ordered by the army, pumping handsome profits into the company. The army needed new Jeeps, because the units produced for W.W. II were now anywhere between five and ten years old and a more modern unit was needed for the harsh terrain of the Korean Peninsula.

The Jeep station wagon models also received the new F-head four engine and the optional Lightning six, as well as the same pointy grille and chrome trim as the Jeepster. Pickup models benefited from the same styling improvement bestowed on the Jeepster and station wagons. Willys was fortunate to receive the large volume of military orders it got for 1950, because they turned out to be the highlight of an otherwise unremarkable year. The company ended the year with a profit of $1.6 million.

The 1951 Willys' line-up debuted in November 1950, and it showed little change from the previous year. The little CJ-3A returned unchanged, not receiving the F-head four that its larger stable mates had added the previous year. Station wagons likewise were mostly unchanged from 1950. As in prior years, the station wagons were available in two-wheel-drive or four-wheel-drive four-cylinder models, and a six-cylinder model offered only in two-wheel-drive. A two-wheel-drive panel delivery was likewise available.

The Jeepster line was unchanged, mainly because there was no real production of 1951 models. Although Willys offered a 1951 Jeepster, all the units sold evidently were leftover 1950 models, although one source at the Jeep plant in Toledo believes there many have been a handful of "real" 1951 Jeepsters, perhaps 9 total, produced from leftover parts. For the three years of production and four years of model sales, only 19,131 Jeepsters were built, instead of the purported 50,000 annually that Willys had hoped for. The Jeepster had thus failed as a passenger car, but Ward Canaday had his hired engineers and stylists working on a "real" postwar passenger car, so the Jeepsters usefulness was coming to an end regardless.

Willys was also working on a vastly-improved military model, something even better than the recently introduced M-38, a larger, more powerful scout car. It was planned to include the F-head four in the new vehicle, as well as a wider body, better ride and handling and improved appearance. Several prototype variations were built, including one that had an extremely wide body. It may well be that if the Korean War hadn't come when it did, the M-38 might have been passed over in favor of continued development of this newer type Jeep. Some of the prototypes were developed in civilian versions as well, since it was a given that a civilian version of the new military vehicle would be produced at some point. Military vehicle and commercial truck sales were of major importance to Willys, forming as they did a major source of Willys' profits. Development dollars earmarked for vehicles in those categories usually received first priority, but civilian vehicles were often derived from the military versions.

The new military vehicle that debuted in 1951 was called, confusingly enough, the M-38A1. It was confusing in that one might reasonably expect a vehicle so designated to be merely a slight variation of the M-38. But the M-38A1 was an entirely new vehicle, and a much better one as well. As planned, it was fitted with the F-head four-cylinder engine. It retained the waterproof 24-volt electrical system introduced on the earlier model. Biggest change was the body. The M-38A1 body was wider, longer and much more stylish than its predecessor. *Popular Science* magazine's article on the new Jeep opened with the line, "Memo to GIs the world over: They're slicking up the Jeep for you." It really was a tremendous improvement, although its doubtful if even its most ardent supporter would have guessed, in 1951, that the vehicle would remain in production, in either military or civilian form, for over 30 years!

Willys had a new source of income in 1951, which was both good news and bad. First the good news—Kaiser-Frazer Corporation, upstart newcomer to the auto business, was purchasing four- and six-cylinder engines from Willys for installation in its all-new small car, the Henry J (as in Henry J. Kaiser, the famed industrialist behind K-F). The purchase agreement was very lucrative for Willys, since it utilized existing production capabilities to build the engines. Although the Henry J engines weren't identical to those installed in Willys' vehicles, the differences were merely details. With over 80,000 1951 Henry J's produced (in an extended model year), this was a substantial revenue source. The bad news was two-fold: the introduction of the Henry J meant that the upcoming Willys compact now had a competitor already entrenched and waiting. Further, by supplying engines for the small Kaiser car, Willys relinquished a sales advantage; it couldn't boast its engines were superior to the Henry J's.

It had already lost the undeniable advantage of being able to boast of being first on the market with a compact car. Nash-Kelvinator, the innovative independent based in Detroit, had introduced the first American compact car, the Nash Rambler, in 1950. With the new Henry J and rumors of a small car soon to come from Hudson, the tiny niche that Canaday hoped his Willys' car would occupy was rapidly becoming crowded.

Still, confidence reigned in Toledo. And why not? The year 1951 ended with Willys reporting its highest-ever sales, $219,861,553, and possessing a solid backlog of Jeep orders. Net profits of $4,585,566 were nearly three times the amount reported for 1951. But there were rumors that the engine deal with Kaiser-Frazer might lead to further deals, including a merger of the two firms. Such rumors were floating around all the independents, not just Willys, but at that time, so far as the public knew anyway, none of the firms had actually taken any action towards merger. In actuality, most of the

Popular Science magazine ran an article on new M-38A1 military Jeep in its July 1952 issue.

companies had already had some sort of talks going on at one time or another.

Ward Canaday had waited a long time to see his firm re-enter the automobile market, and 1952 was the year it would finally do so. He had put up impatiently with situations and men that seemed only to delay the project, and he had personally helped to move the thing forward. Just as his

hands can be seen clearly at the helm of the good ship Willys, his influence on the new Willys' car was sure and certain.

There could be little to question of its engineering; Clyde Paton was a universally respected engineer and if his decision was to build anything in such or so a way, well, who could argue? Besides, Canaday and Ritter were no engineers. Styling, however, was a different matter. It was a rare company president in the 1950s (or 1960s, 1970s and 1980s for that matter) who didn't feel himself to be an expert in the matter of automobile styling. And even if he didn't feel himself sufficiently adroit to comment, he was sure to have a wife, friend, or even a large, important dealer who did feel free to offer opinions on design.

It was a thing that stylists struggled with back then, and it was difficult to deny a direct request from the top to change or alter a design, especially if it was done in a certain manner. William Mitchell, one of the stylists working on the new Willys' car, recalled just such an incident (in *Special Interest Autos* magazine). He had mocked-up a hood ornament for the new Willys' car, decided it was ugly, and tossed it into a nearby trash can. A little later that evening Ward Canaday came strolling into the design area, with Paton in tow. As the talk turned to hood ornament design, Canaday spotted the discarded one among the scrap. When he fished it out of the barrel to see how it would look on the car, Mitchell blurted out, "Oh my God that looks like hell!." Canaday turned to the designer, fixed him with a look and replied "I'm going to teach you a lesson, Mr. Mitchell. I run this company, and I like it, and that's what it's going to be."

The new car, dubbed the Aero-Willys, debuted with the other 1952 Willys' models on October 4, 1951. The Aero, which came in several models and trim levels, was a good looking compact. It was solidly engineered with a combination of good ride, decent power, and crisp handling that surprised and pleased most road testers of the day. Fuel economy was excellent, especially for so roomy and comfortable a machine. It had just a few drawbacks, but they were substantial. For one thing, the new Willys was the newest entry in the compact market, joining the low-priced Henry J and the Nash Rambler.

The Henry J competed on a price and fuel economy basis, though it had been stripped down to the basics to do so and was a rather stark automobile. The Rambler was unique in its appeal; it was beautifully trimmed and only came in premium body styles, such as a convertible, hardtop and station wagon. But Nash's Rambler didn't compete so much on price; its draw was its superior trim and fancier body styles. A big problem Willys had, which was shared with the other independents, was that they were smaller firms with fewer dealers. The public was somewhat wary of placing a major purchase like a car with a small, independent producer. Lastly, many people felt the Willys' car was overpriced.

The rest of the 1952 Willys-Overland line received much less notice than the Aero cars, and that could have been predicted. After all, the greatest percentage of production was slated for military needs plus the new Aero Willys' cars, and the rest of the line-up was mostly carry-over. Naturally enough the Jeepster was not returned to the line-up. It was missed by many people, the ones who loved its unique style and whimsical nature. The Jeepster was one of those rare cars that seem to become collector items almost as soon as they go out of production. Surely a car with that much emotional appeal wouldn't stay out of production forever. A notable event took place in March when the 1,000,000 Jeep rolled off the assembly line.

It was a good year for Willys—the new cars were introduced, the 1,000,000th Jeep was built, and the company looked to the future with hope. The coming year would be Willys' 50th anniversary as a company, an event few people who had grown up with the firm ever thought it would reach, but reach it Willys did, although it had often been a struggle. Still, for all the happiness in Toledo, rumors still persisted that Willys was for sale, and that the person most interested in buying it was a man by the name of Kaiser.

Chapter Four

KAISER AND THE JEEP

1953-1969

Front end styling of CJ-3B looked a bit odd.

The fall of 1952 brought, as would be expected, the debut of the 1953 Willys-Overland line. Everyone at Willys knew that 1953 would be an exciting year, because it was the company's fiftieth-anniversary. In honor of the occasion, all Aero Willys' cars were given gold-colored 'W' emblems to wear on their grilles rather than the usual chromed items. Coincidentally, a new Jeep vehicle was introduced.

The new Jeep was an attempt by Willys Engineering to solve concerns about inadequate power in their smallest civilian product. Although the Go-Devil engine had built a reputation as a powerhouse during pre-war testing and subsequent wartime service, the world had moved on since then. Engines produced by just about every other manu-facturer were becoming more and more powerful. Modern V-8 engines were rapidly moving to the forefront in the auto industry, and even some of the sixes used in cars were now more powerful than the big straight eights of past years. Taken in that context, the Jeep flathead-four was considerably under-powered. An obvious solution was to install the more powerful F-head four in the small Jeep CJ, and that's what Willys' engineers did.

However, because the tall F-head wouldn't fit under the hood of the CJ-3A, Willys had to cobble together a new Jeep with a raised hood and taller grille. This change would allow enough room to accommodate the more potent engine. The result was a vehicle that, at 72-horsepower, was 20% more

Stamina

The Willys-built 'Jeep' has earned a world-wide reputation for *Stamina*. Its built-in dependability and ruggedness are reflected in other Willys vehicles.

When you buy any Willys passenger or utility car, you have taken the first step in getting lower operating costs.

In the 4-wheel-drive models, you have assured yourself of the "go-any-where" ability which characterizes their performance, on or off the road.

These are the qualities *which advanced Willys from 7th to 5th place in the industry* last year.

The Universal Jeep—Gives 20 per cent more power with 72 h.p. *Hurricane 4* Engine. 4-wheel drive puts *action* in *traction*. Ideal for tractor work, hauling, towing, pushing, pulling and as a mobile unit.

2- or 4-Wheel-Drive Station Wagon—Rides six—or provides 98 cubic feet of hauling space. An ideal family and business car. 4-wheel drive takes passengers or cargo where conventional cars can't go.

4-Wheel-Drive Truck—Rugged, agile . . . *Hurricane* powered, gets you through treacherous roads that stop other trucks. Maintain schedules, save money, with this great truck.

2- or 4-Wheel-Drive Sedan Delivery—112 cubic feet cargo space within steel body on 104½-inch wheel-base. Optional 4-wheel drive for rough terrain— ideal for service operations and rural deliveries.

ECONOMY

Willys fielded an extensive product line during its 50th Anniversary year.

68

powerful than the CJ-3A. Yet there was a tradeoff in the new CJ-3B's front end appearance, at least stylistically speaking. The tall grille made it look like a startled pumpkin. The old CJ-3A remained in the line-up for a time, before being phased out as production of the new Jeep ramped up (though the handsome CJ-3A's body wasn't slated to enjoy retirement for very long, Willys had other work for it to do). An addition was also made to the Jeep truck line in the form of a four-wheel-drive sedan delivery (nee panel delivery), built on the wagon body. It was just the thing for hauling supplies out to remote work sites.

A major turning point in the life of the corporation came mid-year, when it became apparent that the rumors of merger with Kaiser-Frazer were more than idle gossip. The Kaisers had expressed an interest in buying the firm, and Ward Canaday likewise expressed an interest in selling. Canaday's price was just over $62 million. Because of Kaiser-Frazer's precarious finances, the other Kaiser interests had to make a loan to their auto making firm to enable it to finance the takeover of Willys-Overland.

There were several reasons why Kaiser wanted Willys, but the biggest one was pride. Henry Kaiser had never failed at anything he tried, but it appeared that the auto business would break that streak. Kaiser-Frazer was struggling, trying vainly to turn a profit, a feat it hadn't been able to do since the golden year of 1948. Merger seemed its only hope of remaining in the auto business. Like Willys, Kaiser sales had slumped in 1949, and since that time, despite seeing a significant increase in Kaiser sales in 1951, the company hadn't been able to return to profitability. Its Henry J auto, after enjoying a fairly good first year of sales, had also slumped in the market and was now a verifiable flop. The outlook was grim; although K-F could hold on for awhile longer, sooner or later it would have to either abandon the business, or merge with a profitable company in hopes that would help turn things around.

None of the likeliest candidates for merger, Studebaker Corporation, headquartered in South Bend, Indiana, and the Detroit-based independent automobile makers—Hudson, Packard and Nash, were interested in merging with K-F. They felt that the company was too closely held by the Kaiser family. That left Willys as a possibility, the best one as things happened. K-F tightly *was* ruled

Henry J. Kaiser wanted to buy Willys-Overland to prop up his auto empire.

by the Kaisers, and it needed to find another company that was similarly run, and for sale. Canaday at Willys must have seemed like the sort of man with whom Henry Kaiser could do business.

The sale was consummated on April 28, 1953. Financially speaking, it was a huge deal. It was, at the time, the largest merging of two automotive firms in history. Although it wasn't known at the time, it was also the first of what would be a veritable rush to merge. By the end of 1954, there would be no independent automaker, save Checker Motors, that hadn't merged with another.

Willys-Overland was renamed Willys Motors, Inc., dropping the venerable (though hardly contemporary) Overland brand. Although offered a position with the new firm, Ward Canaday declined, took his money and left the scene. The little advertising man had certainly fared well in the years since he first joined Willys.

The sales organization, called Kaiser-Willys, existed as long as there was a Kaiser car, which wasn't too long. The Willys car was still enjoying decent sales, although it certainly wasn't setting the world on fire. In truth, the fate of both Willys Motors and Kaiser no longer rested on their passenger cars, but rather on the continued success of the Jeep line. With Henry Kaiser's son Edgar firmly in charge, the merged company set to work consoli-

NOW!

YOUR CHOICE OF TWO GREAT FOUR WHEEL DRIVE UNIVERSAL `Jeep`'s

CJ-5
New Rugged Stamina, New Sturdier Body Design, New Larger Windshield, New Softer Springs, New All-Weather Canvas Top, New Bucket Seats.

CJ-3B
Tested and Proven . . . Famous the World Over as the Work Horse of Farm, Public Service and Industry.

POWERED BY
THE *HURRICANE* F-HEAD ENGINE

MORE POWER AT LESS COST

The *Hurricane* F-head is one of the most efficient engines ever developed. Overhead intake valve and valve-in-block exhaust give better "breathing" and less susceptibility to carbon. Using regular grades of gasoline, the *Hurricane* squeezes more energy from every drop, giving higher horsepower output with greater fuel economy.

See your nearest Willys distributor or dealer or write

WILLYS MOTORS, INC.
— OR —
WILLYS-OVERLAND EXPORT CORP.
TOLEDO 1, OHIO • U.S.A.

(Jeep)
PRODUCT

W

THE WORLD'S MOST USEFUL VEHICLES

— 3 —

CJ-5 was slightly more expensive than the CJ-3B, which remained in production.

Although Willys built cars, such as this Aero Lark Deluxe, Jeeps were still important, as evidenced by the many Jeep vehicles seen in the background.

dating its two organizations into one. In time, Kaiser car manufacturing shifted to the venerable Jeep plant in Toledo, and Kaiser's huge Willow Run plant was sold to General Motors, which assembled Hydra-Matic transmissions there.

An event took place in the next model year that was more significant than the people involved realized at the time. Another new Jeep was introduced, not an unusual event in itself, of course, but this introduction was for a vehicle destined to become the most legendary civilian Jeep of all time, the CJ-5. Style-wise it was obvious that the new Jeep was based on the earlier military M38-A1 model. It sported a wide cowl, neat integration of its tall hood line, smoothly curved fenders and a rounder, more "finished" look than previous Jeep Universals. Mechanical specifications included the F-head engine, three-speed transmission and, of course, four-wheel-drive. It was, in short, a larger and more comfortable Jeep. Its design represented a step forward in technology over the stillborn CJ-4 that Willys had developed in prototype form just as the Korean War was heating up. Perhaps if that war hadn't forced the only-modestly improved M38 into production, the military version of the CJ-4 would have been in production by 1950 or

1951, and perhaps the civilian version as well. As things turned out, Willys simply skipped over the CJ-4 and went right to production of the CJ-5.

The CJ-5 was the best little Jeep yet, more substantial and car-like, yet as rugged as could be. The body was three inches wider than the CJ-3B and its wheelbase was one inch longer. Inside there was more leg and hip room, and softer seats. Although it looked to be just another improved model, like the prior upgrades, the CJ-5 became instead a standard bearer, remaining in production right to the 1983 model year.

It was a good thing that the CJ-5 was such a great vehicle, and that overall Jeep sales were good in 1954, because both the Willys' passenger cars and the two Kaiser lines (the Kaiser and Henry J brands) were down for the count in 1954. Although they were not yet out of the sales fight, there was little doubt that their demise was coming.

Towards the end of the year, big Roy Abernethy, the man Kaiser had put in charge of Kaiser-Willys' sales, left the firm to pursue his passion for selling automobiles at the struggling American Motors Corporation. At AMC he would win wide acclaim for building AMC's dealer body into a mighty sales force, though his later elevation to the

The all-new CJ-5 debuted in 1954. Apparently, early CJ-5s came with a two-piece windshield, as seen in this introductory brochure.

Aero Ace, pictured outside the Willys plant in Toledo. Note the line of new Jeep station wagons in the background.

presidency of AMC would ultimately prove disastrous to that company.

One modest project that Willys was working on in 1954 was a small military Jeep designed to be lighter than standard Jeeps. The military wanted a vehicle that would be easier for helicopters and planes to carry. As designed, the experimental Jeep was 3 ft. 3 in. shorter in length, and weighed about 1200-lbs. less, even though it was equipped with the 60-hp flathead engine. Willys' designer Miguel Ordorica explained how it was done. He said, "I started by examining each part carefully—if I could substitute something lighter for it, I did. If I could throw it away, I did. You'd be surprised how much I threw away." Some of the discarding was questionable, since the tiny Jeep had no dash instruments at all! However, despite its useful design evidently no orders were placed for it. There were improvements to the truck and station wagon lines. Complaints about inadequate power were addressed by the addition of more powerful 226-cid six-cylinder engines (originally developed for Kaiser cars) for 1954.

When the 1955 model year opened, Kaiser-Willys trimmed the number of passenger cars it offered to just three, at the same time face-lifting the Aero-Willys' front-end styling in an attempt to re-

ignite sales. It was for naught, and before the year was out, both Willys and Kaiser cars ended their production runs in the U.S., though both were later assembled in Latin American markets. This ended, for the time being, Jeeps efforts to market cars along with its traditional products.

With passenger cars fading out of the picture, Willys concentrated on Jeep vehicles once again. A new low-priced commercial model was introduced. Called the DJ-3A, it utilized the body of the retired CJ-3A, as well as its flat head four-cylinder engine, but was offered only as a two-wheel-drive vehicle. The DJ-3A came with either left or right-hand drive, since one of Willys' intentions was to offer it as a postal delivery car here in the U.S. Of course, it could also be sold in right-hand drive markets overseas. Available as an open roadster or with optional hardtop or soft-top, the DJ-3A offered rugged construction and dependability in a less expensive package.

Priced at just $1205 for the basic roadster, and marketed as a low cost delivery car or runabout, it enjoyed only modest sales. It did however, allow Willys to sell in a market niche it would otherwise have missed out on. Also introduced into production was a new long wheelbase version of the CJ-5 dubbed the CJ-6. The CJ-6 used a "101" wheel-

Willys gave renewed emphasis to Jeep during 1955.

The Jeep DJ-3A Dispatcher was an excellent low-cost vehicle for routine parking patrol.

base, and was identical in appearance to the CJ-5 from the front bumper to just aft of the door opening. At that point, an extra panel was welded into place on the body, because of the extended wheelbase. It looked very much like a patched-in job—which it was. The CJ-6 (and its later cousin the two-wheel-drive DJ-6) never sold in large numbers in the U.S., in spite of having only a very modest price premium over the smaller CJ-5. It proved popular in overseas markets, where it was often fitted with side-facing rear bench seats and used as a taxi.

For 1956 and 1957, things remained relatively the same in Willys' model line-up, with changes limited to color and trim details. The company began production of a small utility vehicle for the military. Called the Mechanical Mule (M-274), it was designed to be a tough, very low-cost workhorse for off-road only. Weighing only 750 lbs., and powered by an air-cooled 16-hp four-cylinder en-gine, the Mule lacked fenders, springs, even differentials, but was built to be rugged and easily maintained. In all, the company built 4,618 Mules. Work also commenced on a vehicle that resembled the Mule slightly (and has been mistakenly identified in some books as a Mule). This vehicle was larger, heavier, had a 100-hp engine and could be operated on the road as a personnel carrier.

Willys enjoyed good sales and reasonable profits, and few would have blamed it if it became complacent. After all, in the four-wheel-drive market Jeep was the undisputed leader. Although four-wheel-drive vehicles were available from a few other companies, Jeep dominated the market. However, that situation was unlikely to remain the same forever and the company bravely attempted to enlarge Jeeps model range. One big change came in 1957, when Jeep introduced into production a new range of trucks to supplement (and probably eventually replace) its decade-old Jeep pickups.

Aluminum Jeep prototype was tested by the army.

The new CJ-6 for 1955 combined excellent CJ-5 mechanicals with longer wheelbase, and was especially popular in overseas markets.

The new trucks reportedly were designed by Brooks Stevens, the independent designer Willys had hired during the 1940s to design its core products. The idea behind the new trucks was to develop a line of advanced commercial vehicles that would be different from, and better than, competing trucks from the larger producers. What Stevens penned was a futuristic-looking line of "forward control" trucks with styling that imitated the look of heavy duty cab-over trucks.

Called the FC (for Forward Control) series, these new trucks were a very clever design. The high-mounted cab allowed good visibility. To give the FC models a visual tie to the rest of the Jeep family, the center grille panel was shaped to imitate the look of the standard seven-slot CJ-5 grille, and

was painted a contrasting color. Because a cab-over design is inherently space-efficient the 81" wheelbase FC-150 model could boast of a six-foot cargo bed despite being built on what was basically a CJ-5 chassis. Surprisingly, the FC-150's overall length was even a few inches shorter than AMC's tiny Metropolitan car! Equipped with the F-head four, the FC-150 offered modern styling, a spacious interior, full size carrying capacity, four-cylinder economy and Jeep's legendary dependability. The FC-150 was soon joined by a larger FC-170 model on a 103.5" wheelbase, which came with the 226-cid six-cylinder engine. Both were cutting-edge designs with features not available in other light trucks, and both had the potential to start a new trend in truck design.

The Jeep FC-170 featured unique style and high load capacity.

Jeep pickups were always popular with companies that needed a durable off-road truck.

At the very least, the thinking was that they could secure a substantial volume of plus business for Willys. Both, however, proved to be mediocre sellers in the truck market. It was a lesson learned, at one time or another, by most of the independent auto manufacturers: although the public always claims an interest in innovative vehicles, a company should never bring out a product that is too far advanced. The public simply wasn't ready for so different a vehicle as the FC and they stayed away in droves.

Willys continued to offer the trucks in the U.S. market for several years, shipped many to overseas markets, and developed military versions as well, including a van-like personnel carrier. However, it was all just an attempt to earn back some of the development dollars they had spent. Brooks Stevens even commissioned the building of perhaps three van prototypes, based on the FC, to explore the idea of introducing a small passenger van in America. Unfortunately, the timing wasn't right for another radically new idea, and Americans would have to wait another quarter century before they would see an American minivan. The 1958 Jeep line-up was,

in the main, carryover, in part because of the great expense incurred with the previous year's introduction of the new FC truck line. However, by 1959, Jeep was again ready to field some new variations of its Jeep vehicles.

American Motors was enjoying terrific sales of its compact Ramblers, particularly the popular station wagons. As a result, for 1959, Willys decided to try to capture a bit of that booming market segment with a specially packaged version of its two-wheel-drive Jeep station wagon. Featuring special chrome trim and two-tone paint (the height of automotive fashion just then), the special Jeep wagon came lavishly equipped, at least by Jeep standards. Featuring black floor carpeting, four Goodyear white side-wall "Captive Air" tires, vinyl upholstered seats, and a one-piece windshield, it was dubbed the Jeep "Maverick"(or Maverick Special). This name was a reference to the popular TV Western series starring James Garner that was sponsored by parent company Kaiser. Priced at $1995, the Maverick managed to undercut the Rambler's price, though it proved unable to achieve anywhere near the Rambler's sales. Unfortunately, the public still viewed Jeeps

FC-170's four-wheel drive made it perfect for all kinds of hauling.

Good-looking 1959 Jeep Maverick was a specially trimmed two-wheel drive model aimed at passenger car buyers.

Jeeps were purchased by rural mail carriers long before the U.S. Postal Service began using them.

more as utility or farm vehicles than passenger cars, and when shopping for a family wagon most suburbanites chose one from either the Big Three or the little two (AMC and Studebaker-Packard).

A fresh opportunity presented itself for 1959 with the introduction of another new commercial model in Jeep's two-wheel-drive line. The Jeep Gala was a DJ-3A open roadster that Willys dressed up in resort-wear. Initially the vehicle was sold overseas to fancy vacation spots in warm climates, including the famous Las Brisas Hotel in Acapulco; they proved so popular that Willys soon offered them to resorts in America. Included was a candy-striped surrey-style canvas top complete with fringe, and striped seats to match. Three pastel colors were available; pink, green and light blue. Metal side steps, chrome bumpers and wheel discs were included as standard equipment.

Overseas, Jeeps continued to be popular and were now being assembled in some nineteen countries including France, Argentina, Mexico, Japan and Brazil. The Brazilian operation was growing by leaps and bounds, even signing an agreement to assemble Renault cars in its plant. Meanwhile, Mitsubishi Motors of Japan paid Willys a hefty license fee for the rights to build Jeeps for the Japanese market. There was even a small assembly plant in Canada, though production there was surprisingly modest.

Also in 1959, Edgar Kaiser turned over the presidency of Willys Motors to Steven Girard. Edgar, however, wasn't retiring from the company; he was merely moving up the corporate ladder. For 1960 there was yet another new Jeep model, and this was one of the more unusual ones. The U.S. Postal service was looking for a light van-type vehicle for postal route delivery. Willys had already sold many DJ-3As, and even some CJ-5s as postal delivery trucks, but what the USPS wanted now was a bigger vehicle that could carry larger volumes of mail, and be able to perform more duties than simple door to door delivery. They needed something to handle jobs such as bulk pickup from postal drop boxes.

Willys engineered a small step-van, using the DJ-3A's 80" chassis as the base. The body itself was a sturdy steel design, boxy, functional and space efficient. The new Jeep's official model designation was FJ-3. The Postal Service awarded a contract to Willys Motors to built the new van, and Willys later would offer a version of the vehicle to regular customers through its dealer network as the FJ-3A Fleetvan.

Fancy 1960 Jeep Surrey was a two-wheel drive fun machine.

The 1963 Willys line included Dispatcher, Surrey Gala, and Fleetvan, among others.

'Jeep' DISPATCHER · SURREY GALA · FLEETVAN

DISPATCHER DJ-3A

'JEEP' DISPATCHER, DJ-3A

Lightweight, highly maneuverable—turns in a radius of 17½ ft.—the Dispatcher has a cargo capacity of 40 cu. ft., an ample gate opening 35¹¹⁄₁₆ in. high by 36 in. wide and an easy-to-load platform height of just 23⅛ inches. Open body or optional Soft Top, Half Top and Hardtop models with ten standard body colors to choose from. All models have optional vented, folding windshields.

'JEEP' SURREY GALA, DJ-3A

Colorful choice of smart shops, small businesses, resort motels and hotels throughout the world, the Surrey Gala with the fringe on top is economical to buy and operate. Washable curtains, tops and seat coverings made of sturdy weather-resistant fabrics. Three two-tone paint options.

SURREY GALA DJ-3A

'JEEP' FLEETVAN, MODEL FJ-3A

Specifically designed for light-duty, multi-stop operation, the 'Jeep' Fleetvan is efficient, rugged, highly maneuverable and economical. Carries 1,000 lbs. of payload on 81 inches of wheelbase and supports a cargo capacity of 170 cu. ft. Only 154 in. long and 64.7 in. wide, the Fleetvan turns in a radius of 17 ft., important in traffic and the loading area. The driver of the Fleetvan can see an object only three feet high 12 in. from the front bumper. Side door height is 70 in. for easy walk-through.

FLEETVAN FJ-3A

Specialized equipment for Jeeps included a portable welding unit.

The Trenton, New Jersey, Police Department used this Jeep DJ-3.

The Jeep Gala returned for 1960, renamed the "Surrey" and was offered now to American buyers, though its marketing was still aimed at resort hotels and other vacation destinations. Some hotels included the use of a Surrey in their basic room charge; others kept a few Surreys on hand for daily rentals as needed. Willys kept things confused by referring to the vehicle as both the Gala or the Surrey, and sometimes as the Gala Surrey. Regardless of nomenclature used, the little machine is remembered as the cutest Jeep of all.

There used to be a saying that, "Old Willys never die ... they just go to South America," and in 1960, the world saw a perfect example of how that saying came to be. In March of 1960, Willys launched an exciting new passenger car onto the

market—the Brazilian market that is. It had a very familiar look to it, which was only natural since it was a resurrected Aero-Willys sedan. Back in 1955, the company decided to save the tooling for the Willys' car in the event it could be used overseas; by 1960, that opportunity arrived. The government of Brazil was eager to establish a domestic automobile industry and welcomed the idea of a Willys' car with open arms. Although Willys was a small fish in a big pond in America, down in Brazil it was a big player, and its Jeeps had already established a good reputation for Willys. At first the little Willys' car was a duplicate of the final American version, but later it was re-styled and improved. In a long production run that reportedly lasted to the 1972 model year, it eventually even

'Jeep' 1-TON PICK-UP
6000 LB. G.V.W.

'Jeep' 4-WHEEL DRIVE VEHICL
ON THE ROAD . . . OFF THE ROAD . . . POWE

DELUXE TRUCK COMFORT
THE 'Jeep' TRUCK OFFERS YOU THE DELUXE FEATURES OF OTHER TRUCKS *AT NO EXTRA COST*

Wide opening, one step, easy-enter doors. No-slip, no-trip weather protected safety step. Fully insulated padded floor mat covers entire cab floor. Comfortable full width seat covered in attractive, long wearing, washable vinyl. Matching durable covered door panels. Gleaming chromium door and dash hardware. Dual rubber padded arm rests, dual underseat tool compartments. Big push button dispatch box. High level fresh air ventilation for summer comfort.

Big, bright map light that floods entire cab with light. Here's a map light by which you can really read. Inside rear view mirror, full width rear window, and dual tail-lights all standard equipment.

Attractive, easy-to-read instruments. Big, convenient, chromium ash tray. Rheostat control of instrument lighting for night driving comfort. Automatic key starting . . . no searching for a foot starter with muddy, slippery shoes.

— DELUXE FEATURES ARE PROVIDED AT *NO EXTRA COST* IN THE 'Jeep' TRUCK —

GREATER SAFETY
CONVENIENCE and HANDLING EASE

'Jeep' trucks have a proven safety record which is unsurpassed. The millions of miles traveled by 'Jeep' trucks through the world's worst jungles, mountains and deserts have demonstrated the inherent, built-in safety of these rugged vehicles.

Low center of gravity, 4-wheel drive traction, excellent vision, large brakes and husky construction make a 'Jeep' truck one of the world's safest trucks, on or off the road.

The 'Jeep' Truck is easy to use. High efficiency, variable ratio, cam and lever steering takes the work out of parking and turning. 'Jeep' Trucks require less steering effort than many passenger cars. Wide-opening, alligator hood gives complete access to the engine compartment. No reaching and crawling when servicing the engine.

Low bed-height makes loading and unloading simple. The low 'Jeep' Truck cab is easy to enter and leave . . . just one step in or out. No icy, muddy running boards.

Despite its age, the Jeep pickup still offered many advantages to buyers.

84

Three CJ models were available for 1963.

outsold the American version! The combination of strong Jeep and car sales helped Willys Brazil become a major manufacturer in the Brazilian market. It became so strong it could even develop its own Brazil-only Jeep models.

With CJ3-Bs, DJ-3As, CJ-5s, Jeep pickups, Jeep station wagons, the FC-150 and FC-170 Forward Control trucks, and the new Fleetvans, Willys could boast, in 1960, of the most extensive Jeep model line-up in its history. The variations seemed almost endless, with the FC series offered in pickup, stake and cab & chassis models, while the DJ-3A had roadster, convertible and hardtop

models, plus the Surrey variant, CJ's could be with hard or soft tops or no top at all, and station wagons could be had in four- and six-cylinder models, with or without four-wheel drive, or as panel delivery vehicles. In addition, Willys maintained a catalog of specialty vehicles, such as ambulances and fire trucks, that could be built on Jeep chassis. For example, the CJ-5s, trucks and FC-170s were available in fire truck versions, while the panel delivery was offered as an ambulance model and also as a personnel carrier.

The model proliferation was deliberately vast, so Willys could continue to expand sales despite not having redesigned its core product line in many years. The CJ-5's design was by then seven years old, while the station wagon and pickups had first been seen in 1946-1947. Even the FC series, the newest Jeep design (aside from the specialty Fleet-van), was already in its fourth model year. The problem was that competition was about to appear in Willys' market niche.

Also occurring in 1960, American Motors Corporation landed a contract to build a light-weight military car called the Mighty Mite for the U.S. Marines. It was very similar to the one Willys had worked on in 1954. It was an extreme-ly well designed vehicle, and potentially could steal some business away from Willys. In the end, the Marines ordered less than 4000 units of the tiny AMC military car. AMC's president, George Romney, was interested in obtaining further mili-tary contracts, but one of his vice presidents, Roy D. Chapin Jr., had an even bolder vision—he wanted AMC to acquire Willys Motors! Chapin was very enthusiastic about the potential of an AMC-Willys' merger and managed to get Rom-ney to agree to meet with Edgar Kaiser to discuss the idea. Things didn't go the way Chapin hoped, however. Romney chose to concentrate his efforts on AMC's Ramblers, and no deal was forthcom-ing.

Willys was faced with a new rival in 1961, the first real competitor it had faced since before World War II. In January of that year, the Interna-tional Harvester Company, looking to expand its model range downward in the light truck market, as well as draw some sales from the passenger car market, launched its all-new Scout four-wheel-drive vehicle in roadster, pickup and station wagon versions. The Scout clearly was aimed at Jeep's tra-ditional buyers. Built on a 100" wheelbase it was larger and more comfortable than a CJ, yet shorter and more maneuverable than the Jeep station wag-on, and it looked more modern than either. First year sales of over 25,000 units must have worried Jeep executives.

Yet in spite of some negatives, things went tol-erably well for Willys in 1961, with a reported 132,755 vehicles produced in that calendar year. Included were a few commercial versions of the Fleetvan introduced the previous year as a postal truck. Although its price undercut those of other, similar trucks, the Fleetvan failed to sell in signifi-cant numbers.

In 1962, Willys was faced with some nagging problems. Its line of vehicles was getting stale, and complaints of inadequate power were growing. By May, to mollify the power concerns, Willys began offering an all-new and very innovative OHC six-cylinder engine (designed by chief engineer A.C. Sampietro, a man blessed with a considerable amount of European experience) in station wagon and pickup models. The new engine, called the "Tornado OHC" offered up 140-horsepower, a dra-matic improvement over the old Kaiser six. *Four Wheeler* magazine called it "Willys New 140-hp Bomb" and said its high torque peak occurring at low rpms meant the little six "promises much for back country enthusiasts." CJ's had to get by with their old-fashioned F-head fours and optional die-sel engines, FC-150s and FJ-3s also used the F-head four, and the DJ series still used the old flat-head four. The old 226-cid Kaiser six was still available as standard equipment on the FC-170 and as an option on station wagons and trucks.

Independent designer Brooks Stevens, still on retainer with Willys, was asked by the head of Willys Brazilian operations to re-style the Jeep sta-tion wagon for that market. Stevens came up with an excellent facelift that managed to make the old design look modern, and it proved very popular in its adopted country. In fact, it would stay in produc-tion years after the original. As an interesting part of the redesign program, Stevens designed a new Jeepster based on the new wagon styling. It nearly made it to production too, but Willys-Brazil was al-ready selling everything it could build and didn't have any extra production capacity to spare for the Jeepster.

Although Willys still offered the M38-A1 mil-itary version of the CJ-5, the army had already be-gun phasing in a new military scout car, designated M-151 but nicknamed the Mutt. An all-new design, the Ford Motor Company earlier had won the con-tract to build it for the army, but for 1962, Willys won back the contract and began to assemble M-151s in its Toledo plant.

Looking back, though, 1962 can be seen as a very sad year in at least one way; it marked the last time that Willys vehicles would be sold in Ameri-ca. Kaiser Industries Corporation, parent of Willys Motors, apparently decided the time had come to utilize the corporate name on its Jeep line. Kaiser might have listed any number of reasons for doing so, but the most compelling one was that it had re-

This front view of the Brazilian Rural Willys shows how well Brooks Stevens was able to integrate new styling on an existing truck—a handsome look. This vehicle was popular in Brazil and remained in production long after U.S. truck had been dropped.

cently invested a huge amount of money to bring out entirely new Jeep vehicles. An all-new chassis would be the foundation for a new line of station wagons and pickup trucks, as well as a wide-range of specialty vehicles, and Kaiser evidently decided to introduce the new Kaiser Jeep name in conjunction with the vehicles. The first models offered on the new chassis were station wagon versions, which the company named Jeep Wagoneers.

And new they were! An all-new body, new engines, new transmissions, plus exciting new features that put them years ahead of competitors. Everything was different. Where previous Jeep wagons had been narrow-bodied, the new Wagoneers were wide. Where earlier Jeep styling had stressed function over form, the new Jeeps' styling was by contrast freshly modern and very up-to-date, yet still with the emphasis on utility. At the front, a tall, upright grille bore a family resemblance to the rest of the Jeep line, though it carried twelve slots rather than the CJ's seven. At the back and side areas, the windows were much larger, giving a lighter, airier

The M-38A1 military Jeep.

87

Classic line of the 1963 Jeep Wagoneer still looks good today!

Wagoneer for 1963 came with the unique Willys OHC Six engine.

look. These were the largest, roomiest, most comfortable Jeeps yet. Interiors were plainly functional on standard models but much richer and more car-like trim was offered on deluxe models. The Wagoneers were available in both two- and four-wheel-drive models and were offered in both two- and four-door versions. The four-doors would prove to be a major innovation in sport utility vehicles. With them, the company was recognizing that the market for strictly functional vehicles was too limited. The new Wagoneers were clearly the beginning of an effort to move the Jeep product line up-market, and they made every other utility wagon seem old-fashioned in comparison.

The new Jeep's engineering was as radical as its styling. The Wagoneer introduced an optional independent front suspension system, the first ever offered on a production four-wheel-drive wagon. Also innovative was the Tornado OHC six-cylinder engine, introduced the previous year on the station wagon and pickup lines. At 140-horsepower, it

was a very potent engine and was still the only OHC six produced in America. Also new were drive selector lights that let the driver know at a glance which driving mode, two-wheel or four-wheel, he was operating in. All four door windows rolled down for superior ventilation. The tailgate window was a new roll-down type, rather than the old-fashioned transom style, and could even be had with electric assist.

However, perhaps the most historically significant innovation on the Wagoneer was that it offered an optional automatic transmission, a three-speed unit from the Borg-Warner company. This was the first-time an automatic transmission was offered with four-wheel-drive, and it opened up the market to a whole class of drivers that were unwilling or unable to accept the drawback of manual transmission shifting in order to gain the undeniable benefit of four-wheel-drive. Men and women who had grown used to automatic transmissions, and young drivers who had never learned how to

Jeep also exhibited its new Wagoneer at the 1963 Geneva Auto Show.

Remarkably handsome 1963 Gladiator pickup was also a tough workhorse.

drive a stick shift, now could be added to the list of prospective buyers for Jeeps. With an automatic transmission, Jeeps could now appear on the shopping list of mainstream buyers looking for a roomy family wagon.

The company name change to Kaiser Jeep Corporation evidently didn't take place until after the introduction of the new Wagoneers, since early brochures stated the Jeeps were, "Built by—And Only By—Willys Motors, Inc. ...." These catalogs were replaced sometime during the model year, however, by nearly identical ones which identified the company as Kaiser Jeep Corporation. In one stroke, the famous old Willys name was dropped, consigned now to shine only in the pages of history books. Also occurring at that time, the dressier "Deluxe" Wagoneer models were now referred to as "Custom" models.

Gladiator Thriftside used old-fashioned stepside box.

THE INSIDE STORY...

ON THE NEW 'JEEP' WAGONEER!

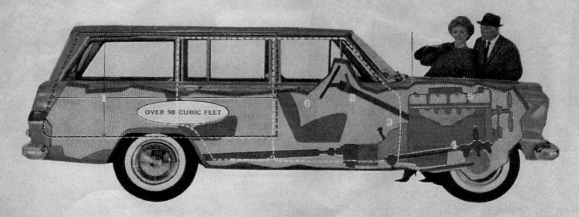

OVER 98 CUBIC FEET

Different? Definitely!

1. Handles Loads Other Wagons Can't! The rear opening is **Higher** (cargo height 3 ft. 5 inches), **Wider** (4 ft. 7 inches), and with tailgate open it has a cargo length of over 9 ft. **2. Automatic Transmission and 4-Wheel Drive.** The Wagoneer is the only station wagon to offer the extra traction and safety of 4-wheel drive, with the extra convenience of optional automatic transmission. **3. Single Selector Knob for 4-Wheel Drive.** Easy to operate. Pull it back when you need 4-wheel drive traction, push it forward when you don't. Unique signal light on the dashboard tells you when you're in 2- or 4-wheel drive. **4. Independent Front Suspension, First in any 4-Wheel Drive Wagon.** Optional independent front suspension with torsion bar action smooths out even the biggest bumps. **5. America's Only Automotive Overhead Camshaft Engine.** The Tornado-OHC engine offers longer engine life, lower maintenance costs, lower gasoline bills than any comparable conventional engine. And it gives you plenty of reserve passing power when you need it. **6. Higher, Wider, Easier-To-Enter Doors.** The Wagoneer's doors swing out a full 82-degrees, making it easy to get in and out. Ample head-room, hip-room, and leg-room assure comfort for six passengers—even on long journeys. **The New 'Jeep' Wagoneer** is the first station wagon ever built to offer the comfort, silence, speed and smoothness of a passenger car—plus the safety and traction of 4-wheel drive. It's the one family wagon you can drive almost anywhere, in almost any weather. The Wagoneer is also available in 2-wheel drive models. **Step in! Size it up! Try it out at your 'Jeep' Dealer's today!**

all new all 'Jeep

KAISER WILLYS MOTORS Willys Motors, world's largest manufacturer of 4-wheel drive vehicles, one of the growing Kaiser Industries.

R5

Advertising gave the "inside story" on 1963 Wagoneer. This ad was produced just prior to the dropping of Willys name in the United States. Note the bottom of ad still lists Willys Motors as the manufacturer.

Tuxedo Park MARK IV

Jeep claimed the Tuxedo Park was a "new idea in sports cars."

Jeep also, in that very busy year, introduced a new line of pickup trucks based on the same new chassis and wearing the same front-end styling as the Wagoneer, though the trucks' front fenders wore more prominent flaring. Called the Jeep Gladiators, the new trucks came in a bewilderingly extensive range of models, in both two- and four-wheel drive. They were offered in two basic series: 120" wheelbase J-200s and 126" wheelbase J-300s, and four body styles, the sleek Townside, the Thriftside—with its narrow bed and flared rear fenders, plus a single rear wheel stake truck, and a dual rear wheel stake truck. Gross Vehicle Weight (GVW) ratings ranged from 4000 lbs. to 8600 lbs. Also available were two panel delivery trucks based on the Wagoneer two-door body, one two-wheel drive model and one four-wheel-drive model. The panel trucks were built without rear side windows, and were equipped with dual rear doors for easily loading and unloading of cargo.

The new line of Jeeps was revolutionary; there is simply no other way to describe them that would adequately summarize their long-term impact on the company and the business itself. The tone of the marketplace was altered, perhaps unnoticeably at first, but irrevocably regardless. Even the public didn't seem to realize it at first, but with the introduction of the Wagoneer, the business itself was making a sea change. The Sport Utility market would gradually become something different over the ensuing years, and companies would have to develop new models to keep pace with it.

The old-style Jeep station wagons and pickups remained in production, but their sales were insignificant when compared to their new brethren. The Wagoneers and Gladiators were the direction Jeep would be taking from here on in. Of course, the CJ-3B, CJ-5, CJ-6, the DJ-3A and Surrey (referred to in the catalog as the Surrey Gala) and the boxy FJ-3A Fleetvan, as well as the rugged FC-150 and FC-170 trucks were still important parts

Evolution

Revolution

The world-famous army 'Jeep' vehicle started it all. Then came the evolutionary changes. Sensible changes. Like more ground clearance. Stronger suspension. Weather proof tops. Fun changes. Like pink and white striped upholstery. Fringed surrey tops. Lively colors. A sports roadster. A station wagon — rugged, durable, designed for work and play.

Then came the 'Jeep' Wagoneer. A revolution! The Wagoneer is so revolutionary, it's hard to recognize your old 'Jeep' friend. It's a station wagon. *And a looker!* You'll be stunned. Slide into that luxurious interior. Beautiful. Comfortable. Visibility unlimited!

Turn the ignition key. You've got an overhead cam engine purring for you. The only one in any American production car. Try that steering. Power.* The brakes. Power again.* The transmission. It's automatic.* Feel that ride. Pure luxury.

And the 'Jeep' heart and spirit are still there. Pull one simple lever and you're in 'Jeep' 4-wheel "Drivepower."† Then there's hardly a hill that can keep you down . . . hardly a mud hole that can bog you down. In fact, there's scarcely any driving situation that can get you down. You're free to go anywhere with the traction to pull you through.

Drop in on your 'Jeep' dealer. He's so enthusiastic about the 'Jeep' Wagoneer he'll be *glad* to give you a test drive. Actually, he gets a kick out of it himself!

*Optional items at slight extra cost.

KAISER Jeep *CORPORATION* Toledo 1, Ohio

†*DRIVEPOWER* is Wagoneer station wagon's new, improved and exclusive 4-wheel drive system.

ALL NEW 'JEEP' WAGONEER

See the Wagoneer demonstrated on "THE GREATEST SHOW ON EARTH," Tuesday nights, ABC-TV Network.

9

This 1964 Jeep ad calls the Wagoneer a "revolution." It was.

of the Jeep line-up. But the emphasis was strongly on the newcomers. As Jeep declared in one early advertisement, "The new Jeep Wagoneer is the first station wagon ever built to offer the comfort, silence, speed, and smoothness of a passenger car—plus the safety and traction of four-wheel-drive. It's the one family wagon you can drive almost anywhere, in almost any weather ." Curiously, that same ad refers to the company as Kaiser Willys Motors. Perhaps at some point, the company had thought about utilizing both names. It's a pity they didn't; perhaps if they had, the Willys' name might still be with us. So 1963 was an important year for Jeep—and a good year for sales. It was going to be tough to come up with an encore, since 1963 was probably the biggest new model launch in Jeep history, but the company was game enough to try.

One can see continuing evidence of a new product philosophy in the 1964 Jeeps. First of all there were the new Tuxedo Park Mark IV versions of the CJ-5 and CJ-6. Jeep called these models, "the new idea in sports cars." The company had called some of its vehicles sports cars in the recent past, namely the two-wheel-drive DJ-3As, but the idea of calling anything with four-wheel-drive a sports car struck

Jeeps were still used by the military. This is an M-38A1.

Jeep testing by the factory was often done outdoors, with emphasis on off-road performance.

Wagoneer panel delivery was a good-looking utility vehicle, and offered large storage area.

Jeep engineers test a Gladiator's hill-climbing ability.

Jeep CJ had many commercial uses.

some people as very strange. But Jeep product planners were thinking of sports cars in a different way from other people. To Jeep, a sports car was an open-bodied vehicle that could take its owner where the fun was—like on the beach, climbing sand dunes or skirting the waters edge, hunting or perhaps rock climbing in the mountains, all while still giving drivers the wind-in the hair experience that was part of the sports car mystique.

But then again, the public had always felt the old Jeepster was a sports car (or maybe a sporty car), and people had been asking for a return of the Jeepster almost from the moment it went out of production. Reportedly, at some point a search of the factory was made in an attempt to locate the tooling for the old Jeepster. Whether or not that's true, the fact is the tooling was gone and however sentimental people might feel about the Jeepster, no one was likely to finance replacement tooling for it.

The Tuxedo Parks were equipped with the standard flathead four-cylinder engine—Jeep didn't have any sort of a high performance engine it could offer, since the OHC six wouldn't fit. But Tuxedo Park trim was much more lavish than any previous small Jeep, including the Surrey. Tuxedo

Parks came with chrome front bumper, chromed hood latches, mirrors and taillight housings, a chrome passenger assist handle, and seat belts all as standard equipment. Six exterior/interior color combinations were available, with convertible tops in matching or harmonizing colors. Optionally available were padded wheel house cushions, chrome wheel covers, spare tire cover, and floor mats. The Tuxedo Parks represented Jeeps first effort to dress up its smallest four-wheel-drive product to appeal to a broader range of buyers. According to Jeep, the little Tuxedo Park allowed buyers to, "Go Where the Fun is ... Have More Fun Going!"

The old Jeep station wagons and pickups returned yet again, and were again basically the same as in previous years, though some models were pruned from the line. A new version of the 230-cid OHC six, with a lowered compression ratio that allowed it to handle low-grade fuel without pinging, was now available. The FC pickups and FJ step vans were also still offered.

No one was expecting any great differences in the Wagoneer line, so they weren't disappointed with the 1964 models. Appearance was nearly identical, and the only news in the drive train de-

(Top) The 1948 Willys station wagon, the fore-runner of today's Sport Utility Vehicles, has classic good looks.

(Right) In the 1950s, Willys bragged of its full line of light-duty trucks.

.Each a Leader in its Field

4-Wheel-Drive Willys Station Wagon . . . only passenger car with all-wheel drive . . . for travel on or off the road in all weather.

4-Wheel-Drive Willys Truck . . . the "go-any-where" truck that gets through mud and snow when ordinary trucks cannot.

Willys Sedan Delivery . . . with the popular and economical *Hurricane 4* Engine for low-cost de-livery. Available with 2 or 4 wheel drive.

Universal Jeep . . . 4 wheel drive, all-purpose workhorse for farm and industry . . . world-famed for ruggedness, versatility.

In Venezuela and Vermont . . . Iran and Indiana . . . Ceylon and California . . . throughout the world, Willys cars and utility vehicles are renowned for modern functional design, for dependable quality and low-cost operation. The varied vehicles pic-tured here—each outstanding in its field—are a proud climax of our first half-century of pioneering in better transportation for work and pleasure.

Military Jeep . . . new, improved model with *Hurricane 4* Engine . . . built by Willys for the armed services.

NAME IN AUTOMOBILES SINCE 1903

(Left) A 1954 CJ-5 shows that early models were equipped with two-piece windshield, soon switched to a one-piece.

(Bottom) The 1957 Jeep FC truck series had unusual styling.

The all NEW 4-Wheel Drive Truck

TURNPIKE PERFORMANCE *Plus* OFF-ROAD TRACTION

Jeep DISPATCHER
MODEL DJ-3A

(Left)
The 1959 Jeep
DJ-3A Dispatcher was
a sturdy, low-cost delivery
vehicle, and came only with
two-wheel-drive.

(Below) Calling James Garner! The
1959 Jeep Maverick was aimed at
suburban dwellers, was well-priced
and attractive.

(Bottom) When the Jeep Surrey Gala
came out in 1959, it was the bright-
est, flashiest Jeep ever made.

$1995.00
ADVERTISED DELIVERED PRICE
Transportation, optional equipment,
state and local taxes are extra

A "MAVERICK SPECIAL"

the new 'Jeep' Station Wagon

Meet America's most useful new vehicle—it's a "Maverick Special," the new 'Jeep' Station Wagon with the built-in budget—costs less to buy, tion wagon with the built-in budget—costs less to buy, less to own and operate, yet has higher *resale* value. You still get 'Jeep' performance, but at a price no other American-built station wagon can match.

The new 'Jeep' Station Wagon unites functional styling and convenience with rugged utility . . . has a new spring suspension system, spacious interiors combined with comfortable seating. Powered by the world-famous 'Jeep' 4-cylinder F-Head "Hurricane" engine. See reverse side for feature details and specifications.

(Top) A Jeep Surrey in its natural setting—waiting at the airport to pick up vacation travelers.

(Middle) Another Jeep Dispatcher, this one served the West Haven Pharmacy.

(Right) Nice advertisement for the all-new 1963 Wagoneer. This is an early ad-note as it still lists the manufacturer as Willys Motors.

meet a history maker...

ALL NEW

ALL 'JEEP'

'JEEP' WAGONEER

Different? Definitely!

The new 'Jeep' Wagoneer is the first station wagon ever built to offer the comfort, silence, speed and smoothness of a passenger car—plus the safety and traction of 4-wheel drive.

The Wagoneer is the one family wagon you can drive almost anywhere, in almost any kind of weather.

It's the first and only 4-wheel drive wagon with optional automatic transmission and independent front suspension.

The 'Jeep' Wagoneer features the power and economy of America's first and only automotive overhead camshaft engine, the Tornado-OHC.

It has the most usable cargo space...both high and wide. It's also available in 2-wheel drive models. Step in. Size it up. Try it out at your 'Jeep' Dealer's today!

Willys Motors, world's largest manufacturer of 4-wheel drive vehicles, one of the growing Kaiser Industries.

(Left) Along with the new Wagoneer came the all-new Gladiator pickup. Note the simple, yet elegant style of grille and hood.

(Below) The Jeep CJ-3 B was an excellent choice for exploring caverns!

(Bottom) Jeep built a number of these two-wheel-drive DJ-5 Dispatchers for the Postal Service.

(Right)
Early 1965 Wagoneer models combined the classic upright grille with the exciting new Vigilante V-8 engine (bought from American Motors). Later in 1965, Wagoneers were given a full width grille.

(Bottom Left) The Jeep Tuxedo Park debuted in 1965. Although they sold poorly, they began a trend towards more sporty features in the smaller Jeep line.

(Bottom Right) The Jeep pickup, always a popular seller in Brazil, had styling unique to that market. This is a 1968 model.

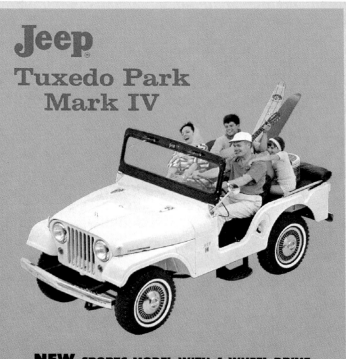

Jeep
Tuxedo Park
Mark IV

NEW SPORTS MODEL WITH 4-WHEEL DRIVE AND 160 HORSEPOWER V-6 ENGINE OPTION

brasileiro nato

O Pick-up "Jeep" nasceu aqui. Foi desenhado e construído por brasileiros, para as condições do Brasil. Tem um motor com a potência exata para o seu trabalho. E carroçaria reforçada, chassi de 5 travessas, caçamba de aço. É o nosso veículo (provado) de entregas urbanas. Ainda mais econômico na operação, o Pick-up "Jeep" tração em 2 rodas custa muito menos que o seu mais próximo concorrente, como resultado do grande volume de produção dos veículos "Jeep". Procure um nosso Concessionário. Marque a hora. E êle irá buscar sua carga, para um transporte experimental grátis. V. tem a prova prática de tudo o que lhe oferece o Pick-up "JEEP".

PICK-UP **Jeep** WILLYS
um produto
veículos de alta qualidade

(Top) The 1967 Jeepster series included these Commando models (l-to-r): Commando Roadster with optional soft top, Commando Roadster with no top, and Commando station wagon.

(Middle) Top of the new Jeepster series was this Jeepster Convertible.

(Bottom) This factory photo is labeled 1969 Super Wagoneer, one of the last of that model built. The picture's setting tells a lot about what the expected market was—wealthy folks who could afford its lofty price tag.

The 'Jeep' Renegade

Here's the ultimate in a rugged off-road
4WD racing machine, possibly the fastest 4WD production
vehicle in the country. It's fast looking, too,
with the special accessory racing stripe and rollbar;
also available with ammeter and electric oil gauge.
Those 8" wheels with 6.70 4-ply "Polyglas" tires give
you the help you need to scramble through the real
tough spots. Looks are backed up with
performance: under the hood is a 160 h.p. Dauntless V-6 engine
package that will muscle you to the lead.
'Jeep' Renegade I — See it at your 'Jeep' dealer. Hurry,
this is a limited production model.

(Left) It is extremely rare to find an advertisement for the limited production 1970 Renegade—and rarer still to find one in color.

(Bottom Left) Holy Toledo! proclaims this advertisement for the Jeepster Convertible— a play on the home of Jeep's main plant in Ohio.

(Bottom Right) This scene from a 1971 Jeep sales brochure captures the essence of the Jeep experience.

Holy Toledo. What a car!
Drives smooth. Plays rough!

Toledo did it...built 'Jeep' ruggedness into a "go anywhere" sports car! Look at those jaunty lines and bucket seats. And that continental spare. It's something else! Make it as sporty as you like. Add hot, new V-6 with automatic transmission; sports console; automatic top; power brakes; even air-conditioning!

Teamed up with these features is the adventure and safety of 'Jeep' 4-wheel drive. Flip a lever—at any speed —and you've got twice the traction,

twice the action going for you. Leave the roads behind. Prowl places no other sportscar would dare go!

Besides the 'Jeepster' Convertible, there's a whole new family of rugged 'Jeepster Commando' models to choose from. Station wagon. Roadster. Pick-up. All in a wide choice of colors. All racy... rugged...rarin' to go!

Smooth ride! Bold performance? You've got

to drive it to believe it! See your 'Jeep' dealer. Check the Yellow Pages.

KAISER Jeep CORPORATION

'Jeepster' Family of fun cars

When Answering Advertisements, Mention MECHANIX ILLUSTRATED

'Jeep'
4-WHEEL DRIVE
Universal
the 2-car car

(Top) Perhaps the rarest of Jeeps, the 1971 Hurst Jeepster. This particular vehicle is a remarkably clean unrestored original that is still in the family of the original owners.

(Above) The 1973 Jeep Wagoneer looked similar to the 1963 Jeep Wagoneer.

(Left) Not too many 1972 Jeep Renegades were built, and they are scarce today.

(Top) The 1975 Jeep pickup offered fancy two-tone paint and an optional travel cap for the bed.

(Bottom) The 1977 Jeep Golden Eagle was an extremely flamboyant package, and proved to be popular with buyers.

1977 Jeep

(Below)
This Jeepney, built in the Philippines for taxi use, was owned by Roy D. Chapin, chairman of American Motors. Philippine Jeepneys are known for their heavy use of custom paint and ornamentation. It is shown at a 1974 auto show.

(Above) The 1978 Wagoneer Limited was the most luxurious four wheeler on the market, and achieved instant success.

(Right) Built in Venezuela, the Llanero was basically a Jeep CJ-7 with a special hardtop and two side-facing rear seats.

(Left) In 1982, Jeep offered these two unique vehicles in overseas markets, but not in the United States. The yellow vehicle is a CJ-10 pickup, the red vehicle is a CJ-8 World Cab.

(Right) The 1982 Jeep pickup was as good-looking as a truck could be.

Built only in 1980, in limited quantities, the Jeep CJ-7 and Cherokee "Golden Hawks" looked similar to the Golden Eagle package introduced earlier, and were a special value model.

(Left) The 1987 Jeep Comanche was attractive, and included a low-price two-wheel-drive model.

(Right) The 1984 Jeep CJ-7 offered a value package that included special wheels and bigger tires, and listed at $8,813.

1984 JEEP CJ-7 SPECIAL VALUE PACKAGE

(Right) The experimental Jeep JJ, for world markets, would have included this small open vehicle.

(Left) Jeep Ecco was a concept of what a future small Jeep might look like.

(Below) The JJ program was studied in the late 1980s, but was dropped by late 1990. It would have included this attractive small Jeep wagon.

Artist concept of what the redesigned 1997 Jeep would look like.

(Left) This 1997 Jeep Dakar concept illustrated what a four-door hard-top Wrangler would look like. According to sources, this vehicle may go into production in the future.

(Right) The Jeep Icon concept also debuted in 1997, and showed a different approach to future Jeep styling.

The 1998 Jeepster concept retained the 'feel' of classic Jeep styling.

King of the Hill—the 1998 Wrangler.

The Power and the Glory—Jeep's stunning 1998 Grand Cherokee 5.9 Limited.

Jeep Grand Cherokee 5.9 Limited in Bright Platinum.

The 1998 Cherokee is still a top-selling SUV.

Jeep Cherokee Sport in Black.

Rugged CJ-5 was a favorite of sportsmen.

CJ was practical as well as fun.

partment was the addition of the low compression OHC engine to the option list. More interesting was the newly released option of air conditioning for the senior Jeeps, the Wagoneer and Gladiator, another sign that things were changing in the four-wheel-drive market.

There was bigger news for the company, however. In a brilliant move, Kaiser Jeep acquired from Studebaker its modern plant on Chippewa Avenue in South Bend, Indiana. Studebaker had announced, in December 1963, that it was moving automobile production to Canada and would no

longer assemble cars in the United States. As part of that decision, the company felt it should no longer build military vehicles either. A novation agreement was signed for Kaiser Jeep to assume an $81 million production contract for 9,359 5-ton tactical trucks for the U.S. Army.

The effect this had on the company was far-reaching, as will be seen. Its immediate consequences, though, was to put Jeep into the medium-duty tactical truck business while at the same time eliminating one of Jeeps big competitors for that business. In May of 1964, the company successful-

Jeep products being tested by factory personnel are lined up just prior to going off-road test area.

ly bid on a multi-year contract for the M44 2-1/2 ton military 6X6 truck, through which it assembled a total of 27,000 units.

There were some big changes in 1965. Several Jeep models went out of production, including Fleetvans, FC-150, FC-170, DJ-3A and the CJ-3B. Why the CJ-3B had remained so long in Jeep's domestic line-up is a bit puzzling, since it offered no real advantages over the vastly more comfortable CJ-5 other than a slightly lower price. From now on the CJ-5 and CJ-6 would be Jeep's sole small four-wheel-drive offerings. Also, with the end of DJ-3A production came the end of the Jeep Surrey model as well.

But as usual, Jeep had new models to introduce. First was a new vehicle to replace the DJ-3A. Built on a two-wheel-drive version of the CJ-5 chassis, the new model was called, rightly enough, the DJ-5. The DJ-5 was a better vehicle than the DJ-3A, larger, smoother-riding and better styled. In addition, a longer wheelbase version, called the DJ-6, was also available and, as one would figure, was a two-wheel-drive version of the CJ-6 model.

The old Jeep pickups and wagons returned for one last model year. They looked very outdated by now, outclassed by the Wagoneers and Gladiators, as well as International's popular Scout. If anyone still had an emotional attachment for the old models, 1965 would be the last time they could indulge themselves.

The Wagoneer and Gladiator lines were improved again, this time by the mid-year addition of V-8 power to the option list. Jeep, not wanting to spend the huge sum of money it would cost to develop its own engine, chose instead to purchase appropriate units from a dependable supplier, American Motors Corporation. The engine was AMC's largest, a cast-iron 327-cid, 250-horsepower unit with 2 barrel carburetor, from its Rambler Ambassador. Jeep called its new engine offering the "Vigilante," and Wagoneers with V-8 power boasted greater smoothness, better acceleration, and a higher top speed than their six-cylinder stable mates.

There were new discussions with American Motors around this time regarding the possibility

Right-hand drive Jeeps were available for special uses, such as postal delivery or parking patrol.

of AMC purchasing Kaiser Jeep. However, this didn't indicate a change of heart by AMC management. What was different now was that George Romney was no longer in charge at AMC—he had left earlier to make a successful run for governor of Michigan. His replacement as AMC president was Roy Abernethy, who, it will be recalled, had earlier worked as Sales VP for Kaiser Willys. AMC vice president Roy D. Chapin Jr. was still every bit as enthusiastic about buying Jeep as he had been years before, and he convinced Abernethy to meet with the Kaiser people to explore the idea. But upon hearing Kaiser's price for Jeep, Abernethy balked. He told the Kaiser executives, "There is no way we can raise that kind of money." Despite an offer made by one Kaiser VP to help AMC find adequate financing, Abernethy chose to pass on the deal.

The synergy created by Kaiser Jeep's entry into expanded production of tactical wheeled vehicles could be seen in the introduction of two new military trucks, the M676 Cargo truck, a diesel-powered vehicle based on the retired FC-170 chassis, and the M715 Cargo Truck, which can most accurately be described as a military version of the Gladiator chassis and body. With the conflict growing in Vietnam, the U.S. Army was eager to upgrade its military truck fleet, and Jeep was in an ideal position to take advantage of the increased demand.

For 1966, Wagoneer received attention from the product planners. The biggest appearance change was in the front-end styling, which went into production in mid 1965. The old upright grille was replaced by a fine new full-width grille that

Wagoneer for 1966 received a handsome new grille.

Super Wagoneer was the most luxurious four-wheeler on the market and set new standards for SUVs.

Hold treacherous curves with twice the "grip" in a 'Jeep' Wagoneer.

Just flip one simple lever for the safety of 'Jeep' 4-wheel drive.

To drive on sharp, slippery curves like this...you need more than driving skill. You need the extra control and confidence that a 'Jeep' Wagoneer with 4-wheel drive can give you. Flip one simple lever— at any speed. You're in 'Jeep' 4-wheel drive. You've got twice the grip on curves. Twice the control in bad weather. Twice the confidence you get with ordinary family wagons. You're less likely to jam on your brakes, far less likely to skid. And you

*TRADEMARK GENERAL MOTORS CORPORATION

A UNIQUE COMBINATION OF LUXURY AND SAFETY.
Your Wagoneer is available with comforts like carpeting, foam-filled seats... and a standard safety package that includes dual brake system, padded dash, 4-way warning flashers, many others...plus the unique safety of 'Jeep' 4-wheel drive.

won't worry about getting stuck in mud or snow. Plus, you've got the extra confidence of knowing that your Wagoneer's built rugged—the 'Jeep' way. Your Wagoneer has the options you expect: V-8 engine or Hi-Torque 6, Turbo Hydra-Matic* automatic transmission, power steering, power brakes, even air conditioning... plus the safety of 'Jeep' 4-wheel drive. Test drive a 'Jeep' Wagoneer today!

KAISER Jeep CORPORATION
TOLEDO 1, OHIO

You've got to drive it to believe it. See your 'Jeep' dealer. Check the Yellow Pages.

Clever advertisement tells it all. Note the bent guardrail in the foreground.

lent the Wagoneer a much more modern, stylish look.

A bold new model also debuted. Called the Super Wagoneer, it was an effort to cash in on the rapidly increasing prestige of four-wheel-drive ownership. Super Wagoneers were the most elegant Jeeps that had ever been seen, including as standard equipment just about every comfort and convenience feature that man could devise. Standard features included a special 4bbl version of the Vigilante V-8 that produced 270-hp; air conditioning, Turbo Hydra-Matic transmission, power steering, power brakes, electric powered tailgate window, and tilt steering wheel. Exterior features included a full-length antique-gold trim panel with a contrasting strip that ran underneath it, gold trim panel covering the tailgate, vinyl covered roof, standard roof rack, "mag" style wheel covers, whitewall tires, and unique fender top ornaments. Inside the Super Wagoneer was plush door panel trim, fancy carpeting, front bucket seats with a 'sports' console, and an acoustic headliner. Tinted glass and a standard transistor radio completed the package.

The Super Wagoneer represented, said Jeep, "... an epoch in station wagon excellence. Here is a grandly conceived harmony of beauty and performance; a union of all the usual (and not so usual) features you appreciate in other fine cars...provided for the first time with four-wheel-drive...." Even more than that, the Super Wagoneer was a statement; an indication that Jeep realized and understood something of the direction that sport utility wagons were heading for, a sign post for other companies to follow if they dared to. There were many scoffers, because the idea of an expensive, luxury four-wheel-drive wagon was just too far-out for most people.

Although the Gladiators were still based on the same senior line chassis as the Wagoneers the pickup trucks did not receive the new front-end styling, remaining instead with the same upright grille they wore when first announced. Jeep was by now consciously trying to separate the two lines in the public's mind.

With the dropping of the old-style wagons and pickups, the Wagoneer became the sole station wagon offered by Kaiser Jeep, and the Gladiator became the sole pickup entry. This was a good move for Jeep, since it placed emphasis on its most modern products.

There was great and welcome news for CJ enthusiasts in 1966. Finally responding to requests for more power, Kaiser Jeep copied a trick that hot rodders had already been doing for a couple years. Jeep engineers found it was possible to fit the compact, lightweight Buick V-6 engine under the hood of the CJ-5, allowing the company to finally offer a real performance engine option on its smallest product. The engine, which Jeep called the Dauntless V-6, displaced 225-cid and offered 155-hp, turning the rugged little CJ into a hot little performer. Owners bragged of doing four-wheel "burnout's" and being able to power their way up just about any mountain with ease. Magazines claimed a 90-mph top speed was attainable (though only for the strong of heart we would guess). After Buick had decided it no longer needed the V-6, Kaiser Jeep bought the engine assembly line and made the engine its own.

Ford Motor Company introduced a new competitor for Jeep when it announced its all-new Bronco for 1966. Offered in roadster, soft-top and station wagon models, like the similar-looking International Scout, the Bronco, with the might of Ford's huge dealer force behind it, had the potential to steal a substantial number of sales from Jeep. Clearly, there would have to be a response from Jeep sometime soon.

In 1967, there came a flurry of actions by the company. Important news was that two of its big overseas subsidiaries were sold by Kaiser Jeep. One of the ventures, Industrias Kaiser Argentina (IKA), which had long been an assembler of Jeep vehicles, and had even built the old Kaiser senior line after it had failed in America, was sold off to French automaker Renault. One of the more interesting vehicles IKA assembled in its plant was a Renault-badged Rambler American equipped with the Willys' six-cylinder OHC engine, a truly international car if ever there was one. Jeep retained an affiliation with IKA and continued to profit by licensing fees and sales of Jeep components.

Also sold was the hugely successful Willys Do Brazil, which boasted production of over 60,000 vehicles in the previous year, including a re-styled and updated version of the Aero Willys' car. The purchaser of the Brazilian operations was Ford Motor Company, which received rights to the Jeep name in Brazil, though it was prohibited from using it on any vehicles outside that country. After a time, the Brazilian products came to be known as "Ford Jeeps."

Happy combo! Racy and rugged. Holy Toledo, what a car!

Leave ordinary, garden-variety driving behind...in this 'Jeepster' Convertible. The rugged rascal only Toledo could build—because that's where 'Jeep' ruggedness comes from.

Settle back in those bucket seats. Take the wheel. And go!

You'll be noticed...thanks to snazzy features like that continental spare. Now, hit the highway and open 'er up! What a smooth performer...specially if you choose that hot new V-6 with automatic transmission.

Then flip one lever...you're in 'Jeep' 4-wheel drive! You've got excitement ...and safety, too...you just won't find with ordinary sports cars. What's your idea of fun? This baby will get you there!

Or, maybe you'd rather choose from the 'Jeepster Commando' models. Roadster. Station wagon. And the sportiest pick-up ever!

The 'Jeepster' family. It's tough. Terrific! You've

got to drive it to believe it! See your 'Jeep' dealer. Check the Yellow Pages.
KAISER Jeep CORPORATION TOLEDO, OHIO 43601

'Jeepster'®
Family of fun cars

A LIMITED NUMBER OF FRANCHISES ARE AVAILABLE IN SELECTED AREAS. IF YOU ARE INTERESTED, WRITE TO: DEALER DEVELOPMENT MANAGER, KAISER Jeep CORPORATION, TOLEDO, OHIO 43601

Commando ad showcases special convertible model as well as one of Jeep slogans: Holy Toledo!—a reference to the home of Jeep's main plant.

Jeep line undergoes testing in 1966. Note the two-door Wagoneer in background has the old-style grille, while the four-door Wagoneer has the newer style. Evidently this photo was taken around the time of the changeover to the new style.

Commando roadster could be ordered with a removable soft top.

In America, the Wagoneer and Gladiator lines returned for 1967 with only minimal changes. The OHC six-cylinder engine was dropped reportedly due to concerns about noise, reliability and cost, and was replaced by an American Motors engine, the sturdy, quiet and silky-smooth 232-cid six. The AMC 327-cid V-8 remained available as an option. There was likewise little new in the CJ and DJ series, nor was much expected since the V-6 engine had been added earlier, and that seemed to be big enough news to tide folks over for quite a while.

The biggest news for 1967 was the announcement of a completely new line of Jeep vehicles, the Jeepster series. The new Jeeps came partly in answer to continued requests from long-time Jeep customers for a return of the classic Willys' Jeepster, but mostly in reply to the growing threat from the International Scout and Ford Bronco. The Jeepsters were certainly a measured response.

Kaiser Jeep had to invest a fair amount of money in bringing out the new Jeeps. That old story that a search was made to try to locate the original Willys' Jeepster tooling somehow doesn't ring true, but even more curious is the commonly held notion that the tooling *was* found and that the new Jeepster was based on the chassis and body of the old, though somewhat modified. Regardless of how many times that story has been seen in print, rest assured that the old tooling was not used for the new Jeepster. A simple comparison of the two shows that the frames, bodies, engines, transmissions, interior, tops and related hardware are different. Just as a 1968 Chevy Malibu shares no parts with a 1998 Malibu, the two Jeepsters were related in name only.

Even the concepts were different. The Willys Jeepster was meant to be a sporty phaeton, a different sort of car, but still a car nonetheless. The Kaiser Jeep Jeepster was meant to be an altogether different type of machine—a sports utility vehicle. To illustrate a major difference, consider that the Willys Jeepster had been offered only in two-wheel-drive, like any other car of its era. In contrast, the new Jeepsters came only as four-wheel drive vehicles—no two-wheel-drive models were offered because this meant to be a sports vehicle for both on- and off- road.

Having stated the above, however, it should be noted that the new Jeepster's styling was most certainly meant to be reminiscent of the old. Built on the 101" wheelbase chassis of the CJ-6, the new Jeepster had its own unique body. Front fenders appear to have been modified CJ units, but virtually everything else was completely new. The hood was wider than the CJ models and, in combination with the similar yet wider grille and the gently rounded fenders, carried a distinct family resemblance to the CJ line. The well-shaped body lines cleverly concealed the vehicle's CJ-6 origins. The Jeepster was meant to be a more civilized small Jeep, sort of in-between the rugged CJ's and the plush Wagoneers. It's believed the Jeepster's styling was created by Kaiser Jeep stylist James Anger, whom many believe also had considerable input on the original 1963 Wagoneer design, though he is not generally credited for it.

The Jeepster came in two series. Jeepster Commandos could be had as an open roadster, a roadster with soft top, a hardtop station wagon, a soft top pickup and a hardtop pickup. Non-optioned Commando roadsters were stark; front bucket seats were standard, but the rear seat was optional, as was carpeting, radio, wheel covers, power brakes etc. The standard engine was the Hurricane Four, a terribly under-powered mill for a supposedly sporty car. But the powerful V-6, now rated at 160-hp, could be ordered, and with it GM's wonderful Hydra-Matic transmission. With the V-6/automatic combination, one got a smooth, powerful Jeep that looked good and felt sporty to drive. Because of its long wheelbase, the Jeepster rode very well; its steering was unassisted and rather slow, but not excessively heavy. Jeepsters came with standard steel doors that had vent wings and roll down windows—things a CJ owner would consider real luxuries.

Jeepster Commandos could be outfitted for just about any job. With a steel roof and standard rear seat, the station wagon was an ideal family car/hunting car, a much better compromise vehicle for the family than a CJ. Equipped as a pickup truck the Jeepster Commando could work in tight places, yet carry a fair amount of cargo. As a roadster or soft-top, it offered a better ride and more interior room than a CJ, while still providing the same open air experience.

A separate model in the Jeepster series was called simply the "Jeepster Convertible." It was not a part of the Commando line of Jeepsters, but a separate sports model. This was a high-line version, trimmed and equipped for the person who wanted the ultimate Jeepster or who counted themselves

For 1968, a new low-price convertible model was added to Commando line.

among the persons calling for a return of the "classic" Jeepster. The standard paint scheme aped the Willys' model, with its main body color set off by a contrasting color contained in a fancy chrome molding that began at the cowl, ran along the body sides a few inches below the top of the door skin, and wrapped around the back end, very similar to the old Willys. The Jeepster came with standard front bucket and rear bench seating, a manually operated convertible top with glass rear window, (as distinct from the balky removable soft tops used on the Jeepster roadsters and also on the CJ's), Continental spare tire with cover, color coordinated front and rear floor mats and interior trim, chrome-plated bumpers, hood latches and hood hinges, and hub caps. A Custom trim package added, among other things, deluxe upholstery, thick pile carpeting, wheel trim rings, and a power-operated top with boot. Unlike the Willys, however, the new Jeepster came with roll up windows and, as mentioned, four-wheel-drive.

Jeep launched the new Jeepster with a very large advertising campaign and managed to generate a great deal of interest. The motor press was especially attracted to the new Jeep. "Sports car, off-highway utility vehicle; vacation-trip carryall—the 'Jeepster' is all these things" wrote Jim Dunne in *Popular Science*. Dave Epperson, writing in *Car*

Life, stated "The 'Jeepster' Sports convertible seemed eminently roadable and off-roadable." Alex Markovich, writing in *Popular Mechanics*, said, "One thing's for sure. This car will take you where the action is."

The Jeepster was positioned right between the CJ and the Wagoneer, like the Scout and Bronco were. It was the most car-like small Jeep yet, and it was a good looking machine as well. With a big-money advertising kick-off and a generally positive reaction from the press, the Jeepster enjoyed decent first-year sales.

One other event taking place in 1967, missed by most of the people who were watching Jeep back then and even missed by many historians since, was the formation of a new special division within the company devoted to the research, development and production of Government vehicles. Named the Defense and Government Products Division, it was fated to evolve into a separate entity someday, and become famous on its own. In 1967, however, it's formation was a strong indication of how significant military sales had become to Kaiser Jeep. They were of critical importance to the profitability of Jeep operations, and counted for an inordinate (and some might argue unhealthy) percentage of Jeep's annual production.

Jeepster convertible was fancier, more expensive, than Commando convertible.

Taken altogether, 1967 was a great year for Jeep. The company reported record sales of $470,731,000 and record operating profits of $14,530,000. But an area of genuine concern was that sales to the government totaled $302,103,000, or in other words 64% of dollar volume. Another concern was that unit sales of non-government-destined Jeeps totaled only 61,300 worldwide. It all pointed up to the fact that despite all the new prod- ucts launched since 1963, Kaiser Jeep was simply not growing in the civilian market— it was highly dependent on government sales.

The year after a major new product launch usu- ally held little new in the way of innovations or product improvements at Jeep and 1968 didn't change that pattern. A low-priced Commando con- vertible was added to the Jeepster line. It offered Jeepster buyers a vehicle with a real convertible top (as opposed to the removable soft-top available on the roadster), at a price tag that was lower than the full-dress Jeepster convertible. The Commando's top itself was different from the Jeepster Sports Convertible; however, the Commando's top was full length, since the Commando lacked the abbre- viated "trunk" seen on the Jeepster.

The company dropped the two-wheel-drive models of the Wagoneer, forsaking the two-wheel- drive wagon market for the time being (which, as things worked out, was quite a while). A few mod- els were trimmed from the Gladiator series, too. But the Wagoneer line gained a new Custom V-8 series to fit in between the basic Wagoneers and the full-boat Super Wagoneer. Sometime during the year the AMC 327-cid 2 bbl. engine used in the non-Super Wagoneers was replaced by a 230-hp

Jeep XJ001 was a fiberglass-bodied one-of-a-kind experimental Jeep sports car, had a V-8 engine and four-wheel drive.

The Great Jeep Escape vehicles for 1969 included this unusual CJ with its own house trailer.

350-cid V-8 purchased from Buick. The Super continued to use the 270-hp AMC engine to the end of the season.

For the second year in-a-row, Kaiser Jeep Corporation reported record high sales and operating profits. Sales totaled $476,983,000, up over $6 million from the previous year, and profits came to $15,016,000, up $486,000 from 1967. The company explained that the record profits for the two years were due to the "High-volume pro-duction of military vehicles...." The main plant for military vehicle production was the ex-Studebaker factory in South Bend, but for 1967 and 1968 production had been augmented by the manufacturing of 1-1/4 ton trucks (M715 cargo trucks and M725 ambulances) in the main Jeep plant at Toledo, Ohio. The company also revealed that since buying the Studebaker plant in 1964 it had received an astounding $1 billion in government contracts for military trucks. Dollar sales to the

An elegant trailer deserves an elegant tow vehicle--and Jeep Wagoneer was the best there was.

U.S. Government were down slightly to $297.5 million for 1968, accounting for 62% of sales volume.

The company also reported that although shipments of Gladiators and Wagoneers were up in 1968, Jeepster sales had fallen, resulting in an overall decline of 3% for Jeep retail sales in America. The company explained that Jeepster sales were down in comparison to the high levels of 1967, which they further explained, was due to the special marketing effort that accompanied their introduction. However, the falling Jeepster sales reflected two more simple truths—the product hadn't been as well received by the market as Jeep might have wished—and Kaiser Jeep had become more a military supplier than a retail-oriented manufacturer. The company even went so far as to warn stockholders that, "The profitability of Kaiser Jeep Corporation in 1969 will be dependent on economies being effected at Toledo and continued high-volume military production at the South Bend plant."

Another concern, if anyone cared to think further about it, was that nearly one third of Kaiser Jeep's aforementioned profit had come as royalties on Jeep vehicles produced and sold overseas under license agreements. While royalties are not in themselves a bad thing, in Jeep's case it can possi-

bly be interpreted as an indication of complacency or stagnation. Jeep was not expanding its own business overseas as much as it should have, despite the potential indicated by healthy royalties. Jeeps that year were being produced in thirty-two foreign countries.

Kaiser Jeep had some plans for the future, however. It seemed to be searching for a product niche or several niches, where it could finally expand its presence in the retail market. For the final year of the sixties, there would be new models aimed at very specific market areas.

In the styling studio, Jeep designers were hard at work on a new concept in four wheeling, a true sports car. Dubbed the XJ001, it might be considered Jeep's Corvette, because surprisingly enough it was a fiberglass-bodied two-seater equipped with a potent V-8 engine, stick shift, bucket seats and tachometer. Unlike any Jeep that had ever come before (or since, for that matter), it wouldn't be ready for public scrutiny for another year.

For 1969, Jeep took aim at the outdoorsman, a reliable prospect it had successfully targeted many times before. For 1969 however, there was going to be a new wrinkle in Jeep's approach to hunters, fishermen, and the like. Jeep wanted to expand its appeal and to do so it would attempt to get the prospect's spouse interested in the great outdoors. After all, if the wife (and in that decade the spouse of an outdoorsperson was more likely to be a wife than a husband) became interested in camping, fishing and hunting, she was more likely to okay the purchase of a vehicle that would enhance those pastimes—like a Jeep, for instance. And what better way to win the wife over to Jeep, than by finding a way for her to bring many of the comforts of home along with the family when they traveled?

Thus were born the so-called "Great Jeep Escape" recreational vehicles. Of these, there were three. First and most intriguing was the Jeep Camper for the CJ-5. The Camper was a completely self-contained two-wheeled unit designed to be fastened to the back of a CJ-5. Able to sleep four, the camper featured a table with two bench seats (which pulled out to make a bed), a wardrobe, toilet, three burner stove, small sink, an ice box, and another bed in the area over the Jeep's cab. More comfortable accommodations could usually be had in the Jeep Gladiator with a Camper that slid into its bed. There were a wide variety of campers available though, including small, low

Jeepster Commando was offered in several models for 1969.

'Jeepster' Commando Convertible

'Jeepster' Commando Convertible

'Jeepster' Commando Roadster

profile caps that would keep two fishermen warm and dry, though without offering any real interior comforts aside from an overhead light, sliding windows and space for two sleeping bags. But going further up the product range led to large fancy units with deluxe interiors boasting full stand-up height inside. There was even an inexpensive soft-top enclosure to turn the pickup into the lowest-cost "camper" imaginable.

But the class act of Jeep's recreational fleet was the Wagoneer towing a vacation travel trailer. Used in this way, the Wagoneer could literally bring all the comforts of home and then be unhooked at the campsite and used for into-town transportation.

This historic vehicle, called the "462," began a trend to high-performance Jeep CJs

Jeeps coming down the assembly line in Toledo. Note the second CJ in line has a two-piece windshield; it may be an export model.

Jeep had other product news for 1969, aside from the campers. The company took a big step when it further pruned the Wagoneer line by discontinuing the two-door models. It wasn't a great loss, since the four-door models had always been much more popular. The end of the two-door Wagoneer also meant the end of the panel delivery truck too, as might be expected. The Super Wagoneer was phased out of production that Fall, evidently after a small run of 1969 models were produced, so the Custom Wagoneer was now the top of the line.

There were no substantial changes in the Jeepster or Jeepster Commando series for 1969. The Jeep Universal (CJ-5/CJ-6) series likewise was returned mostly unchanged, save for one very significant model. What was significant about the new CJ model was it's targeted audience. Instead of being a high-roller like the Super Wagoneer, or a dressed-up "family" Jeep like the Tuxedo Park (which were dropped), or even a sporty retro-look beach cruiser like the Jeepster, the new limited production Jeep "462" was aimed squarely at off-road racing enthusiasts. It was equipped with the 'Dauntless' V-6 engine, a swing-out spare tire carrier, big (for the time) Polyglas tubeless tires, electric ammeter and oil gauges, and full wheel covers. To emphasize its sports nature, it came fitted with a roll bar, an unusual feature back then. Although it looks tame today, in its time the '462' was considered a hairy machine. The '462' apparently didn't sell in large numbers but it was very well received and gave Jeep an indication that perhaps sports-oriented Jeeps were the wave of the future. Although not successful in the conventional way of thinking, the '462' is significant because it led the way to what would be the most exciting Jeep of the coming decade.

But the future was getting complicated for Jeep. Out in Detroit, Roy D. Chapin Jr., by now Chairman of American Motors Corporation, was still interested in folding Jeep into his struggling car firm. Chapin had ascended to the top post at AMC in 1967, after former president Roy Abernethy was forced to retire in the face of disastrous sales. Chapin had his hands full saving AMC from financial ruin in 1967 and 1968, and additionally lacked the wherewithal to purchase Jeep. But in 1969, with his car firm still struggling but coming back from the brink (and even managing a small profit), Chapin approached Edgar Kaiser again. Edgar was just as interested in selling Jeep as before. Exactly why he wanted to sell is difficult to understand, since Jeep made up about half of Kaiser Industries sales and profits and was the single largest division of the company. But the Kaisers had expanded into several businesses more to their liking over the years, and their current emphasis was on the Pacific Rim and the business of raw materials. Perhaps they wanted to finally exit the automobile business to concentrate solely on these other interests. It certainly seemed a good time to sell Jeep—although it was coming off of the two best years in its history, its future was uncertain.

American Motors stated, in its 1969 annual report to the stockholders, "We have reached an agreement to purchase the KAISER Jeep CORPORATION for $10 million in cash, 5,500,000 shares of American Motors common stock and approximately $10 million in negotiable five-year serial notes." As the company noted it wasn't a done deal, since it had to be voted on by the stockholders at the annual meeting in February 1970.

The sale terms totaled approximately $70 million. What American Motors was getting for its money was a line of trucks and sport utility vehicles, two items its product line lacked. In addition, the company would increase its presence in overseas markets. Although in many countries it was already allied with Jeep in joint manufacture of vehicles, there were many other countries where Jeep had an established sales network that possibly could add AMC cars to its line-up. AMC had similar circumstances where its existing overseas dealers could add Jeeps to their sales mix. Besides that, AMC was gaining 1600 Jeep dealers in the U.S., some of which could be expected to add AMC cars to their operations. American Motors executives also expressed the hope that Jeep's vast experience bidding on government contracts

would help the company secure fleet sales of AMC cars to Federal agencies. Besides all the aforementioned, AMC was also getting the military business that had been the backbone of Jeep operations and profitability. Although it couldn't be known how that would fare in the future, the government-destined vehicle business had a healthy backlog of orders and was well positioned to win whatever military business went out for bid. Taken overall, the possibilities at Jeep were very promising.

Roy Chapin negotiated a reasonable price when he purchased Jeep. The cost was considerably less than his predecessors at AMC had faced, mainly because in the period since that time, Jeep had sold off its Argentinean and Brazilian operations. These were its two biggest overseas subsidiaries. It's possible too, that the price was affected by the uncertainty over future military needs.

But several sources felt AMC was making a very large mistake buying Jeep. One of the more vocal was Gerald C. Meyers, who in 1969 was AMC's Vice-President-Product Development Group, but who previously had been VP-Automotive Manufacturing. Earlier, Chapin had sent Meyers to Jeep to look over the company and report back on what sort of prospect it was for purchase by AMC. Meyer's opinion was that, while the military operation looked intriguing, the retail (or commercial) business was a loser. He felt Kaiser Jeep had more problems than AMC could handle just then. The magazine *Dun's Review* was much less mannerly with its opinion it called the Jeep buyout, "Chapin's Folly."

But in the end, it didn't matter what Gerry Meyers, *Dun's Review*, or the man in the moon thought of Roy Chapin's idea. It was up to AMC's stockholders to vote on the idea and they seemed to like it, though that could be viewed only as a sign of how much they trusted Chapin's judgment.

It's very easy nowadays for armchair quarterbacks and assorted other sages to nod confidently and laud Chapin's wisdom in purchasing Jeep, but in 1969, history had not yet proved him right or wrong. If he was correct in his judgments, AMC stood to make some decent money. However, if he was wrong, there was every chance that both AMC and Jeep would go right down the tubes...along with Chapin's reputation, of course. But then again, no one ever said the automobile business was easy.

Chapter Five

Building a New Jeep Company

1970-1979

Jeep vehicles rolling down the assembly line in Toledo.

There are a number of methods with which one can measure the overall success of a business. The most common ones, obviously, are sales and profits—the more you have of both of these, the better you're doing. Another measure, used more often today than in years past, is the price a companies shares are trading for on the stock exchange. The popularity of this method merely reflects the greedy era we live in nowadays, since it places the greatest emphasis on the stockholder, rather than products, customers, or employees. Along with these useful yardsticks, the automobile industry has its own set of measures unique to the business—unit sales of vehicles, and market share. An additional, albeit less tangible, measure of the success or failure of a company is its image in the marketplace—a factor difficult to grasp, troublesome to define, and very hard to quantify, but an altogether vital piece of information that should be entered in the ledgers under a special category marked "Blue Sky."

By certain measures, the Kaiser Jeep Corporation of 1969 was a successful firm. Its vehicles had a worldwide appeal, with annual Jeep production that hovered just north or south of the 100,000 unit mark during the 1960s. The sixties also saw the company set sales and profits records on more than one occasion, and Jeep held a goodly share of the market for civilian four-wheel-drive vehicles as well as a big piece of the tactical wheeled vehicle market. As far as image is concerned, the answer would seem obvious—the Jeep name was known throughout the world.

But there were a few clouds in the picture. Although total Jeep volume was fairly good, retail sales in the U.S. were nothing to brag about—in 1969, according to the *Automotive News*, they totaled only 36,017 units, compared with 38,486 reported the previous year. Kaiser Jeep, you see, was heavily dependent on sales to the military. It also had a hefty reliance on sales of built-up Jeeps for export, as well as sales of completely knocked-

down kits (known in the industry as CKDs) for assembly overseas. Kaiser Jeeps' dollar volume was good, and so were its profits; what it lacked was a solid domestic retail base. The overseas trade, plus military and other government sales, made up the bulk of its business. A serious concern was that military sales were strongly influenced by the Vietnam war, and when that conflict died out, the military business would likely suffer a sudden drop. And there was one more concern as well.

For as all business leaders know, there is one other way to measure the success of a company, and that is to compare it to its peers. Ideally, one should compare a company's rate of growth in comparison to its peers over a set course of time. Looking back one can see two companies that were similar to Jeep—the GMC (General Motors Coach) Division of General Motors, and the International Harvester Company. GMC is the truck division of GM. Its purpose is to enable GM's non-Chevrolet dealers to offer a line of trucks through their stores. Although it generally doesn't sell as many trucks as Chevrolet, over the years, GMC has acquired more of a truck "image" than Chevrolet has. Internation-

Jeep was pitched as a sporty, 'fun' car for active people.

The man who bought Jeep from Kaiser, Roy D. Chapin Jr. Standing is AMC president William Luneburg.

al Harvester Company (which today is known as Navistar International) was a long-time truck manufacturer, stronger in the heavy truck segment than in the light duty market. Although by the sixties it was primarily a truck and agricultural equipment manufacturer, in earlier years its product line even included passenger cars.

Looking through the pages of the *Automotive News,* we see that in 1959, Jeep sold 30,626 units at retail in the U.S. In the same year, GMC retailed 33,745 and International (IHC) retailed 48,792 vehicles. As the decade of the sixties opened, the numbers ran like this: Jeep 31,385; GMC 45,761; IHC 48,729. Fast forwarding now to the final year of that decade, one sees that Jeep retail sales had risen only to the 36,017 mentioned previously, up about 15% from 10 years earlier, while GMC retail sales more than doubled to 101,189 and IHC had managed to climb to 63,480, or about a 30% increase. Judged by that comparison Jeep hadn't kept pace with its peers.

Of course, the product lines were not identical company to company—Jeep had no large or medium trucks like IHC and GMC, and those two firms had nothing quite like the CJ-5, though IHC's Scout was a contender. However, all three companies did have four-wheel-drive station wagons and pickup trucks, and all three competed for the truck

buyer's money. During the 1960s, GMC had managed to move past IHC, while Jeep was merely standing still. The total truck market had more than doubled in the ten years from 1960-1969.

So viewed in that context, Jeep was becoming an also-ran in the retail market. Its vehicle's image was good—Jeeps were known as rugged machines. Yet they were also known as being not particularly comfortable or plush (except of course the Wagoneer), not especially powerful, and containing more than a fair share of outmoded technology. The Universal (CJ-5) for instance, still used as its standard engine the F-head four-cylinder. That engine was nothing more than a revision of the WWII era flat-head four, which itself dated back to the Willys' cars of the 1930s—clearly an engine far past its prime. The optional V-6 was much more powerful and modern but it was not a particularly smooth-running engine.

Jeep's reputation for strength, durability and go-anywhere capability was important, but the market was evolving, and customers were demanding more than just the traditional fare. In order to grow in the 1970s, a company would have to offer all the established virtues for which four-wheel-drive vehicles were known. The company would also have to offer a good dose of the popular comfort and convenience features seen on passenger cars.

Kaiser Jeep seems to have realized this, and even took some steps to address the concerns. However, the firm's efforts simply were not enough—as evidenced by its humdrum standing in the retail market. Whether that failure was due to inadequate funding, poor research, or simply because the company was making easier money in other segments is arguable. The fact is, Jeep wasn't taking full advantage of the opportunities in the market.

American Motors chairman Roy D. Chapin Jr., however, saw great possibilities. As a life-long automobile man, with strong experience in sales and marketing, Chapin felt his company was capable of taking Jeep to new levels of sales and prosperity. His then-vice president of Product Development, Gerry Meyers, wasn't thrilled with the idea. He later recalled for *Ward's Auto World,* "I was against (purchasing Jeep) because I knew too much...their problems were many fold. I thought that we had a plateful to begin with and didn't need any more."

With the purchase of Kaiser Jeep, Chapin at last would be able to put his ideas into practice—and heaven knows the man had been forced to wait long enough for the chance. Chapin would then finally learn if he had been right or wrong. It was left to Meyers and his staff to come up with new Jeep products with which to lure buyers.

To simply continue the traditional way things were done at Jeep wouldn't work—as the previous decade proved. The new decade needed a new strategy, new products, a new ethic—almost a whole new company. Jeep had to become more than merely a producer of commercial vehicles that were also available to the retail market—it had to focus on the great opportunities the retail consumer market offered. The retail business had to become Jeep's primary market.

There was nothing that AMC could do to enhance the Jeep product in time for the 1970 model season. The deal closed months after the new-model announcement day, so that year's line-up reflects the thinking of the Kaiser people. There was very little change seen in the various models at introduction time, but sometime after that several important modifications appeared. The Wagoneer received a new grille sometime during the year—early 1970 sales catalogs picture Wagoneers with the same grille used the year before, while later catalogs show a more elegant one. Side marker lights were better integrated in the new styling. The addition of an electric sunroof to the Wagoneer option list was big news in June 1970. The new sunroof came with a full vinyl top offered in a choice of colors.

The Gladiator trucks also got a new grille midseason. Like the Wagoneer, the Gladiators shown in the early 1970 sales catalogs wear the same old grille—in Gladiator's case, the upright style first seen on the 1963 models. Gladiators in the later 1970 catalog are pictured with a new grille—the one just replaced on Wagoneers. That was a smart use of existing tooling and the effect it had on Gladiator styling was very positive—the new grille significantly freshened the Gladiator's appearance. Jeepster Commandos likewise were unchanged for 1970. Unlike its bigger siblings, the Commando didn't receive any mid-year upgrades other than having side marker lenses placed in the fenders rather than on the side of the hood.

The Jeep Universal (CJ-5) looked the same as before, though it too got its side lamps changed from the hood sides to the fenders. There was one surprise—a limited edition model available early in the model year. The new model was the Renegade I. The company said it was "...the ultimate in a rugged off-road four-wheel-drive racing machine, possibly the fastest four-wheel-drive production vehicle in the country." The Renegade clearly showed some influence from the earlier 462 model. Stretching things a bit further, Renegades could even be viewed as an evolution of the Tuxedo Park concept—though unlike the failed Tuxedo Park, the Renegade struck a nerve in the American consumer. Like that earlier 462, the Renegade came with a roll bar, optional ammeter and oil gauge and 160-hp "Dauntless" V-6 engine. Unlike the 462, the Renegade provided a great deal of visual confirmation that it was a sports four-wheeler. In other words, it had the looks to go with the performance. Renegades were offered in several loud colors, including Wild Plum. The Renegade I also included 8-inch wide wheels mounting 6.70 four-ply tires— very big treads in those days—and a special accessory racing stripe (with the Renegade I logo) on the hood sides. Interest in the hot-rod Jeep was astonishing! Although production of the 1970 Renegade I was very limited, the high level of excitement it created meant it would undoubtedly return the following year.

Despite the modest improvements in the Jeep line-up, retail sales took another dip in 1970. The problems confronting Jeep were many, as Meyers had said, but one of the biggest was that Jeep's distribution system was a weak link. Although a number of Jeep dealers sold the product successfully, for too many others Jeep was just an additional, minor part of their businesses. Many sold other lines of trucks and cars built by the Big Three auto makers, some sold farm equipment or lawn and garden tractors, and others were simply glorified gas stations. In addition, the low level of retail sales in recent years hadn't encouraged Jeep dealers to invest much in expanding their businesses and many dealer showrooms were cramped or old fashioned.

To counter these problems, and expand the size of the dealer body, American Motors was encouraging many of its existing passenger car dealers, (of which it had over two thousand), to take on the Jeep line. Meanwhile, AMC representatives worked to bring the existing Jeep dealers up to standard.

Roy Chapin's people were everywhere, integrating and overhauling Jeep as rapidly as possible. Although AMC did indeed have its hands full with its own problems, it had to get Jeep into shape, or it might end up sinking the whole ship. In Detroit and Toledo, Jeep and AMC engineers worked on fitting Jeeps with as many suitable off-the-shelf AMC parts as possible. Manufacturing engineers worked to streamline Jeep's stamping and assembly processes and improve quality. Marvin W. Stucky, an AMC executive, was named Vice-President, Product Development Group/Jeep, in the spring of 1970. Stucky's first efforts focused on improving Jeep's ride and handling, while reducing noise and vibration. Over the longer term, Stucky wanted to incorporate AMC's engines into all Jeep models. That would provide meaningful economies of scale, but to do it meant some expensive alterations would have to be made.

In the meantime, however, AMC was feeling the effects of the Jeep purchase like a hangover. As the annual report clearly showed, the company overall lost $56.2 million, a staggering loss for that decade. Worldwide Jeep sales for the 1970 fiscal year, (we should note here that AMC's fiscal year ran from October 1 to September 30) including government and overseas deliveries, totaled 93,171 units, down about 6,000 from the previous year. But Chapin and AMC president William Luneburg assured stockholders that the situation would improve. They wrote in the annual report that "...Jeep can be and will be a major profit contributor to American Motors."

That wasn't easy to visualize in 1970. With the parent company (a chronically weak parent at that) losing big money, it must have seemed like wishful thinking. In all likelihood some investors must have thought that maybe the folks at *Dun's Review* were right after all. When considering the situation in retrospect, it is important to momentarily forget the size and vitality of today's Sport Utility market and realize that in 1970, what Chapin was espousing—a hearty, prosperous business based on SUVs—was a little hard to swallow.

A major change to Jeep's business components was coming. The Defense and Government

Wagoneer got an electric sunroof, as demonstrated by this leggy lady, in June 1970.

The 1970 Gladiator pickup was even more handsome this year, and could be ordered with interesting side-mounted spare tire.

Products Division, set up by Kaiser in 1967, the reader will recall—was renamed the General Products Division. This was a prelude to a further, even more significant evolution that we will detail later. It assumed the functions of the prior division and was assigned an objective of diversifying into non-governmental fields. In 1970, it introduced a new postal vehicle, the Dispatcher 100, based on the DJ-5 chassis.

As the annual report noted, the four-wheel-drive segment of the truck market had grown by almost 500 percent in the prior decade—though it still came to less than 140,000 units a year. The company felt the rate of growth would continue or even accelerate during the 1970s. The report further stated that the long-range goal for AMC was to, "develop vehicles that are completely new to Jeep."

This historic vehicle is the first of the Jeep Renegades—the 1970 Renegade I. Note the extra wide wheels, big (for the time) tires and Renegade I hood stripe.

Jeep Renegade was a real performer, as this 'airborne' photo confirms.

The report didn't state that the short-term goal was to make Jeep profitable again, but that was the obvious objective. The report noted that "...Jeep, as a whole, was operating profitably in the fourth quarter," although that didn't exactly mean what some people may have thought. Jeep was operating profitably as a whole—just as it had often done in the recent past. However, what was really needed was to have Jeep's *retail* operations running profitably, and that was going to be quite a trick, if indeed it could be done.

For the first year of the new decade, the peer group's results were as follows: Jeep, 33,984 units sold at retail in the U.S., IHC 68,939 in the same period and GMC 89,675. Jeep management's performance during the 1970s will be seen when we examine the results at two five-year checkpoints, 1974 and 1979.

Since AMC didn't take control of Jeep until the middle of the 1970 model year, the changes and improvements it could make to the Jeep line even for 1971 would have to be of a modest nature. There simply wasn't enough time to tool up for radical change. What did appear, when the tight timeline is considered, was a great deal more than most people would have expected. Looking back, 1971 stands out as one of the more interesting years in Jeep's long history.

The 1971 Jeeps debuted in the fall of 1970. As in the prior model year, there was little change at first. However, new features appeared during the year. At introduction both the Wagoneer and Gladiator lines carried as standard equipment the AMC 232-cid six—the same engine Kaiser had been purchasing for some years—and the Buick V-8 as an option. Early in the year, AMC's bigger 258-cid 150-hp six became the standard power plant, and AMC's 304 and 360-cid V-8s replaced the Buick engines on the option list. There were few appearance changes. In fact, a close inspection of the sales brochures reveals that many 1970 photos were reused in the 1971 catalogs.

With no changes to its engine line-up for 1971, the Jeep Universal's focus was on simple appearance enhancements. Some of the Universal (CJ-5) models in the catalogs wore new sport stripes on their hoods, along with optional dress-up items like full wheel covers and whitewall tires to improve their looks. The DJ-5 two-wheel-drive model was still available. It was not shown in the regular brochures, but appeared in the salesman's fact-finder guide book with a price tag of $2382.

The 1971 Hurst Jeepster was produced in limited quantities.

The limited production Renegade returned for 1971, with some important upgrades. Introduced at the Detroit Auto Show, the new model, now dubbed the Renegade II, had beautiful aluminum alloy wheels fitted in place of the plain white wheels of the Renegade I. Production records are vague, but it appears that a total of 600 Renegade II's were built for 1971—200 painted Baja Yellow, 200 painted Mint Green, 50 painted Riverside Orange, and 150 painted Big Bad Orange (same color as used on Big Bad Javelins). Like its predecessor, the Renegade II was a big hit with the public, and the available units sold quickly.

AMC product planners were discovering that specially-trimmed Jeeps were easier to sell than standard units and fetched a higher price. Two specially-trimmed Jeepster Commandos joined the Renegade II in the showroom. The SC-1 was the tamer of the duo. It was a sporty version of the Commando station wagon, painted butterscotch gold with a white top. It came with a standard V-6 engine, radio, roof rack and special trim. A sporty stripe adorned the hood and body sides.

The second limited production Jeepster was likewise a Commando wagon, but unlike any station wagon seen before or since. This was the famed Hurst Jeepster Special, a product of the joint thinking of Jeep product planners and George Hurst, of Hurst Performance Products fame. The Hurst Jeepster featured a red and blue rally stripe that ran across the cowl and down the sides. It also featured a hood-mounted air scoop/tachometer combo, wide-tread tires and a choice of either a Hurst Dual Gate shifter with automatic transmission or a Hurst T-handle shifter for the standard 3-speed manual transmission. No one knows exactly how many of these ultra-rare Jeepsters were built, but an educated guess made by a former Hurst company employee is 100 or less.

Other new Jeeps were in the wind. In AMC's Detroit headquarters, stylists were busy designing a new compact pickup truck, called the "Cowboy." Based on a modified AMC Hornet compact car, the "Cowboy" looked to be a strong contender in the growing market for small trucks. At the time, Japanese brands dominated the small truck market. An ongoing debate was whether or not the use of a modified passenger car shell would dilute the value of the Jeep brand. It was an undeniable worry.

There was big corporate news. In what stands out as a turning point in how Jeep foresaw its role in the new decade, the General Products Division (neé Kaiser Jeep's Defense and Government Products Division) was further restructured and became a separate, wholly owned subsidiary called AM General Corporation. The new company was charged with finding and growing new markets, while maintaining its position as the world's largest producer of tactical wheeled vehicles. With a line of commercial trucks ranging from 1/4-ton postal delivery vehicles up to 5-ton military trucks, AM General became a truck company in its own right, distinct and different from Jeep. Its importance to Jeep history is simply this: AMC recognized that the business of manufacturing Government-destined vehicles was vastly different from the business of competing in the retail market, and thus what had been one company must now become two. From this point on, our narrative will no longer include military and postal products, since as of 1971, they were under the jurisdiction of a separate, though corporate-related, enterprise. They were no longer Jeeps.

One should pause to consider the momentous consequence of the corporate restructuring. With that one act, the military/government vehicle operation, which after all had once been the very soul of Jeep, was spun off by itself, and its vehicles would no longer even be known by the name they had helped make so famous. From that moment on, the business of Jeep Corporation, and the purview of the men and women who oversaw its daily functions, would be the selling of sport utility vehicles and four-wheel-drive trucks in the retail market.

Looking at the numbers, 1971 can be seen as a year of transition. AMC as a whole reported net earnings of $10 million, undoubtedly much of

For 1971, Jeep Wagoneers received AMC's 258-cid six as the standard engine, with AMC 304- and 360-cid V-8s optional.

which came from automobile sales. The company noted that the downward trend in Jeep's share of the four-wheel-drive market had been reversed. Retail sales for the fiscal year were reported to be 37,124, compared to 30,551 for the comparable period in 1970, approximately a 22% increase. Unit volume no longer included government-destined vehicles, since those were now figured in AM General's sales. AM General declined to report unit sales, switching instead to reporting sales by dollar volume. This was a more accurate measurement considering the wide-range of prices and profit margins between the 1/4-ton postal trucks and the giant 5-ton military trucks. Like Jeep Corporation, AM General reported increased sales.

Jeep's international sales were good and getting better. Major overseas markets for AMC/Jeep vehicles were Venezuela, Argentina, and Iran, all three of which had manufacturing or assembly operations for both AMC cars and Jeeps. Listed among the subsidiary and affiliated companies were some familiar old names: Willys Motors Australia, Willys de Venezuela, Jeep Caracas (also in Venezuela), Jeep Overseas, based in Switzerland, Vehiculos Automores Mexicanos (VAM) in Mexico, IKA-Renault, which sprang from the old Indus-

trias Kaiser Argentina, and Turk Willys Overland, headquartered in Istanbul, Turkey.

Like the prior year, 1972 stands out as an important year in Jeep history. It was in 1972 that AMC began to enact the greatest changes seen in Jeep vehicles in 10 years. First of all, the CJ line received major attention. Deciding it was time to ditch the hoary old F-head engine, VP Marvin Stucky ordered that AMC's wonderfully smooth 232-cid six-cylinder engine be fitted as standard equipment in CJ's. Rated at 100-hp (for 1972, AMC used the much more modest net horsepower ratings, rather than the gross ratings of prior years), it was quieter and more powerful than the old 75-hp F-head, and required less maintenance as well. Optional was AMC's 110-hp 258-cid six, and, debuting for the first time in a production CJ vehicle, an optional V-8, AMC's 150-hp 304-cid engine. The F-head four was retained for export vehicles, recognition of the need to offer a four-cylinder engine in many overseas markets.

The sixes were in-line engines, too long to fit comfortably under the CJ's hood, so AMC stylists redesigned the CJ with a longer 83" wheelbase versus the previous 81". This required a good deal of retooling, but surprisingly enough, the company

138

Renegade II was the sportiest, most expensive CJ for 1971.

chose to keep the CJ's appearance the same—no re-styling was done, save what it took to accommodate the longer wheelbase. Gerry Meyers later told *Ward's Auto World* that it was AMC's deliberate intention to retain the CJ's traditional look, saying, "If you want to call that anti-Detroit, go ahead." As Meyers explained, "...it's very important for Jeep that we hang onto the name—the image of the vehicle—while improving the ruggedness, durability and overall off-road aspects."

There were other improvements as well. CJ's new open-end front axle allowed a shorter turning radius. Brakes were improved, too, and a higher capacity heater-defroster was added. Front and rear axles were heftier, a new recirculating ball steering system replaced the old cam and lever style, and suspended brake and clutch pedals replaced the floor mounted pedals— eliminating the annoyance of water splashes. Power steering and power brakes were new options. A clever option was a choice of either a tailgate or fixed rear panel. The advantage of the fixed panel was the elim-

ination of a source of rattles, and the ability to mount the spare wheel directly to the back of the vehicle.

The Gladiator name was retired, and the vehicles formerly called Gladiators were now referred to simply as Jeep Trucks. The Universal name was downplayed—the model was referred to simply as the 'Jeep,' while the rest of the range carried the Jeep label as well as their model names—Jeep Wagoneer, Jeep Truck, etc. Evidently AMC hadn't come up with a proper model name to replace the Universal designation.

The popular Renegade model returned, though it was known simply as the Renegade, not Renegade III as might have been expected. It was even more of a powerhouse than in previous years, because it now came with a healthy 304-cid V-8 as standard equipment. As in past years, the Renegade didn't appear in the regular sales catalogs, since it was available on a limited production basis only. For 1972, three colors—Renegade Yellow, Renegade Orange, and Renegade Plum were offered.

The Jeepster name was dropped, and the vehicle was now known simply as the Jeep Commando. It too, received a longer wheelbase, lengthened to 104", and also got the new higher capacity open-end front axle and improved brakes. Yet a bigger change to the Commando was its front-end styling. The stylist responsible, according to one former Jeep product planner, was Jim Anger, a onetime Kaiser Jeep designer. Commandos were re-styled to look bigger, classier and more like a family wagon. Slab-sided fenders eliminated the family resemblance to the CJ, while a cleverly-styled hood managed to integrate the new front look with the old (and tall) cowl. Commandos likewise received the 232-cid six as standard equipment, a major improvement in itself, and the new optional 258-cid six and 304 V-8 engines. Brighter interiors and flashier exterior colors completed the comprehensive list of improvements to the Commando. Station wagon, pickup and roadster models were again offered.

There were no important appearance changes to either the Wagoneers or the truck line, since both had been recent beneficiaries of styling updates. The pickup line now featured a model with an 8000-lb. Gross Vehicle Weight (GVW)—it came with AMC's 360 V-8 as standard equipment, as did a 7000 GVW model. Wagoneer's boast was that it came with four doors—versus the three doors found on Chevy and GMC Surburbans. Also pitched was Wagoneer's greater luxury and higher level of standard equipment. AMC summed all the new improvements under the tag line, "New '72 Jeep Guts—guts to do more for you than ever before."

In corporate news, AMC reported total sales of $1.4 billion, almost double the total of just three years previous. It was partly the result of buying Jeep (which at the time of the purchase was a decent sized company, with dollar sales volume a little more than half the size of AMC's), and partly the result of improving business results. The companies net profit of $30.2 million was AMC's best since 1964, and the outlook for the future was exceedingly bright. Jeep sales, it was noted, were up 25 percent over 1971. Also noted was that over 400 new Jeep dealers had been signed, although the total number of Jeep dealers had remained about the same. AMC was weeding out the less than effective Jeep dealers and replacing them with better financed, more motivated new dealers. About 540 dealers handled both AMC cars and Jeep vehicles. A boost in Jeep production, planned for 1973, would raise it to double the level it had been when AMC acquired Jeep.

So 1972 ended on a high note, and the outlook for 1973 was even rosier. There was ample reason

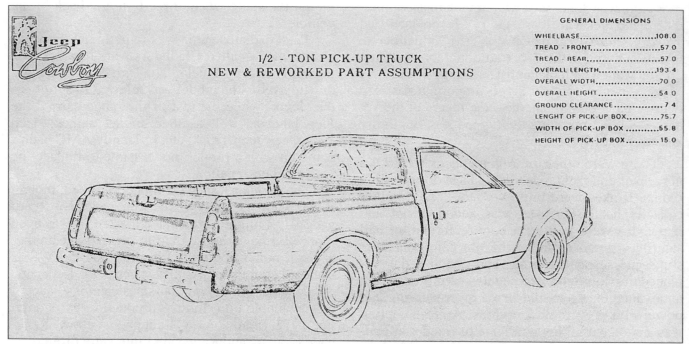

1/2 - TON PICK-UP TRUCK
NEW & REWORKED PART ASSUMPTIONS

GENERAL DIMENSIONS

WHEELBASE	108.0
TREAD - FRONT	57.0
TREAD - REAR	57.0
OVERALL LENGTH	193.4
OVERALL WIDTH	70.0
OVERALL HEIGHT	54.0
GROUND CLEARANCE	7.4
LENGTH OF PICK-UP BOX	75.7
WIDTH OF PICK-UP BOX	55.8
HEIGHT OF PICK-UP BOX	15.0

Original proposal for Jeep Cowboy, a small pickup based on AMC Hornet automobile.

Commando for 1971 looked much the same as prior years.

for feeling confident. The 1973 Jeep line featured additional refinements, which included the introduction of the most revolutionary improvement in four-wheel-drive mechanisms in history. The "Jeep Guts" theme carried over from the year before—the sales brochure was headlined "Jeep '73—tougher guts, brighter looks!"

The standard Jeep, the CJ-5—which AMC still referred to simply as "the Jeep," returned with minimal changes. A fuel tank skid plate was made standard equipment, as were tougher tires. The sales brochure did highlight the sporty Renegade this year—(a purple one no less)—though that model wasn't available until January of 1973.

There was another intriguing new Jeep sports package for 1973 (short-lived though it was). Called the Super Jeep, it was a CJ-5 equipped with the big six engine, four-speed heavy duty transmission, plain white wheels and a wild psychedelic tape stripe treatment. Not a lot is known about the Super Jeep but, according to one source, it was created in response to a shortage of the alloy wheels needed to produce Renegades.

Commandos returned basically unchanged. The prior year's re-styling hadn't brought about any big increase in Commando sales, though sales did go up a bit. Competition in the four-wheel-drive station wagon market was tougher than ever, and the big Chevy Blazer, introduced in 1969, was taking a large chunk of the sales total.

The big news for 1973 was the introduction of a revolution in four-wheel-drive technology—Jeep's remarkable Quadra-Trac system. Quadra-Trac was developed to eliminate every inconvenience and annoyance attached to four-wheel-drive vehicles. Ever since the invention of four-wheel-drive, drivers had to be cautioned not to operate the vehicle's four-wheel-drive when driving on hard dry surfaces. This was because a vehicle's four wheels travel at different speeds whenever the vehicle is traveling in any direction except straight forward or backward. An easy way to understand this phenomenon is to drive a car in a circle over freshly fallen snow—you'll see four separate arcs where the wheels have traveled. A closer examination will reveal that the arcs are of different lengths, since each wheel traveled a slightly different distance—and therefore, a different speed as well.

In a conventional auto this variance is compensated for by the differential—it makes up the difference (hence the term differential). Before the development of Quadra-Trac, a four-wheel-drive vehicle having power going to all four wheels always needed some slippage under the wheels to allow for the difference in wheel speeds. Otherwise the build-up of drive train torque stress (called "axle wind-up") would cause excessive tire wear, and in worse cases a drive line component failure—usually an expensive one. However, with the revolutionary Quadra-Trac, one could drive on any road surface, at any speed, without undue wear to tires or front end components. This was because Quadra-Trac employed a third differential, located near the center of the vehicle, that directed power automatically to the wheels that had the best traction.

Quadra-Trac had some significant ancillary benefits too. Besides allowing owners to drive on all surfaces, it also eliminated the need for front hubs. Those were the tricky little dials on each front wheel that allowed the wheels to turn without driving the front axle, which in turn provided easier steering, better fuel economy, and reduced wear. With Quadra-Trac the four-wheel-drive operated continuously, with the third differential automatically directing the proper amount of power to the wheels as needed. Quadra-Trac came with a high range (for normal driving) as standard, and offered a low range for severe off-road use or snow plowing. Quadra-Trac truly was the first fully automatic four-wheel-drive system offered on a production vehicle. An even more important benefit of Quadra-Trac was that its traction was generally superior to conventional four-wheel-drive, especially for on-road driving.

AMC's statement that, "Someday every four-wheel-drive vehicle may have a system like it. The '73 Jeep Wagoneer has it now," remains one of the most prophetic declarations in automotive history. Today many four-wheelers do indeed have a similar system—that is known generically as "All Wheel Drive" to distinguish it from the conventional part-time systems still offered on many vehicles.

For the company as a whole, 1973 was a fabulous year. The annual report stated that, "Sales of Jeep vehicles in 1973 were at record levels, reflecting the continued rising demand for four-wheel-drive vehicles." It noted that Jeep was now fully integrated into AMC and, privately, management was acknowledging that Jeep was operating at a profitable level. The break-even point for Jeep retail sales was somewhere in the vicinity of 50,000 units per year, and in fiscal 1973, Jeep sales rose by 44%, to 67,000 units in the U.S. Also noted was the fact that the four-wheel-drive market had increased 30%, so Jeep clearly was now outpacing the market. Overseas sales were up as well.

One bit of fallout from AMC's increasing prosperity was the decision not to enter the compact

Jeep CJ-5 with optional V-6 engine was especially good off-road.

For 1972, CJ got a longer wheelbase—apparent here in the longer front fenders—plus standard six and optional V-8 engines.

pickup truck market. The prototype "Cowboy" compact pickup, based on the AMC Hornet, had been developed with an eye towards challenging the widely popular Japanese mini-trucks. However, record Hornet sales (and forecasts for further sales increases) meant that AMC's production capacity might be strained, so the program was shelved.

Looking at the dealer group, the company noted that although 600 new dealers had been signed since 1970, the total Jeep dealer count was down by about 170. However, it was noted that the average Jeep dealers' sales rate had climbed from 19 per year to 46. The goal of strengthening the Jeep dealer group was thus being reached.

Elsewhere in the company, efforts were being undertaken to prepare for even further sales increases. Jeep's Toledo stamping operations were upgraded as were various component parts manu-

Despite its low ride height, Jeep truck offered superior ground clearance.

Jeep Renegade for 1972 was more powerful than ever, with standard 304-cid V-8.

facturing facilities in the AMC system, all with an eye to increasing production. For there was to be another big product announcement from Jeep for 1974—and a smaller one that would prove to be almost as important.

For 1974, one look at the cover of the Jeep sales catalog would tell anybody just what the hot new product was—it was a sport utility wagon called the Jeep Cherokee. Jeep claimed it was, "All-new in the truest sense...." However, one has to wonder what the author of that prose was thinking, for the truth was the Cherokee wasn't all-new, not by any stretch of the imagination. Basically, the new Cherokee was a two-door Wagoneer with updated styling. What was different were the rear side windows. While the old two-door Wagoneer looked very utilitarian, the new Cherokee had an aggressive, sporty appearance. The rear side win-

dows didn't have the thick posts of the old Wagoneer, instead they were one piece interrupted only by a front vent. The Cherokee used the old Wagoneer grille (same as used on the trucks) but looked fancier and much more youthful. Cherokee was aimed directly at the Chevy Blazer, the "poster car" of the burgeoning Sport Utility wagon market, a market that clearly favored vehicles that were larger and heavier than the Jeep Commando, International Scout and Ford Bronco.

The Jeep Cherokee was smaller than the Chevy Suburban/Blazer, but its size was perfect for families wanting something bigger than a Commando. An interesting phenomenon is that Cherokee didn't compete with the Wagoneer. Buyers considered the Wagoneer a more luxurious, "mature" vehicle—sort of the Buick of four-wheelers, and viewed the Cherokee as young and hip.

The 1972 Commando pickup was a handsome, useful truck.

Is there any vehicle better-looking than a Jeep?

Jeep Wagoneer's four-wheel drive was good for getting to off-road vacation spots.

Various elements that Chapin's people had put into place—things like Quadra-Trac, modern six-cylinder and V-8 engines, better interior trim, and a much stronger dealer group, all worked in harmony to make the Cherokee a huge success. Overnight, it became the four-wheeler to buy, and Jeep dealers had waiting lists of buyers.

There was other product news. Jeep finally decided to highlight the CJ-5 and CJ-6 nameplates, rather than calling its littlest product just "the Jeep." The change helped position the Jeep brand properly, and put additional emphasis on each of its individual models. Windshield's on CJ's were now painted body color, rather than black as in prior years. As for other product news, CJ-5 enthusiasts got some that was really exciting. The popular Renegade model was now a regular production offering. Renegades could be ordered in standard Jeep colors, and also were offered in exclusive Renegade Yellow and Renegade Plum colors. The DJ-5 model was dropped, ending Jeeps two-wheel-drive offerings for the time being though, like its several attempts at retailing passenger cars, Jeep would return to the two-wheel-drive market someday. AM General, however, continued to offer the DJ-5, both for mail fleets and as a low-cost military car.

Jeep trucks benefited from brighter looks and new trim packages. One that stood out, the Pioneer package, included two-tone paint, wood grain accent trim and a beautiful interior, making these the plushest pickups Jeep had ever offered. Designations for the truck models were completely revised—the new designations were J-10 for 1/2-ton models and J-20 for the 3/4 ton jobs.

The Wagoneer was made even more handsome by the addition of a new grille with inset turn signal lamps. Wagoneers had evolved into the "class" of the four-wheel-drive field, with standard equipment that included Quadra-Trac, automatic transmission, V-8 engine, power steering and power disc brakes. It had moved up-market from simply being a family wagon. The new Cherokee would take its place in that segment, while Wagoneer would hold the top spot in Jeep's lineup, and in the four-wheel-drive market.

The introduction of the new Cherokee in the popular price range, and the steady upgrading of the Wagoneer to the luxury level reflected product planning and marketing of the highest order. The effect it had was very positive—as reported in the annual report, for the fiscal year Jeep sales rose 8 percent to 72,000, setting another record. Addition-

SHOCKING TRUTH ABOUT SHOCKS!

OFF-ROAD

ARGUS IND

VEHICLES AND ADVENTURE

JULY 1973 75¢

**COMPARING AM's SUPER JEEP, CJ-5, COMMANDO
HOW TO DRIVE OFF-ROAD - PART 3
OFF-ROADER'S BUDGET TOOL KIT**

Off-Road magazine featured the limited edition Super Jeep on the cover of its July 1973 issue.

ally, according to the trade paper *Automotive News*, retail sales for the calendar year reached 96,835! When studying Jeep's steadily increasing sales, it's very important to remember that AMC was working with the same vehicles it had inherited from Kaiser. The only difference was that AMC was applying its considerable expertise in product planning and marketing to upgrade and adapt the vehicles to satisfy the customer's needs.

In international news, AMC reached an agreement to form a joint venture company in Korea to manufacture Jeeps for the local market. Known as

Shinjin Jeep, the new firm was capitalized at $3 million, with each side controlling 50% ownership. The partnership approach that AMC used for expanding Jeep production overseas was deliberate—it reduced the amount of cash the company had to spend to get a new production site going. Additionally, it was believed that a local partner would have a better understanding of the local market, and a strong desire to see Jeep succeed in it. Although many of the overseas affiliates and partnerships were relatively small ventures, in sum, the international market was a strong one for Jeep. The annual

The 1973 Commando wagon was a good compromise between CJ and Wagoneer.

Rugged Jeep truck for 1973 could carry a camper unit just about anywhere.

The '73 Jeep.
We've got the guts to make it even better.

"We've got the guts" said this 1973 Jeep CJ advertisement.

report for 1974 stated that, "Outside of North America, one-third of all world production of four-wheel-drive vehicles in 1974 carried the Jeep trademark...." AMC became a $2 Billion company in 1974—helped substantially by Jeep sales.

As far as peer comparison goes, in 1974 (the mid-point of the decade), the raw numbers as reported in the *Automotive News*, were thus: GMC 143,885, IHC 74,302, and Jeep 96,835. Analyzing the numbers we see that GMC had increased by 60% since 1970. IHC, however, increased only by about 8%, a sign that the appeal of its light duty vehicle line was dwindling. Jeep, now in its fifth year under AMC ownership, had managed to almost tri-

ple its sales from 1970. That this was achieved at all is evidence of the expertise of AMC management. It is extraordinary that it was accomplished while selling almost the same line of vehicles as in 1970.

The 1975 Jeep line-up showed still more refinements. The Jeep CJ line was upgraded with a new electronic ignition and an improved exhaust system. A new option was the Levi's interior, with seats covered in a denim-look material. Big news was the availability of dealer-installed air conditioning—probably shocking many old-time CJ enthusiasts, but times had changed and the public was demanding it. As before, the V-8 powered Rene-

Jeep continued to pitch Quadra-Trac for 1974 with this interesting ad.

gade was a popular choice among Jeep buyers. The Cherokee was back, looking every bit as appealing as the previous year. Not much was new, but it didn't matter. As *Four Wheeler* magazine said, "We don't think you'll find a better all-around, dual purpose 4x4 anywhere."

The Jeep truck line was even prettier this year—the Pioneer package now included full wood-grain side panels, and J-10 models could now be ordered with aluminum alloy wheels. Wagoneers offered a new wood-grain side treatment and added CB radios and radial ply tires to the options list.

The economic recession in 1975 made it a tough year for the auto industry. American Motors suffered a loss of $27 million in fiscal 1975—but that

New Cherokee

It's a Jeep and-a-half

The newest Jeep₈ vehicle has arrived. Jeep Cherokee. Heir to a tradition of quality and rough road dependability, Cherokee takes up where Jeep CJ-5 leaves off. Youthful and sporty, with the extra room that lets you pack along what you used to leave behind.

Cherokee really stands out where the pavement ends because the famous Jeep 4-wheel drive was specifically designed into Cherokee—most of the competition are merely converted two-wheelers. With greater ground clearance and a higher load capacity than any other sports utility vehicle in its weight class, new Cherokee makes a big difference in the boondocks.

Jeep Cherokee combines this rugged performance with sporty good looks—plus exciting options like Quadra-Trac,™ Jeep's automatic 4-wheel drive, automatic transmission, power steering, air conditioning and power front disc brakes.

New Jeep Cherokee is the get-away machine *your* family has been waiting for. It's a Jeep-and-a-half.

Jeep ◢ **Cherokee**
From A Subsidiary of
American Motors Corporation

According to this ad, 1974 Cherokee was "a Jeep-and-a-half."

was mainly because of a big drop in car sales. Wholesale sales of Jeeps (in other words, sales to Jeep dealers) during fiscal 1975 came to 69,289, the second best performance in Jeep history. Retail sales for the calendar year were 85,111, down from 1974 certainly, but likewise the second best year for Jeep sales. The company noted that Jeep buyers were less effected by the recession, because of their higher income level. This came as a surprise to many marketers who had guessed that Jeep buyers came from the lower reaches of the economic pecking order; but the truth was that Jeep owners had the sort of demographics most companies would kill for. In April the 400,000 Jeep built since the acquisition of Jeep Corporation came off the Toledo assembly line.

In overseas markets business was a lot better— Jeep sales were up 43%! In fact, the company boasted that since purchasing Jeep in 1970, they had managed to more than double the volume of overseas sales. As before, nearly 1/3 of four-wheel-

If it takes more than a Jeep CJ-5...

Clever ad shows Cherokee's advantages vs. CJ.

get a Cherokee.™

It's a Jeep and-a-half

Meet Jeep Cherokee, the family man's answer to the sure-footed Jeep CJ-5. With a higher load capacity than anybody in her sports utility weight class, our newest vehicle will haul your family, your gear—even your canoe, strapped to its rugged steel roof—and look good doing it. Options like Quadra-Trac™

Jeep ▲ Cherokee
From A Subsidiary of
American Motors Corporation

Jeep Corporation's automatic 4-wheel drive, automatic transmission, power steering, air conditioning and power front disc brakes bring the spirited Jeep Cherokee new ease and comfort on the roughest trails.

Want more room in the great outdoors? Get a Jeep Cherokee: It's a Jeep-and-a-half.

152

Renegade became a regular production offering for 1974.

drive vehicles of all brands sold outside the U.S. and Canada wore the Jeep brand. These were a combination of Jeep exports and units built overseas. In fact, about 1/3 of all Jeeps produced were being sold abroad.

For 1976, Jeep hit the ground running, introducing a new CJ model that was big news indeed. The CJ-7 had a ten-inch longer wheelbase—93.5 vs. the CJ-5's 83.5. The ten-inch increase was not much as far as appearances or cost was concerned, but it solved nearly every problem or shortcoming that had kept the CJ line from reaching its full sales potential. With the added chassis length, the CJ could now be fitted with an automatic transmission—which was absolutely crucial to increasing sales. To maximize the benefit, Jeep engineers included the renowned Quadra-Trac automatic four-wheel-drive system on all automatic-equipped CJs.

Those ten extra inches of wheelbase gave the CJ-7 a much smoother ride, better handling, and more stable cornering. It offered both front and rear seat passengers greatly increased room and even provided space for groceries and small packages behind the rear seat—something the CJ-5 couldn't offer. Besides all that, it made entering and exiting the vehicle much easier. CJ-7 also offered an op-

tional fiberglass hardtop that was much more stylish than any of the creaky metal tops available on CJ-5s. Yet despite the improvements, the appearance of the Jeep wasn't greatly altered—it still looked rugged and sporty. As Jim Alexander, one of Jeep's product planners, later noted, the CJ-7 (not the Cherokee) was the real replacement for the old Jeepster Commando. It offered a combination of traditional Jeep styling and removable top, with automatic transmissions and greater comfort and convenience. The price for all this improvement was about $100 more than a CJ-5. The CJ-6 model was dropped from the domestic market, though it remained in production for export sales.

The Renegade package returned in a somewhat watered-down form. Both the CJ-5 and CJ-7 could be purchased with the Renegade package, which now included a sports steering wheel, courtesy lights, a day/night rear-view mirror and a dressier dashboard. However, the Renegade option no longer automatically included a V-8 engine. Renegades came with the standard 232-cid six, and a buyer had to pay extra for the V-8 or the other engine option, the 258-six. The Renegade obviously was now a dress-up package, not a combination performance/appearance model.

For 1975, CJ offered a Levi interior.

Cherokee added a new sports model to its line-up for 1976. This was the Cherokee Chief, known internally as the wide-wheel model, because of its wider stance and bigger wheels. The Chief was another clever example of using existing parts to create new products. The Chief used the standard Cherokee body (based, as it was, on the Wagoneer), added the flared fenders like those used on Jeep trucks, sporty body striping, wider axles, and bigger tires mounted on wider wheels, to create an aggressive looking SUV that became the gold standard for that market segment. Public response was so great, that exultant Jeep dealers once again had waiting lists of buyers. The rest of the Cherokee line also did well, the "S" package being particularly popular. Cherokee received stronger frames, as well as new springs and shock absorbers. Jeep Wagoneers and trucks also got upgraded frames

Cherokee 'S' for 1975 was a tremendously popular vehicle.

and suspensions. The Wagoneer's wood-grain body panels were smaller this year and looked less expensive—a curious move, but one that buyers didn't seem to mind, since they bought every Wagoneer the company could build.

There was some concern among company executives that the CJ-7 might cannibalize sales of the CJ-5. It's true that CJ-5 sales did decline somewhat for the year, but CJ sales in total showed a dramatic climb. The company's goal of strengthening its dealer base was also being achieved. By the end of fiscal 1976, there were 1,608 Jeep dealers in the U.S., 1,049 of which also carried the AMC car line. Retail sales for the calendar year were 107,487—another record year. Despite the excellent Jeep numbers, AMC lost $46.3 million for the year, as its passenger car sales continued their downward slide. With little new planned for their 1977 passenger car line, any hope for the coming year being profitable would be up to Jeep.

Despite having had three major introductions (Quadra-Trac, Cherokee and CJ-7) in just four years, Jeep still managed to come up with exciting new products for 1977. In the CJ line, there was a new dress-up package called the Golden Eagle—an attempt to lure even more buyers to the Jeep brand by offering an exciting trim package. The Golden Eagle included gold-tone sport wheels and body

striping, dressier interior trim, and a huge decal of an American eagle appliquéd on the hood. Bold, conspicuous, or just plain outrageous—you be the judge—the Golden Eagle was an attention-getter and a sales success.

There was a new Cherokee four-door wagon for 1977. Although it was nothing more than a Wagoneer with trim differences, the Cherokee four-door appealed to different buyers than the Wagoneer—and thus increased Jeep's market coverage. The truck line now included a sporty package called the Honcho, using the same formula as the other packages—wide wheels, sporty striping, nicer interior trim. Jeep advertised it with a clever line: "Jeep Honcho—Mucho Macho." The Golden Eagle package was also available for pickups, so the Jeep truck line was considerably strengthened. Wagoneers received only detail changes, but were offered this year in just a single model equivalent to the former Custom series.

As expected, 1977 was another great year for Jeep. By May, the Toledo plant was cranking out 600 units per day, compared to the 175 units a day it was building when AMC took it over. The product mix was much better too, with about 18% of J-10 trucks ordered with the very profitable Honcho package, and 25% of CJ's built with the Renegade package. The plant was working voluntary overtime

Although the 1975 J-20 was a heavy-duty work truck, the Pioneer trim package gave it a touch of elegance.

nearly every Saturday. In March, Jeep unveiled a prototype diesel-powered CJ planned for Europe.

Jeep's parent, American Motors, was still struggling with poor car sales in 1977. In an attempt to sway public opinion (and reassure investors), AMC management hit the road with a traveling auto show that featured concept cars—ideas for the future. Called Concept 80, the group included a mock-up of a new CJ, considerably smaller than even a CJ-5. Dubbed Concept Jeep II, the new Jeep looked like a modern version of the old Jeep CJ-2. In May, Gerald C. Meyers was named president of AMC, succeeding the retiring William Luneburg. Meyers was the executive who had been against the purchase of Jeep (as the press delighted in reminding him, by the way), but now was one of Jeep's biggest boosters. Roy D. Chapin Jr. remained on as Board Chairman, and his apparent successor, R. William McNealy, was Vice Chairman.

Towards the end of the calendar year, AMC announced a joint venture to manufacture Jeeps in Egypt. A new company called Arab American Vehicles would be co-owned, 51% by the Arab Organization for Industrialization (representing the United Arab Emirates, Saudi Arabia, Quatar and Egypt), and 49% by AMC. A new plant would be built near Cairo at Heliopolis, Egypt, with a planned capacity of 10,000-12,000 Jeeps. Because it had a licensee assembling Jeeps in Israel, AMC was on the Arab blacklist. Ordinarily this would have precluded it getting the Egypt deal approved, but the lure of a Jeep factory proved too much for the Arabs, and the deal was made.

In October, Gerald Meyers became CEO of AMC when Roy Chapin relinquished that post while still retaining his position as Board Chairman. Chapin was interested in retiring but the board felt that, in light of the companies precarious financial condition, the transition to a new management should perhaps be gradual. Promoting Meyers was a surprise move, and not surprisingly, Chapin's heir apparent, R. William McNealy resigned. Although AMC never released any official word why McNealy left, insiders claimed he had displeased the board when he advocated betting everything on Jeep and elimination of the AMC car line. If true, he wasn't alone. One New York stock analyst predicted that, "AMC is very likely to become the Jeep Manufacturing Corporation of Toledo, Ohio."

Things were not as bad as all that, not yet anyway. For the fiscal year AMC reported a profit $8.2 million. Car sales took another big drop, but wholesale sales of Jeeps rose yet again, to 153,485 worldwide. Jeep's abundant profitability was dragged

Wagoneer for 1975 had stylish woodgrain trim.

The new CJ-7 was a longer, roomier CJ, and was the first CJ that could be had with automatic transmission.

The CJ-5 was still available for 1976, as was the hot-selling Renegade package.

The 1976 Cherokee Chief, built on the wide-wheel chassis, was popular with young families.

down by the huge losses on passenger cars, and it was only the strong performance of AMC's other operations, including a particularly profitable year for AM General, that moved the company into profitability. In international markets, the company reported plans to increase production at its Venezuela Jeep plant, and boasted that Jeep vehicles had captured nearly 75% of four-wheel-drive sales in Iran.

For 1978, the four-wheel-drive market continued its rapid growth. Although Jeep didn't hold as large a share of the market as it once had, its growth had been phenomenal notwithstanding. Most of the press chose this year to focus on AMC's new Concord luxury compact car—a sign that reporters still considered automobiles more important than Jeeps. The 1978 Jeep line-up showed continuing improvements and a few new editions that were both pleasant to the eye and profitable to the corporation.

A motto first used in the back section of Jeep's 1976 sales catalog (and featured more prominently in the 1977 catalog) received more play for 1978. "Jeep Wrote the Book on Four Wheel Drive" captured the essence of Jeep's heritage and capability in a way that earlier slogans—"Tough Jeep Guts," or "Toughest Four Letter Word on Wheels" hadn't.

It was important in the rapidly expanding four-wheeler market to remind buyers that Jeep had more experience building four-wheel-drive vehicles than anyone else.

For 1978, CJ's received minor changes in trim and options, as did the Cherokee line. Despite increasing sales, Jeep pickup trucks were still the weakest part of the line-up, so they received another new trim package, a low cost option called the "10-4 Package"—a play on CB radio operator's slang. The 10-4 package included spoke wheels, roll bar, two-tone body striping and a 10-4 decal on the side.

The big news for 1978 came early in the calendar year, with the introduction of the glamorous new Wagoneer Limited. The Wagoneer Limited was the most luxurious four-wheel-drive vehicle America had ever seen. Standard equipment included the 360-cid V-8 engine, automatic transmission and Quadra-Trac used on regular Wagoneers, plus leather bucket seats (the first four-wheeler to offer leather upholstery), aluminum wheels with whitewall radial tires, roof rack with wood-grain accents, air conditioning, AM/FM/CB (or tape) radio, tinted glass, tilt steering wheel, and many other trim and convenience items. The Limited was similar in concept to the old Wagoneer Super of earlier

Cherokee 'S' for 1976 was more elegant, less sporty than the Chief.

The 1976 Jeep J-10 pickup offered an attractive package in two-tone paint option.

Looking like it had stolen its hood decal from a Pontiac Firebird was the sporty Golden Eagle package for 1977.

The 1977 Jeep Honcho was "Mucho Macho."

AMC Styling Vice-President Dick Teague with the Concept Jeep II.

years, but was much more elegant. With its advanced Quadra-Trac and modern engine, it was the "Rolls-Royce" of four-wheel-drives. With a price tag of about $11,000, the Limited was sure to test the limit of price sensitivity in the SUV market.

Rumors were flying that the struggling AMC would merge or become affiliated with another company. They were becoming so shrill that at one press gathering an apparently flustered Frank S. Hedge, vice-president of public relations angrily told a reporter, "I won't reiterate anything. I can't speak for the corporation," apparently forgetting for a moment that as head of public relations it was his job to speak for the corporation.

By mid-year the company announced big news—in an effort to solve the twin problems of too much passenger car production capacity and not enough Jeep, it was retooling the small AMC plant in Brampton, Ontario, Canada to build Jeep CJ's. It would mean an additional 50,000 Jeeps could be built each year. AMC of Canada President William S. Pickett told reporters the production equipment would be new—nothing was being sent up from Toledo.

The increased production was very much needed, for if any complaint could be made about AMC's handling of Jeep since its acquisition, it would be that it hadn't raised Jeep production as quickly as it raised Jeep demand. The new plant could go a long way towards improving AMC's profitability, since it would increase availability of its hottest selling products. At the same time, it was reducing the passenger car break-even point—the number of car sales needed for operations to break even profit-wise. Roy Chapin explained it to Dave Smith of *Ward's Auto World* this way, "...once you get skin-

Jeep set a new record for production in 1978. Driving the 150,000th Jeep built that year off the assembly line is Ohio Governor James A. Rhodes, with AMC President Gerry Meyers in the front passenger seat.

nied down to a level where you can exist, the upside, when it comes, is a very profitable thing...once you get your fixed costs down so you can make money at a lower level...it's a beautiful business."

It was a beautiful business for AMC, which in 1978, reported a profit of $36.7 million. In October of 1978, Gerry Meyers took over as Chairman of the Board, as Roy D. Chapin Jr. reduced his role in the company to board member and consultant. The company reported some news that was a bit surprising—by year's end it had more Jeep dealers than car dealers—1,999 Jeep dealers vs. 1,846 for passenger cars. Of the total, 1,517 carried both lines.

Jeep sales set yet another record as the company delivered 153,000 units to its U.S. and Canadian dealers. The annual report stated that by year's end Jeep sales had exceeded year-ago periods for 37 consecutive months—a stunning record. The report also stated management's belief that, "The four-wheel-drive market should remain strong in the years ahead, because it has become increasingly diverse, reflecting basic changes in buyer needs and preferences." Plans were announced to expand Jeep production at Toledo as well.

Since passenger car sales had fallen further, and the normally robust AM General subsidiary showed a loss for the year, it's logical to assume that the main thing propping up AMC's profits were the ever-increasing Jeep sales. One can't state that as fact even after a careful reading of the company annual report, because AMC lumped Jeeps and cars together under a category called General Automotive.

The outlook for 1979 was good. Gerry Meyers told *Ward's Auto World*, "Over the last nine to 12 months, there has been a large vocal group of people who are saying recession is just around the corner, but it hasn't happened. It is something to be on the lookout for, but so far the evidence is not that we are on the front edge of a recession." In answer to a remark by Ward's editor Dave Smith that, "some people are beginning to say that the four-wheel-drive market is starting to peak out," Meyers replied "Baloney—absolute baloney."

For 1979, Jeep was in a position of great strength. Both the CJ-5 and CJ-7 were offered in base, Renegade or Golden Eagle form. The 258-cid six became the standard engine as the old 232-six went out of production. The 304 V-8 remained a popular option. Cherokees were available as two-door or four-door base models or with the Cherokee 'S' package, or could be had with the Golden

This young lady seems thrilled with her 1978 Cherokee four-door.

Wagoneer Limited was the most luxurious four-wheel-drive that money could buy.

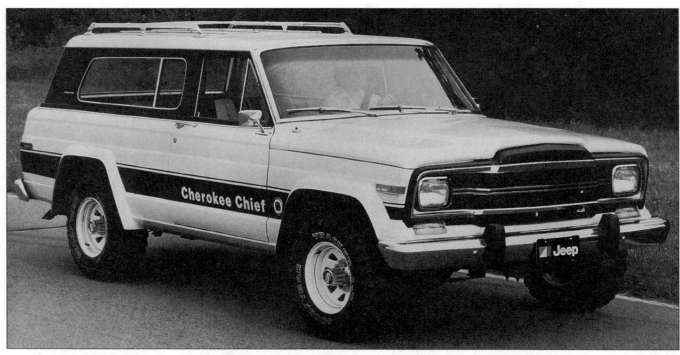

Cherokee Chief for 1979 was even better-looking, and very popular.

Cherokee four-door was a sporty, family wagon.

Eagle or Chief packages in the wide-wheel two-door body. New on the Cherokee were square head lamps set in a new, cleanly styled grille.

Wagoneer returned for 1979 with a new grille, and a stronger emphasis on the Limited model. The Limited had surprised nearly everyone; despite its high price tag it sold out and now had a waiting list of buyers. Jeep J10 and J20 pickups also got a new grille along with detail refinements. In celebration of 25 years of Jeep CJ-5 production, a special lim-

It's doubtful anyone in 1954 thought the CJ-5 would still be on the market in 1979. To commemorate the anniversary, Jeep offered this limited production Silver Anniversary CJ-5.

ited issue Silver Anniversary CJ-5 model was announced. Specially trimmed and painted its own shade of silver metallic paint, the commemorative CJ was a handsome tribute to the enduring appeal of the basic Jeep model.

Early in the year AMC announced it had reached an agreement with Renault. The deal allowed AMC the rights to distribute the fuel-efficient line of Renault cars in the U.S. and Canada. Renault, in exchange, would invest in AMC and would have the right to distribute Jeeps in France and Columbia. As originally structured, the deal was a win-win situation all the way around. AMC would get financial aid plus a line of badly-needed high gas mileage cars; Renault would overnight become a major automotive importer in the U.S. as well as earn a bit of extra money from sales of Jeep in France. The old Hotchkiss company which once assembled Jeeps in France had relinquished that role many years previous.

By February 1979, the company was reporting that the Brampton plant was running an overtime schedule, while Toledo had been running at capacity for many months. It was announced that Jeep production would soon be added to the main AMC plant at Kenosha, WI. Further, a new $27.5 million paint facility was planned for Toledo, a move that would allow a 50% increase in Toledo's output by 1981. Plans were announced to double Jeep pro-

duction in Venezuela, to 14,000 units annually. AMC's new president, Paul Tippett, was bragging that within three years AMC would be producing more than 350,000 Jeep per year.

By May of 1979, Jeep sales were running an astounding 41% over 1978's record pace. Seemingly all the company had to do to sell more Jeeps was to build more—demand apparently was limitless. Assembly in China was also being studied. However, in the third quarter report to the stockholders, in August 1979, there appeared the first indication of a possible problem. Sales were still up, hitting a record $798 million for the quarter, $2.3 billion for the 9 month period. Jeep deliveries to dealers set a record for the first three quarters, as expected. Yet in the third quarter, Jeep sales failed to exceed the prior year's quarter for the first time in many months. That in itself was nothing to fret about; after all, no one really believed Jeep could go on increasing sales forever. But the reasons behind the stumble in Jeep sales was rooted in the economic crisis brought about when extremists took control of Iran, shut off oil supplies to America and created a gasoline shortage. Soon, consumers who had been aching to drive home a new V-8 powered Jeep Cherokee (capable of perhaps 10-14 mpg) were suddenly more interested in small, economical cars.

Jeep, with its strong standing in the market, was able to roll with the first punches. As Paul Tippett

165

later explained, "Three days after we saw this thing coming, we had promotions running on the CJ's...." Jeep was able to prop up sales by tapping into the built-up demand they hadn't been able to satisfy before. With demand down, Jeep dealers were forced to work a little harder for each sale. So work they did, (helped by a strong backlog of vehicles customer-ordered before the crisis), and in the end they were able to deliver a good sales year. The sales problem was greatest in the Cherokee line. This was the unkindest cut of all, because although CJs were the spiritual heir of Jeep's heritage, and Wagoneers were the single most profitable Jeep product, when all was said and down, the Cherokee was Jeep's bread and butter model, the most important model in terms of sales volume. And Cherokee sales were decimated.

Much of this managed to slip past industry observers. That was because AMC's fiscal year still ran from October 1 to September 30, and thus its annual report showed a rosier picture than it would have, had it continued to the end of calendar 1979. Sales, you see, did not bounce back by year end. Instead, they got worse. Much worse.

This particular fiscal year ended up being a plum for American Motors. Sales hit $3.1 billion, a new record, and net earnings came to $83.4 million, also a record. Working capital was strong and stockholders' equity was good. A startling event took place—Jeep out sold AMC passenger cars with 207,642 Jeeps worldwide as compared to 207,557 cars. That had been expected for several months, though it is unlikely that AMC (or anyone else for that matter) ever considered it possible when they first got together in 1970. A great many things had changed in the intervening nine years.

If one compares Jeep in relation to its two peers, GMC and International Harvester, using 1970 as the base year, 1974 as the mid-point and 1979 as the final year, one can easily view how each progressed in the 1970s—a decade which proved pivotal to the light truck industry. As already stated, at the beginning of this chapter, according to the *Automotive News,* Jeep retail sales in the calendar year 1970 were 33,984, GMC's were 89,675 and IH's were 68,939. Jeep clearly was the runt of the group. By 1979, GMC sales were 236,750—up 264%. International didn't fare so well—its sales in 1979 were 23,464, and it would soon exit the light truck field. Jeep retail sales in calendar 1979 were reported at 145,214—up 427%. Jeep, then , not only outpaced the market, it had outpaced its peer group—and vindicated Roy Chapin's extraordinary vision. Where, one might ask, was *Dun's Review* now?

Taken as a whole, the decade of the 1970s was a golden era for Jeep, one in which it achieved greater prosperity than ever before, while at the same time earning a reputation that was second only to its legendary war record. Jeep was one of the icons of the 1970s, a symbol of America itself. But however hard it was for anyone to believe, the problems in Iran were going to shape American industry for years to come, in particular the transportation industry. In 1979, Jeep had passed through the last great year it would enjoy for many a day. Ahead was a decade of uncertainty, of threats and disappointments, an era that would see Jeep struggle mightily to reinvent itself for a new age, even as it came under the control of a foreign government. AMC had successfully created a new Jeep company—now that company would be tested to see if it could survive the coming conflict. No one ever said the automobile industry was easy, and Jeep was about to learn exactly how hard it could be.

Chapter Six

A STRUGGLE TO SURVIVE

1980-1987

The 1980 Jeep Sportside pickups came only in Custom trim, and were meant to be sporty, personal trucks.

The world was a very different place in 1980. Even though a recession had begun, interest rates still managed to hit record highs—delivering a double blow to the struggling economy. The light truck market (both two-wheel-drive and four-wheel-drive), which had peaked in 1978 at 3,770,550 units, fell to 3,227,537 in 1979, and would sink to 2,227,472 during 1980—a drop of over 40% in just two years. With fuel concerns uppermost in everyone's mind, interest in Japanese trucks reached new levels. Yet even as four-wheel-drive sales continued to drop in the fall of 1979, Jeep management seemed confident things weren't going to get too difficult, and that the extraordinary demand that Jeep had enjoyed for so long would soon return. Certainly, the 1980 Jeep product line was geared to address concerns about fuel economy.

The 1980 Jeep CJs received a new four-cylinder engine as standard equipment, the first Jeep available (in America) with a four since 1971. The engine, nostalgically dubbed the "Hurricane" was a 2.5 liter (151-cid), the sturdy though unremarkable Iron Duke supplied by General Motors. Most Jeeps now featured standard four-speed transmissions, and all non-Quadra-Trac Jeeps got free-wheeling front hubs as standard. These moves represented Jeep's determined effort to improve real world fuel economy. Since Quadra-Trac was fairly fuel-thirsty, an all-new Quadra-Trac system was announced. Its viscous fluid coupling was smoother and quieter than the cone-clutch friction system it replaced. Also new was an optional automatic transmission/part-time four-wheel-drive combination available on CJs, Cherokees and trucks.

CJs were available with the popular Golden Eagle and Renegade packages, plus a new-for-1980 line-topping Laredo package. Laredo combined sportiness with luxury, including the fanciest inte-

167

The 1980 Renegade was still popular with CJ buyers.

The 1980 Jeep CJ Laredo was a beautiful package.

rior ever seen on a CJ. On the exterior, the Laredo was flashy without being outrageous—a handsome chrome grille and chrome bumper graced the front, tasteful striping was applied on the body sides and rear, and a bold Laredo decal rode on the hood's sides.

The Jeep truck was also given a Laredo option, as well as the popular Honcho package. The 10-4, Golden Eagle and Pioneer models didn't make the cut, and were dropped. Wagoneer and Wagoneer Limited models returned with refinements. The 360 V-8 and Quadra-Trac continued as standard equipment. However, to make certain the fuel economy concerns of even the affluent were being addressed, the Wagoneers could now be ordered with the 258-cid six-cylinder, and either a four-speed or automatic transmission combined with part-time four-wheel-drive.

Pickup trucks were seen as one possibility to increase sales, since truck sales in the past had been hampered by a shortage of production. A new program dubbed "TST" for Time to Sell Trucks—had already begun to focus retail attention on possibilities in the pickup market.

The big truck news for 1980 was the availability of a new wide rear fender model called the Sportside. Envisioned as a sporty personal truck, the Sportside came only with custom interior trim, white-spoke wheels, outline white-letter tires, black and chrome grill, and a rear step bumper. A Honcho Sportside model included all that, plus special decals, denim bucket seats, roll bar and wood side rails for the pickup box.

There were signs that things would be okay. In January, Robert Irvin of the *Automotive News* wrote that, "...AMC has made the sort of comeback which seems to be long-lasting." In February, that same trade paper ran a picture of the 1,000,000th Jeep produced by American Motors, as it came off the assembly line in Toledo. The first quarter of fiscal 1980, which ended Dec. 31, 1979, even showed an operating profit for the company of $12.8 million, although, that figure was a drop of 32% from the prior year—inspite of a 10% sales increase. The sales increase, however, had been fueled by increased interest in AMC cars, due to fuel economy concerns, and the introduction of a new four-wheel-drive car called the Eagle, and also to increasing sales of Renault cars by AMC/Jeep dealers. Company President Paul Tippett assured the Detroit Auto Writers Group (DAWG) that the company was in good shape. He said, "Now we're in a position where we can take some lumps and not get in the soup."

There were problems. Buyers who purchased CJs with the four-cylinder engine often reported gas mileage of 20 mpg over the road, and 17 in town, both of which were excellent numbers. However, six-cylinder buyers were more likely to report 14-17 mpg and V-8 buyers coming in at 12-15 mpg—not encouraging in a fuel tight market. Even more worrisome—in a poll by Mike Lamm of *Popular Mechanics* magazine, fully 60% of CJ buyers experienced a mechanical problem with their Jeeps.

The constantly increasing Jeep production of the late 1970s, fueled by a market that was simply ravenous for four-wheelers, had taken a toll on quality. Besides mechanical problems, paint quality had also gone downhill. That problem, however, was being addressed. A new $30 million paint facility at Toledo would become operational during the year.

With all the troubles in Iran, someone was bound to recall that Jeep had an assembly plant there. When *Ward's Auto World* asked about it, chairman Meyers replied "We build Jeeps there, and we were still in production up until yesterday...It isn't a sizable facility but volumes have been good...." Anyway, as Meyers noted, GM owned the plant—for Jeep it was simply an assembly point.

Other big news in 1980 was Renault's investing $150 million in AMC, gaining an immediate 5% ownership of the firm with the possibility of expanding that to 22%. The money was to be used to finance tooling to build a line of Renault cars in Wisconsin.

In mid-1980, Jeep's product planners developed a pair of limited-production Jeeps to create some excitement in the market. The CJ Golden Hawk, available on both the CJ-5 and CJ-7, included a tri-tone stylized Hawk decal on the hood, tri-tone striping on the body, gold-colored wheels, tan top and high-back seats, fog lamps and a host of other trim bits. The Cherokee Golden Hawk featured similar decals and stripes, a black tubular brush guard and bronze tone glass on the rear side windows. (See color section) Bold and eye-catching though they were, the Hawks failed to sell in large numbers. The market simply wasn't there.

Despite a difficult economy, the 1980 Jeep product line was the best in years.

Jeep wasn't the only one suffering. Its old peer and competitor International Harvester was struggling with poor sales, and by the end of the year would announce the discontinuation of its Scout sport utility vehicles—IH was leaving the light truck market.

Early in the fiscal year, AMC car sales increased in response to the new interest in fuel economy. With Jeep sales on the downturn and cars on the upswing, the Brampton, Ontario plant was converted back to car production. By mid-year, however, even car sales were struggling due to the record high interest rates, high unemployment, and inroads from Japanese cars. Jeep sales, which had been propped-up by a high backlog of ordered vehicles, hit the skids. Cherokees, which only a few months earlier had long lists of waiting buyers, suddenly became a drug on the market. In fact, for 1980 Cherokee production was about one-fifth of 1979s pace—7,614 vs. 39,183! When Cherokee sales dropped, AMC, despite Paul Tippett's pro-

nouncement to the contrary, did indeed find itself in the soup. The company soon found out exactly how dependent on Jeep sales it had become. Huge losses began to pile up and new partner Renault had to step in with more money. In an agreement signed September 23, 1980, Renault agreed to invest $220 million in AMC, increasing its ownership to 46% of the company—this being less than two years after management had assured AMC stockholders Renault would have no substantial equity position in the company.

AMC decided that beginning with 1980 it would change its fiscal year to run January-December, like the other auto makers, so from this point on that is how it's stated. For the fiscal year/calendar year AMC lost a staggering $197.5 million—a mind-numbing amount of money. While factory wholesale sales of cars in the U.S. and Canada were flat, at 203,251 for the twelve months ending Dec. 31, 1980, unit sales of Jeep fell an unbelievable 57%, dropping from 156,825 to 67,312. Compar-

All 1981 Jeep truck models, including this stylish Sportside, received a re-styled roof line.

ing the old fiscal year with similar cut-off dates for 1980, the drop was 77,359 vs. 175,647 in fiscal 1979. Overseas, Jeep sales suffered less—they dropped less than 10%.

What happened was that the severe economic situation, arriving as it did almost overnight, had kicked out two of the three legs of AMC's stool. With cars and Jeeps both struggling, only AM General was profitable and it just wasn't enough to off-set the gigantic losses generated by the rest of the company. Now, suddenly, AMC not only had to

For 1981, Cherokee offered this good-looking four-door Chief.

develop new cars, it also had to develop an all-new line of Jeeps—vehicles that would be so fuel-efficient and right for the decade that they could sell even in the hard times America now faced. The un-spoken fact was that in the ten years AMC had owned Jeep, it had yet to "develop vehicles that are completely new to Jeep," despite so stating in the 1970 annual report. It was a do-able thing, design-ing new Jeeps, but it would cost an ungodly amount of money. With no income coming in, Renault seemed like the only choice, and Meyers and Tip-pett took it. Thus, a line of all-new Jeep vehicles would debut in 1983. Hopefully, they would arrive in time to save the company.

However, 1983 was three years off, so Jeep's product planners and market wizards would have to make the best of what they had until then. There had been many changes on the 1980 models, and there would have to be more in 1981.

There was an emphasis on aerodynamics for 1981—certainly something that Jeep designers had never worried about before. Improved aero-dynamics would yield better real world fuel econ-omy, so all senior Jeeps now came with an undercarriage air dam, and most of those models also had suspension changes to reduce ride height. The 258-cid six-cylinder engine was redesigned to reduce weight by utilizing a new lighter weight block, plastic valve cover and lighter components. More fuel-efficient rear-axle gears were fitted to all models.

A new Wagoneer package debuted, called the Brougham. Positioned between the Custom and the Limited, the Brougham offered nicer interior trim than the Custom, plus a roof rack, floor mats, power tailgate window, digital clock, and lighted visor vanity mirror. All Wagoneers now came with fuel-saving radial tires and the 258-cid six as standard equipment. The Custom (and Brougham package) came with a four-speed transmission, while the Limited included Quadra-Trac. All Wagoneers could be ordered with the optional automatic transmission/part-time four-wheel-drive option, however. For the first time, Wagoneer sales catalogs listed the fuel economy ratings—15 mpg city and 22 highway for the standard six.

The Cherokee line was hurting the most, so it received a great deal of attention for 1981. New this year were radial tires standard on most models, as well as the 258-six, four-speed manual transmission and part-time four-wheel-drive. All models got a handsome new grille. The Chief package was now available on four-door Cherokees, as was the Laredo. The old Cherokee 'S', Golden Eagle and Golden Hawk packages were dropped. The new four-door models were not built on the wide-wheel chassis, however, because the wide wheels created additional drag, which cut fuel economy. It is also possible that fender extensions wouldn't have looked right on the small rear wheel openings.

To give the sales people something to talk about, Jeep trucks received a beautiful new grille, lowered ride height, and, at last, a re-styling of the roof that eliminated the 'lip' over the cab. The Honcho and Laredo packages returned. Like the other senior Jeeps, most trucks got the 258-six as standard equipment, though the J-20 still came with a standard 360-cid V-8.

The CJ-5 and CJ-7 special packages were trimmed down to just two: the ever-popular Renegade and Laredo. All came with the four-cylinder/four-speed combination as standard (Renegade certainly wasn't a muscle car any longer), but the 258-six and 304 V-8 were still available. The base power train was rated by the Environmental Protection Agency at 22 mpg in the city and 27 mpg

The Jeep Scrambler, new for 1981, was a sporty compact pickup.

highway—the best fuel economy of any American-made four-wheeler, and considered a great achievement, because the Jeep was every bit as rugged and sturdy as always.

However, the biggest product news for 1981 was the Scrambler, a new pickup designed to do battle with the popular small Japanese trucks. The new truck was not the Hornet-based Cowboy that product planning put together in 1971. Deciding to build it on the CJ chassis neatly eliminated any concern about diluting the Jeep image, and made it easier to tool up, since the Jeep was a body-on-frame design rather than the more complicated unibody of AMC's passenger cars. With a wheelbase of 103.5 inches the Scrambler, also known as the CJ-8, was about the size of the old Commando pickup, and even had a fair resemblance. The new truck, however, was a fully modern machine and shared all the advances brought forth on its CJ siblings. The standard equipment was the same as the CJ's, and the optional appearance package mirrored those on the CJ-5/CJ-7, with the Scrambler SR package equivalent to the Renegade, while the SL package equaled the Laredo in content. Base priced at $7288 and offered as a basic open roadster with optional soft-top or hardtop, the Scrambler represented a great opportunity for Jeep to expand into a part of the market that was still doing well—one of the few bright spots in a dismal retail world. Gerry Meyers was optimistic, and the *Automotive News* quoted him in June 1981, "You haven't heard anybody recently question our future; you won't."

In August 1981, Jeep announced the opening of a new facility in Australia—a big market where Jeep had always been a small player. The new plant would build Cherokee and J-20 trucks, while still importing CJ-7s from the U.S. It was hoped that this latest attempt would make Jeep a larger factor in Australia's growing four-wheel-drive market. In other overseas news, Jeep International tried to help peddle some fleet units overseas by running ads in the *New York Times* offering, "Jeeps To Go." "We sell them here, and you get them there," stated the advertisements.

In the U.S., all the tactics Jeep tried didn't move the needle—the market was as dry as a desert and as merciless as Attila. The company ended fiscal 1981 with another loss, $136.6 million this time. When the annual report appeared, stockholders couldn't help but notice that Meyers, the man the French government had given a medal to the year before for strengthening Franco-American relationships through the AMC-Renault deal, was no longer with the company. Paul Tippett had been elevated to board chairman and CEO, and dapper little Jose Dedeurwaerder became president. A long-time Renault employee (and past manager of a European facility that assembled AMC products), Dedeurwaerder was obviously the power behind the throne.

Wholesale sales of Jeeps to dealers fell slightly, to 63,216, in the U.S. and Canada, but rose nearly a third overseas to 41,412, meaning that Jeep overall had a tiny increase. But 104,628 total units simply wasn't enough. The problem was that Jeep had become so big it needed to sell a great many units to break even, but buyers now wanted products that were smaller and more fuel efficient. For Jeep, unfortunately, those were still far in the future.

The Jeep Scrambler was a flop, with only 7,840 produced. There were several reasons why it sold so poorly, but the biggest was that Jeep failed to market it as a truck. Advertisements stressed its sportiness, fuel economy and versatility, but failed to supply the basic information that Scrambler was a small, fuel-efficient American-made alternative to Japanese trucks. Most shoppers thought it was just another CJ-7. Scrambler base prices didn't even include a top, so it didn't really seem to be a pickup truck. The five-foot bed, a foot shorter than most others, also turned off many buyers. Another problem was price—although $7288 was reasonable for a four-wheel-drive truck, Scrambler didn't have a low price two-wheel-drive model like the imports, and that was a big part of the market. It was too bad, because with superior ride and handling (because of its long wheelbase), in addition to adequate carrying capacity, the Scrambler was a great little truck.

This advertisement from the *New York Times* illustrated Jeep's problem in 1981—too much product stacking up waiting for buyers.

The 1982 CJ-7 Limited was the most luxurious small Jeep ever, and has not been surpassed in all the years since it debuted.

The 1982 Laredo was no longer the top-of-the-CJ-line, but was luxurious regardless.

CJ-5 Renegade was most fun with the top down. Note this vehicle is equipped with Jeep's optional saddlebags—small triangular-shaped storage pouches fitted to the rollbar.

There were some bright spots in 1981. A new pickup was developed for overseas markets. Combining a CJ cab with a J-10 chassis, the CJ-10 boasted a payload capacity of 3000 lbs. (See color section) Another new overseas model, the CJ-8 World Cab, was based on the new Scrambler, but had a full hardtop that turned the little truck into a sport utility wagon. (See color section) Jeep Venezuela, the largest assembler of Jeep vehicles outside the U.S., reported a great year, taking 50% of Venezuela's 10,000 unit four-wheel-drive market. The Egypt operation received a new order for CJ-6s and also negotiated a contract to assemble cars (BMWs, reportedly) for another company. Additionally, a new operation, Jeep Africa, was created to try to penetrate a market where Jeep had thus far found little success.

Another of Jeep's competitors bit the dust. Plymouth discontinued its Trail Duster SUV at the end of the model year, a victim of the disastrous state of the four-wheel-drive market. When the 1982 model year arrived, Jeep had nothing new—only refinements of the existing products. The biggest news was a new luxury trim for the CJ-7, the Limited. Jeep product planners felt that buyers stepping down from big four-wheel-drive wagons might be interested in a vehicle with the luxury they were used to in

a smaller, more fuel efficient package. AMC was using the Limited name for its highest trim level in cars and on the Wagoneer, so the nomenclature fit the CJ. The model itself didn't quite seem to square with the rough and ready CJ image. However, the CJ Limited was a pleasant mixture of luxury appointments and engineering refinements. To begin, the Limited included power steering and brakes, AM/FM radio, monochromatic paint, a color keyed hardtop and wheel lip extensions, special mirrors, special bucket seats with cloth trim and improved ride package. With a price starting at $11,552 the Limited's sales were certain to match its nameplate.

New this year was a five-speed manual transmission available on all models except the J-20. Senior Jeeps so equipped were EPA rated at 18 mpg city and 25 mpg highway. This was an incredible improvement from just three years earlier. CJs were rated 23 mpg city/28 mpg highway. Quadra-Trac was replaced by Selec-Trac, a similar system which included a switch inside the vehicle that enabled drivers to disconnect four-wheel-drive and run in rear drive only. This allowed for better gas mileage. Roy Lunn, VP of product engineering called it "...a logical step forward in the evolution of sophisticated four-wheel-drive systems." A variation of the AMC Eagle's

Select Drive system, it included a low range the four-wheel-drive cars lacked. Both systems required that the driver stop the vehicle before changing the drive mode.

Cherokees and Wagoneers were little changed, but offered several new colors. These were probably the best put-together Jeeps in history, since they benefited from a less-frenzied assembly line, as well as constant improvement since the market collapse of 1979. Also, they were now being painted in Jeep's new state-of-the-art paint facility (which went on-line in mid 1981).

There was a new special edition CJ named the Jamboree. Commemorating the 30th anniversary of the famed off-road expedition of the same name, the Jeep Jamboree included special hood decals, chrome wheels and bumpers, electric winch, fire extinguisher, grille and brush guards and more. Offered only in Aztec Gold paint, just 2,500 were built. (See Chapter 10)

The Pioneer name was reintroduced on a trim package for J-series trucks. It was less fancy than the earlier version, consisting mainly of interior trim upgrades plus body side moldings and decals. Priced at under $600, it was meant to be a low-cost upgrade from the basic truck. Interestingly, a Pioneer option for Cherokees is listed in the Jeep salesman's specification book, but doesn't appear in sales brochures that year.

In July, the *Automotive News* ran a spy photo of the next generation of Jeeps—the downsized XJ model that Jeep was pinning all its hopes on. Designed to offer nearly identical interior room as a Cherokee in a smaller, less fuel-thirsty package, the XJ was going to be the most important new Jeep since 1940. Towards year's end a new four-cylinder engine, a 150-cid AMC-designed unit, debuted in AMC Eagles and Jeep CJs. Its significance

was two-fold—the fact that cash-short AMC would invest the huge sums needed to produce it showed the importance of four-cylinder power in those fuel-desperate times and, even more significantly, it was going to be the standard engine for the new Jeeps that were by then just a year or so away.

As was expected, 1982 ended with a bigger loss for the company, $153.4 million, $17 million more than 1981. It couldn't be avoided; sales were still in the basement, the economy was still in a funk, interest rates were high, and little AMC was tooling up for an all-new line of Renault cars (the Alliance) and the new Jeep wagons, plus the new four-cylinder engine and goodness knows how many other component parts. With over $490 million in losses in just three years, it was also obvious that operations would have to return to profitability soon, or there wouldn't be any company left to sell those new products.

For 1983, Chevrolet introduced its new S-10 Blazer—a downsized, fuel efficient four-wheel-drive wagon with a 4 cylinder engine as standard and a small optional V-6. Midway through the year, Ford brought potent new competition to the market with its downsized, fuel-stingy Bronco II. Powered by a small V-6 engine, the Bronco II, like the S-10 Blazer, was what the market was buying just now, while

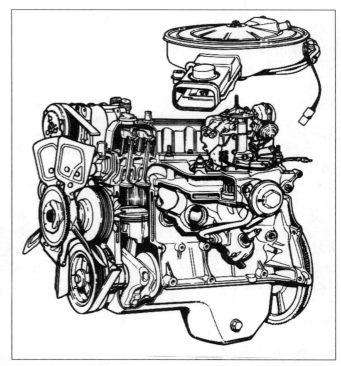

AMC introduced its new four-cylinder engine into production in mid-1983.

The 1983 Cherokee Laredo still looks good today.

The 1984 Jeep Cherokee Chief was typical of the all-new compact Jeep SportWagons, and proved popular with buyers.

big, conventional 4x4s gathered dust in the show-rooms. Almost all of AMC's attention for 1983 was focused on launching its new Alliance car—Jeep's turn at bat was still a year away. However, Jeep deal-ers had to be make a living in 1983, so the line re-turned with still more refinements.

Advertising for Scrambler at last began to em-phasize that it was a truck. Not much was altered to its base equipment list, however the base Scrambler was still an open roadster. Cherokee four-doors now came only in Pioneer trim, though the two-door was still offered in base, Chief and Laredo versions.

The economy was gradually improving, and in-terest rates began to float down from their lofty peak. Paul Tippett, in an interview with the *Auto-motive News*, spoke of "... a year and a half ago when we had 20% interest rates and the costs of carrying inventories was higher than it is now. But it's still high. It's 11%. So it's a major factor."

In May 1983, Jeep made history again when a deal was announced creating a joint venture com-pany to produce Jeeps in China. For the incredibly low investment of $8 million in cash and $8 million in technological expertise, Jeep gained a 31.6 per-cent share in Beijing Jeep Corporation. This was the first time an American vehicle maker was invit-ed to participate in the huge China market. The co-

partner, Beijing Automotive Works, was building 20,000 units a year of a four-wheel-drive military vehicle based on an old Russian design. The Chi-nese hoped partnering with Jeep would produce a new design to replace their outdated truck as well as teach them about production efficiency.

August of 1983 brought news. Renault re-vealed it had taken over VAM, Jeep's Mexico affil-iate, but would continue building Jeeps there for the Mexican market. AMC announced it had sold AM General, the former military vehicle branch of Jeep, to LTV for $190 million, or about $120 mil-lion more than AMC had paid for it *and* Jeep. Roy Chapin must have smiled broadly. AMC also re-vealed a troubling loss for its third quarter, $78.87 million. However, behind that bad news was a sil-ver lining. Much of the loss could be attributed to the expense involved in bringing its long anticipat-ed new Jeeps to market, and now they were only days away.

The year ended with good news and bad. The bad news was very grave indeed—the company lost $146,730,000, marking the fourth year in a row of losses. Company officers stated in the annual report that the year "...was one of substantial progress...." However, after four years, investors were under-standably impatient. It's true the fourth-quarter had

Do compact SUVs get any better looking than this? The 1984 Wagoneer was part of the advanced new Jeep line.

produced a profit, a slender $7.4 million, but in the auto industry the fourth quarter is traditionally the most profitable, since it reflects sales of the first vehicles of the new model year, when dealers are building up inventories. Everyone realized that such a slim profit margin meant the company could easily slip right back into losses.

Jeep wholesale sales to dealers for calendar 1983 were up over 22,000, because of heavy ordering of the all-new 1984 sport utility wagons, which offset a drop in overseas sales. Total sales for AMC were $3.27 billion but, as in the recent past, most of that was from cars, not Jeeps. If Jeep was ever going to regain its past sales levels, it would do so only if the new Jeeps were successful.

Unspoken, but ever present in management's mind, was that if the new generation of Jeeps should fail, the corporation would likely go out of business. AMC had held on for four years just for this moment, when the new Jeeps would ride in to the rescue. The company had sold off valuable assets, had gradually even sold itself to the French, just to reach this fall of 1983. Everything Jeep had ever been, or ever would be, was riding on the success of the new Jeeps.

The automotive press wondered if AMC had the skill to design a completely new Jeep. After all,

they had yet to do so in 14 years of owning Jeep, and hadn't even designed an all-new car since the 1975 Pacer. Paul Tippett was asked what his feelings were about a report that Nissan would soon be building its own sport utility vehicles (SUV) in America. Said Tippett, "If they build them in this country and don't have an undervalued yen, I'm willing to take 'em on." Auto writers had seen spy photos of the new Jeeps, heard rumors and even got a few tidbits of information deliberately leaked by company executives, but had to withhold judgment until they had something more substantial. They got that in August when the company showed the new models.

The last time an all-new Jeep wagon had been introduced, Willys Motors was still around, Studebaker dealers were still peddling Larks and Avantis, and few people had ever heard the name Toyota. The world had changed a lot in the intervening years and the auto market had changed considerably too, and changed again in response to the economic upheaval of recent times. However, the new Jeeps were designed specifically for the new era.

There had been many discussions about naming the new Jeep wagons. Some executives wanted bold new names that would show that these were all-new vehicles. Others felt it important to retain

178

The Wagoneer Limited became the Grand Wagoneer in 1984, and was still the most luxurious four-wheel drive vehicle in America.

the old, accepted Jeep nameplates that were so familiar to buyers. In the end focus groups and marketing clinics decided the issue. Out of hundreds of possible names, a list of fifty was shown to various test groups, and the results were conclusive—buyers preferred the existing Jeep names.

The new Jeep line, called the XJ series while under development, consisted of the sporty Cherokee, available in two-door and four-door wagons, and the Wagoneer, offered as a four-door wagon only, built on the same body as the Cherokee four-door. Prices started at $9995 for the two-door Cher-

It's not known how many of these 1984 Custom Wagoneers (offered at $15,995) were sold, but it's doubtful the number was very high. Buyers wanted luxury in their SUVs.

okee and $10,295 for a four-door, right in line with the competition from GM and Ford. Chrysler had no similar model (nor would it have for another 14 years). The Wagoneer and Wagoneer Limited were better trimmed, carried more standard equipment, and were priced and aimed at a higher income buyer. AMC marketing VP Joe Cappy said the new Jeeps were, "... designed to have broad appeal in a changing market." Twenty-five percent of the four-wheel-drive market was expected to be the new 'compact' types.

The new Sportwagons, as Jeep liked to call them, included a great deal of new technology. Foremost (in keeping with its Nash/AMC heritage) was the introduction of a new type of body construction which Jeep termed Uniframe. Still in use today, Uniframe was a major advance in four-wheel-drive design. Basically a version of unibody (or unitized) construction, in the Jeeps it included a stamped steel frame member that was welded to the undercarriage. Combining two items, a light metal frame with the steel underbody, allowed Jeep to provide superior rigidity and lower weight. The bodies were built to a new standard of fit and finish for the industry, using 29 new Cybotech robots in the framing operation. As George Maddox, vice president for manufactur-

For 1985, Jeep Wagoneer and Cherokee could be ordered with a fuel efficient Turbo Diesel engine.

ing explained, "We have taken a number of steps to assure that the new Jeep SportWagons will have the highest possible degree of quality."

Also revolutionary was the front suspension, which Jeep called Quadra-Link. Many companies were going to independent front suspensions on their four-wheelers, to provide a smoother, more car-like ride. Jeep engineers, however, still preferred a solid front axle since it guaranteed superior off-road durability. Quadra-Link provided the best trade-off between those two opposing goals. Its coil springs and four locating arms gave maximum handling control and a ride comparable to independent front suspensions while ensuring the robust strength that a solid front axle provides. An added benefit was constant ground clearance that bettered the Ford and Chevy designs by over an inch.

In truth, the Jeep XJ sport utilities bettered the competition on every front. The long wheelbase allowed full five-passenger seating, a first in the compact sport utility market. The Jeeps offered greater interior room, as well as more cargo capacity than the Ford/GM competition. For the first time ever on a Jeep vehicle, the heating/air conditioning system was completely integrated into the

instrument panel—a vast improvement over earlier designs. A new part-time four-wheel-drive system called Command-Trac allowed shift-on-the-fly capability, a unique feature at the time, while Selec-Trac was still the only two-wheel-drive/four-wheel-drive full-time system available. Most importantly, the Jeep was the only maker to offer both two- and four-door SUVs—the other major companies still believed that the heart of the Sport Utility market was a two-door, but Jeep believed otherwise.

Twenty-one inches shorter, six inches narrower, four inches lower and nearly 1,000 lbs. lighter than the former Cherokee, the XJ's retained 90% of the interior room of the old models. Yet they were able performers even when equipped with the standard AMC four, and provided fuel economy figures of 24 mpg in the city, 33 highway with the four-speed transmission. Even the most fuel-thirsty power train, the V-6 (purchased from GM) with automatic produced 26 mpg on the highway. This result was better than many compact cars of just a few years earlier.

The new Cherokees offered two dress-up packages, the Chief and Pioneer, while the Wagoneer

The Cherokee Chief, this a 1985 model, was always popular.

and Wagoneer Limited models catered to luxury and near-luxury buyers. Out in Derby, Connecticut, one visionary Jeep salesman was telling his customers the new Cherokee was so advanced that Jeep would still be selling it in the year 2000. He was right. The former Cherokee was dropped from the line, but the old Wagoneer Limited was renamed Grand Wagoneer and continued to attract the most discriminating (and wealthy) buyers. Priced now at $19,306, the Grand Wagoneer occupied a pedestal no other vehicle could even approach.

The new SportWagons were sure to be a volume seller, so Jeep decided to prune the rest of the line to reduce complexity in its manufacturing operations. The CJ-5, that legendary performer that had first joined the civilian line in 1954, was dropped. Its sales appeal had diminished considerably and now it was time to put it to rest.

The balance of the Jeep line offered only detail changes, as the company put all emphasis on successfully launching the new Cherokee/Wagoneer. Just in case anyone out there wanted a full-size Jeep wagon at a cost lower than a Grand Wagoneer, a special mid-year offering, the Custom Wagoneer,

consisted of the full-size Wagoneer body with plain trim and a $15,995 price tag.

During 1984, the Australian Army was spotted testing new Jeep CJ-10 pickups—the first time Jeeps were under consideration by the Aussies since World War II. But the testing received little notice in the press, because all eyes were focused on the Cherokee/Wagoneer twins. Early into the model year, Jeep executives breathed a collective sigh of relief. The press loved the new vehicles, dealers were ec-

It had been many years since a two-wheel drive Jeep wagon had been offered in America, but this two-wheel drive Cherokee—introduced in mid-1985—proved surprisingly popular.

The 1985 Jeep Renegade was still popular with buyers for good reason—it was a sporty vehicle.

The 1985 Jeep J-20 pickup was a heavy-duty workhorse, and looked similar to the original 1963 model.

Cherokee Pioneer 4-door

JEEP
TECHNOLOGY.
Only in a Jeep!

The road to work and play is not always paved. That's why there are Jeep vehicles. Vehicles built to be tough and reliable. But all this toughness didn't just happen. It was designed and engineered. And through it all, Jeep's two priorities dominated from the drawing board to the production line: technological quality and innovation.

The kind of quality that translates into fit, finish, reliability and durability. Innovation in the form of an impressive ride.

Quality Engineering.
Take Jeep Cherokee, for instance. Cherokee was specifically conceived as a 4-wheel drive vehicle. But it is Cherokee's other technological innovations that made the critics take notice. Here's why:

Quadra-Link Suspension...a solid front axle combines four locating arms and coil springs for extra ruggedness off-road and on-road smoothness with ground clearance that's the best in its class.

UniFrame Construction...frame and body shell are welded to create a solid unit. The result is an extremely rigid body with improved vehicle strength.

Selec-Trac...only Cherokee offers this unique all-surface system that lets you "shift-on-the-fly" from 2-wheel drive to 4-wheel drive at any speed from the driver's seat. Perfect for off-road or when weather or road conditions dictate.

Turbo-Diesel...Jeep Cherokee offers the only inter-cooled turbo-diesel engine in its class. Only in a Jeep!

Spring Special Pioneer 2-door

Take advantage now of a Spring Special Cherokee Pioneer Sportwagon. Contrasting dark blue and ice blue metallic clearcoat exterior with blue denim and sheepskin trimmed interior. The finishing touch is added with styled wheels and trim rings.

This spring Cherokee comes in a new 2-wheel drive model. With all the rugged and durable advantages that are standard in Jeep...and with a price starting at $9,195,* this new Cherokee is even more economical to own.

**Jeep J-10/J-20—
Built to Work. Built to Last.**
If you had to pick a "do-it-all" pickup, it would be Jeep. These trucks are heavy-duty! Their 7.8 foot long cargo boxes have payload capacities of more than 2 tons. And with an optional towing package, these trucks can tow trailers of up to 8,000 pounds. High ground clearance yet low loading height make loading these pickups a cinch. And J-20 has a heavy-duty cooling system, front stabilizer bar, fuel tank skid plate and tinted glass, standard. Ford F-250 and Dodge W-250 don't. Best of all, these trucks are built with the same 4-wheel drive technology Jeep is famous for. This translates into 4-wheel drive Jeep toughness.

Cherokee Pioneer and Spring Special Pioneer offered buyers better trim at a reasonable price.

static and the public was snapping them up enthusiastically. In fact, before the year ended, the Jeeps were named "4X4 of the Year" by all three leading off-road magazines: *4 Wheel & Off-Road, Four Wheeler,* and *Off-Road.* They were the first four-wheel-drive machines ever to earn that 'triple crown' distinction. For the fiscal year, Jeep dealers bought 193,428 vehicles worldwide, as compared to the 113,443 they bought in 1983. José Dedeurwaerder noted that Jeep production had to be raised to a daily rate of 824 units, the highest in Jeep history.

The company managed to produce a profit for the year, $15.5 million. It wasn't much, but it represented the first full year profit since 1979. Net sales for the year were $4.2 billion.

Since 1984 was the mid-point of the decade, it may well serve to take a look at Jeep's position compared to its peers. As was already explained, IH really was no longer a peer (its Scout line of compact SUVs had been discontinued after the 1980 models), so the company was competing only in the large truck market—an area Jeep has thus far

AMC President Jose' Dedeurwaerder introduced the handsome new Jeep Comanche pickup for 1986.

The Wrangler was greatly improved over CJ-7.

avoided. Jeep sales total had been about half that of GMC's in 1980, and the situation was about the same for 1984, though thankfully both companies' sales had about doubled. The good news was that after four turbulent years things seemed to be heading back to normal, and Jeep had emerged in roughly the same spot it had previously been in. With the four-wheel-drive SUV market now rebounding, the race was on to see how each would place by the end of the decade. The market was ripe now, ready for the picking, and the company that did the best job of providing customers with the products they wanted would gain the greater share of the harvest.

Jeep seemed to be ready for just about anything in 1985, offering twice as many four-wheel-drive models as any competitor, foreign or domestic. The XJ Jeeps had done extremely well in 1984, and the line was strengthened for the new model year. A new 85-hp Renault-built 2.1 liter turbocharged diesel engine was available in all states except California. With a five-speed transmission the turbodiesel was rated at an astounding 31 mpg in the city, and 36 mpg on the highway. Compared to the 10 mpg common in 1979, it was an achievement of note.

Shift-on-the-Fly capability was now available on Selec-Trac four-wheel-drive, another innovation of great merit. Cherokees now could be had with a new Laredo package, inspired by Laredos of the recent past, on both two- and four-door models.

Grand Wagoneers and pickups returned with little change—they got the improved Selec-Trac system, standard on the Grand Wagoneer, optional on J-10. Trucks were available in base or Pioneer trim, while CJs and Scramblers got high back bucket seats added to their standard equipment.

When spring came, the factory even added a few special models. The Spring Special CJ included unique striping, white spoke wheels and came in red or bronze 'micatallic' paint, while the Spring Special Cherokee had two-tone blue paint, blue denim and sheepskin interior, and styled wheels.

An historic mid-year model was the two-wheel drive Cherokee—the first two-wheel drive Jeep in over a decade, and the first-ever two-wheel-drive Cherokee. Available in base and Pioneer trim, in both two- and four-door models, the two-wheel-drive Cherokee was aimed at buyers Jeep hadn't been able to attract before. These were people in

warm weather states interested in a sport utility wagon, but unwilling to pay the tab for four-wheel-drive. GM dealers had been harvesting this market pretty handily; now Jeep would be able to share in it.

AMC announced plans to move production of the CJ-7 back into the Brampton, Ontario Canada plant, to make room in Toledo for manufacture of a new compact pickup based on the Cherokee. Canadian Jeep production was scheduled to begin on January 6, 1986.

The company ended 1985 with a dreadful loss, $125 million on sales of just over $4 billion. However, the fault wasn't Jeep's. Retail sales of Jeep vehicles in the U.S. were a record 181,389, up over 27,000 from the prior year. Sales of Renault cars had stumbled and were now drenching the books in red ink. It was hoped that a new intermediate car, plus two new Jeep models coming in 1986, would stem the losses.

Rumors were rampant that AMC was about to go under. Renault, under new management, apparently was reevaluating its stake in AMC. Because Renault had lost $1.4 billion in 1984, it certainly was a believable rumor. In response to the rumors, AMC's José Dedeurwaerder showed reporters a letter from Renault's new president Georges Besse pledging continued support for AMC.

Cherokee production began in China, and by year's end it was revealed that in the near future compact pickups would also be produced by Beijing Jeep. Jeep was celebrating 40 years of heritage in 1986. For the new model year the company showed improvements to most of its models and also announced its long-awaited compact pickup. Engineered on a modified Cherokee platform and using Cherokee front-end sheet metal, this was as handsome a pickup as anyone could ask for. Advertisements stated "There's a new truck on the road. It's called Comanche. It's made by Jeep. It's worth a look." Comanche was entering a highly competitive part of the market and in order to compete, it would have to offer both two-wheel-drive and four-wheel-drive models. The base sticker price for the two-wheel-drive version was $7,049, making it the lowest priced Jeep that year. The four-wheel-drive's base sticker price listed at $8,699.

What was missing was a short-bed price-leader to match the Japanese competition plus the Ford Ranger/Chevy S-10 trucks, many of which offered models priced around $6000-$6800. This first year only long-bed versions were available. Comanches

New Jeep Wrangler for 1987 was easy to spot because of its unique grille and square headlamps.

came with the same engine line-up as the Cherokee—base 2.5 four, optional 2.8 V-6 and 2.1 turbodiesel. With the Comanche's introduction, the poor-selling Scrambler, which had once held so much promise, was dropped. Few people noticed; even fewer cared.

Cherokee offered a new "Off-Highway" package for 1986. Consisting of premium high-pressure gas shock absorbers (painted yellow), big P225/75R15 tires, spoker wheels, skidplates, a high ground-clearance suspension and a 4.10:1 axle ratio, the Off-Highway Cherokee was purpose-built for rough terrain. Wagoneers got a new grille treatment this year, one that looked remarkably like the 1965 Rambler Ambassador, with a horizontally split grille and stacked head lamps. Grand Wagoneers also got a new grille, rich but rather busy-looking, and also got a stand-up hood ornament, a classic styling cliché of the 1980s, but one that was still in great demand. CJ-7s received only detail changes. J-series trucks got a thorough interior redesign, with a very elegant new instru-

ment panel, because the Grand Wagoneer, with which it shared many parts, also needed one. However, the J-trucks exterior styling remained the same, because their sales had fallen to such a low point there was little sense in spending much money to update them. After so many years of production, the J-trucks hadn't much excitement left in them.

Throughout the previous summer there had been rumors that a replacement for the CJ-7 was coming. By the fall, AMC executives verified the rumors had some basis, though they first claimed that a new Jeep, called the YJ, would complement, not replace the CJ. By December of 1985, four months into the 1986 model year, AMC announced it would cease production of the CJ in January.

Stories about the new Jeep YJ began to circulate, many based on misinformation put forth by company executives. The new Jeep would be smaller; it would share styling features and engineering with the Cherokee. The YJs would be much more stylish than CJs, wider and lower, too.

GET YOUR HANDS ON A PIECE OF HISTORY

"Get Your Hands On A Piece Of History" was the advice of this brochure announcing the final production of CJs.

They would be plusher, and ride better. José Dedeurwaerder said they would be, "...like a CJ convertible." Named the Jeep Wrangler, it would be built in Canada alongside AMC's Eagle automobile. Interestingly enough, the Wrangler name was owned by someone else in Canada, so up there it was marketed under the name Jeep YJ. Wrangler went on sale May 13, 1986. It wasn't all that much different in appearance from the CJ-7, in fact, at first glance it looked like nothing more than a CJ-7 with a bent grille and rectangular head lamps. It was however, much more than appearances would indicate.

A reporter for the *Automotive News* claimed the new Wrangler shared no components with the CJ, but that was incorrect, because it used the same engines as before. The Wrangler was a completely redesigned machine, and it certainly was more civilized. Its suspension design was borrowed from the Cherokee, and the stance was both low and wide. Compared to the CJ-7, the Wrangler was

slightly wider, but about an inch shorter in length. Wheelbase, at 93.4 inches, was the same as the CJ. Wranglers came with standard half-metal doors, a soft-top (removable, not convertible, despite what AMC's president had predicted), a one-piece swing-away tailgate that also served as the spare tire carrier. The instrument panel was all new and greatly improved over the CJ.

Perhaps in an effort to divorce it from the CJ line, Wrangler didn't offer a Renegade package. The CJ-7 was retired when the Wrangler arrived, a victim of the changing times and a glut of personal injury lawsuits by lawyers who evidently were shocked to learn that a tall, short-wheelbase, light-utility vehicle would actually handle differently than a long wheelbase, low-slung passenger car. These lawyers rejected the idea that people who refused to wear seatbelts had any responsibility for their injuries. No matter, AMC made sure the CJ marched off into history in style. A small brochure was produced touting the history and heritage of

Chrysler's Lee Iacocca engineered the buyout of Jeep, one of the shrewdest deals of all time.

"An American legend has come home again. Jeep, and the people of AMC, are now part of Chrysler. That's good for us. Good for you. And good for America."

Lee Iacocca

"When we bought American Motors, we got an American legend. Jeep. The most rugged, most versatile, most loveable four-wheel drive vehicle ever built.

"It hit the beaches at Normandy and slogged through the mud of Anzio. It fought through the jungles of Guadalcanal and the snows of Korea. For more than forty years, Jeep has been as tough as the spirit that made America great.

"Now I'm proud to tell you that the legend lives, at Chrysler.

And don't worry. We won't fool around with an American institution. Jeep will stay Jeep. That's a promise.

"Only one thing will change, for the better. The most American brand of all will be back where it belongs. With an American company. Jeep Wrangler, Cherokee, Wagoneer and Commanche will be built by Chrysler, sold by Chrysler, and serviced by Chrysler. At 1400 Jeep dealers across the country.

"When you've said you want to be the best, it helps to have the best going for you. We do. Jeep."

CHRYSLER MOTORS

CHRYSLER · PLYMOUTH · DODGE CARS · DODGE TRUCKS · JEEP

We just want to be the best.

In the 1980s, the Cherokee Limited was one of the most coveted vehicles in the world for its combination of luxury, style and performance.

the Jeep CJ, and offering buyers "The Last of The Jeep CJs," a special Collectors Edition commemorating the end of CJ production.

Jeep had an outstanding sales year for 1986, 207,514 retail sales in the U.S., a new record. However, its parent company, AMC, went in the opposite direction, reporting its worst passenger car sales ever. Plummeting sales of its Renault models, plus huge expenditures for a new car plant in Canada, a new intermediate car, and all the new Jeep models of the recent past, had pushed AMC to the brink. In a stock prospectus that July, the company said it was in "... a very tight cash position." They weren't kidding. Working capital had decreased from $190 million at December 31, 1980, to $3 million at December 31, 1985, and had since decreased to a negative $21 million at March, 31, 1986. The company, according to the prospectus, had long term debt of nearly $1 billion. For the fis-

cal year, AMC showed a loss of $91,319,000 on sales of $3,486,472.

The options available to Renault just then were to either sink more money into the firm, which seemed to be a bottomless pit, or declare bankruptcy and see its huge investment go for naught, or sell the company to someone who thought they could do better. In the meantime, though, the compact four-wheel-drive market was strengthening, and Jeep's 1987 models were on the market.

For 1987, Jeep introduced an historic new engine, an in-line six-cylinder to replace the V-6 it had been buying from General Motors. Based on the existing AMC block (which dated back to 1964), but reduced to a 4.0 displacement, the Power-Tech Six produced a whopping 173 horsepower and 220 lb. of torque, an awesome display of might. Jeep put some expensive technology into this engine to make it that powerful: sequential multi-point fuel injection, automatic altitude compensation and fast-burn combustion. The new Jeep engine was perhaps the first of the new generation of high-output/high fuel economy engines that would characterize the 1990s. Compared to the GM V-6, the Jeep mill produced 50% more horsepower and 47% more torque. Overnight, Jeep became the performance standard for the SUV market. Jeeps equipped with the new engine boasted acceleration times of 0-60 mph in 9.5 seconds—fantastic performance for a light duty vehicle back then, and yet fuel economy was also said to be improved. As an added benefit the increased power gave Cherokees and Wagoneers a 5000 lb. towing capacity. The factory expected that 80% of Cherokee, Wagoneer and Comanche buyers would opt for the 4.0—a significant boost to AMC's profitability since the engine was produced in-house, not purchased from a vendor.

Jeep was pushing its truck models again and even issued a separate sales catalog for them. There was much to talk about, but the biggest news was the arrival of a new short-bed Comanche, the SporTruck. Priced at just $6495, which included bold striping on the sides, wheel trim rings and steel-belted tires, it was perhaps the best value in small pickups in America. Also new was a "Comanche Chief" version that borrowed styling cues from the Cherokee Chief. The J-series trucks were advertised as "Thoroughbred Workhorses,'" a highly descriptive and completely accurate label. The J-trucks looked old-hat compared with the sleek pickups from GM and Ford. Only diehard Jeep lovers were still buying them, but the trucks were the noble keepers of an old tradition, and it was sad to see them slowly fading away.

Grand Wagoneers got an interesting new standard tire. Made by Michelin, the tire was designed to automatically seal small punctures. The smaller Wagoneers still came with the four-cylinder engine standard, but the 4.0 was optionally available, and probably installed in most Wagoneers that year. The Wagoneer sales catalog for 1987 was very attractive, including as it did the Wagoneer, Wagoneer Limited, and the Grand Wagoneer all in one booklet.

For 1987, Cherokees were much improved, getting the hot new six-cylinder engine, plus a new four-speed automatic transmission jointly developed by Warner Gear and Japanese manufacturer Aisin Seiki. With this highly advanced transmis-

sion and the potent new 4.0 engine, the XJ Jeeps rocketed to the forefront of four-wheel-drive innovation—staying, as usual, several years ahead of the crowd. Cherokee also got a new model, the luxurious Cherokee Limited, a cross between the sporty flavor of the Chief, and the all-out elegance of the Wagoneer Limited. It managed to appeal to a segment of the population who wanted as much luxury as could be had in a Sport Utility Vehicle, but who viewed the Wagoneer as too dignified to be cool. In spite of all the problems the parent company had, and a market that was remorseless, Jeep was still in the ring, fighting it out for sales.

AMC had a new president. Joe Cappy, an AMC executive who replaced José Dedeurwaerder in mid-1986, was a talkative sort, always good for a controversial quote or two. At the end of 1986, Ward's Auto World speaking about labor problems at Jeep's Toledo plant, pointedly asked Cappy if he was prepared to move Jeep production out of Toledo if labor negotiations remained stalemated. Cappy replied "I don't know what I'll do, but only a stupid person would do business down in Toledo if they don't have a competitive contract. I may be many things, but my mother did not raise a stupid kid."

AMC's president expressed confidence that Renault would continue to stand behind the company, but events were about to spin out of control. On November 17, 1986, Renault Chairman George Besse was shot down outside his Paris home, a victim apparently because of his stature as a leading capitalist. With AMC's protector now dead, the way was clear for others at Renault, who had been calling for an end to its AMC investment, to push their agendas. Selling AMC would relieve the French firm of a huge liability, assuming a buyer could be found.

Out in Michigan, Lee Iaccoca of Chrysler Corporation was ready to make his move. Iaccoca himself stated that the three big plusses AMC had were Jeep, a dealer organization and a new car plant in Canada—and he listed Jeep first. By March, a deal was announced—for approximately $1.1 billion, Chrysler would purchase American Motors Corporation, the last independent automobile company in America. Within months, both the Renault and AMC car lines would be discontinued, a new car line called the Eagle would emerge to replace them, and AMC would be renamed the Jeep/Eagle Division of Chrysler.

The news reassured some skeptics that Jeep was at last in the clear. However, a glance at the last AMC financial statement, a Proxy Statement/Prospectus dated July 2, 1987, reveals that AMC had a net profit of $23.4 million for the first quarter. This was a healthy return, and one which came back-to-back with a profitable fourth quarter in the prior fiscal year. It is reasonable for one to believe the company had turned the corner and was now on the road to recovery; some executives even felt it might report record profits for the year.

The immediate result of the change in ownership was that the new owner took an inventory of Jeeps strengths and weaknesses. The most glaring weakness was in the large pickup line, and so the venerable, old J-10 and J-20 trucks, those noble veterans first offered in the fall of 1962, were discontinued at the end of the 1987 model year.

Two watershed events had occurred; Jeep was once again the stepchild of a new owner, and another grand old automobile maker had breathed its last. Whether or not Chrysler realized it, they had taken over a company that had been irretrievably altered by its former owner. American Motors had taken a small, ill-equipped agricultural truck builder and transformed it into a major force in the burgeoning, consumer-oriented SUV market—a company that could, and did match the big firms sucessfully, product for product. It was now up to Chrysler and its management to bring Jeep to the next level—to increase its production capacity, attract new and larger dealers, and introduce new products and features that would boost Jeep sales to new records. A new era was fast approaching.

Chapter Seven

CHRYSLER TAKES THE WHEEL

1988-1992

Lee A. Iacocca knew Jeep was one of the most respected brands in the world.

Because of the long lead times inherent in the automobile business, Chrysler wasn't able to exert much influence on the design of the 1988 Jeep product line. Then again, it really didn't need to. The financial numbers of 1987, and sales figures for both 1986 and 1987, spoke volumes—Jeep had already turned the corner. Partly it was the result of a good economy, and increasing interest in sport utility vehicles (SUVs), but mostly it was simply

that Jeep was building great products and the public knew it.

The 1988 Jeeps offered mostly detail improvements, but there were a few surprises as well. The most dramatic was a new pickup—the sinister-looking "Eliminator." Built on a short-bed Comanche chassis, the "Eliminator" included as standard the potent 4.0 engine, five-speed transmission, tachometer and aluminum wheels. With the Pioneer, SporTruck, Chief and Laredo trim packages, the Comanche line was both broad and exciting. The Wagoneer base model was dropped, leaving the Limited as the sole 'small' Wagoneer. The Grand Wagoneer, favorite of wealthy horse owners and others who needed a plush tow vehicle, returned with its classic styling intact.

Wranglers received many new features, most attractive of which was the Sahara trim package. This included khaki-colored wheels and soft-top, special body striping, and fog lamps with neat little mesh screens. Offered in either coffee or khaki paint, the Sahara was the first specialty Jeep with a

The 1988 Comanche Eliminator was perhaps the first true high-performance pickup, and a fast machine.

193

To counter inroads made by low-priced Asian imports, Wrangler 'S' debuted with a price of only $8,995, and could be ordered in white, black, yellow, coffee, or red.

Jeep was a sponsor of the 1988 U.S. Olympic team, and offered these special Olympic Edition Jeeps to celebrate.

desert theme, and was the sportiest of the Wrangler line. Other Wranglers were the base and Laredo models. Small Japanese four-wheel-drive machines, particularly the Suzuki Samurai, had gradually eaten into Jeep's market. Wrangler sales in 1987 weren't encouraging—only about 30,000 were retailed in the U.S. Jeep and Renault agreed to explore the possibility of a joint venture to produce a smaller, less expensive vehicle by sharing development costs. However, in the meantime Jeep came up with its own response—a new budget model called the Wrangler 'S'. Introduced mid-year, the Wrangler 'S', available in a limited choice of colors, could be had only with the base 2.5-liter four-cylinder with a five-speed stick, but otherwise was much like the other Wranglers except its price—$8995. Though that was still a tad above the Japanese four-wheelers, any sort of comparison would prove the larger and more rugged Wrangler was far superior.

Mid-way through the year, Jeep introduced special Olympic Commemorative Editions in the Cherokee, Comanche and Wrangler series that featured unique striping, aluminum wheels and an Olympic decal. Jeep was an official sponsor of the Olympics and wanted to make some hay out of it.

In September, it was announced that Jeep production capacity at the Toledo, Ohio, and Brampton, Canada, plants would be increased to 403,000 units—a substantial increase and sure sign Chrysler was aiming for much higher sales. A reporter noted that Jeep production had already been boosted three times since the Chrysler buy-out. Chrysler also had big plans to increase export sales of Jeeps.

Chrysler spotted other areas of great potential. In fact, as Chrysler grew more familiar with its Jeep operations, it discovered some surprising facts—such as, that Jeep buyers had the highest demographics in the company. This is not hard to imagine, since poor people couldn't afford to buy Grand Wagoneers, not at the then-price of about $25,000. Top-line Cherokee and Wagoneer Limiteds weren't all that much lower in price, either. The Jeep buyer, it turned out, was what every marketer was chasing just then (and now for that matter)—young, hip and well-heeled.

The company also saw vast possibilities for expanding sales by offering Jeep models to its Dodge dealers. As discussed, modifications would be made to the existing Jeep vehicles to differentiate them just enough so that they could wear Dodge nameplates and be sold by that division's much larger dealer body. Dodge, at the time, was selling a re-badge version of the Mitsubishi Montero as the Dodge Raider, though not with any notable success. If the front-end styling of the Wrangler could be altered enough so it didn't look like a Jeep rip-off, Dodge dealers could sell it as a Dodge. It might not sell any better than the Raider, but it would be more profitable, since it would be built in the company's own plant.

Likewise with the Cherokee. Dodge dealers didn't have anything to compete with the hugely successful Ford and GM offerings, so a re-badged Cherokee was sure to be welcome by them. Dodge dealers were ecstatic with the idea. Then again, as the saying goes, the door swings both ways. Chrysler was also planning to offer a version of its hottest product, the Dodge/Plymouth minivan, through Jeep/Eagle dealers. Whether it would be badged as a Jeep or an Eagle was problematic, (though Eagle evidently was the more likely) but its model name was going to be the Commando—and it would have four-wheel-drive. Upon learning of this part of the tale, Dodge dealers were up in arms and it took a great deal of soothing words by Chrysler executives to calm them down and win back their trust. Plans to share Dodge and Jeep products were shelved. The year went well for Jeep, with 253,454 retail sales in America, a new record and up from an already impressive 208,440 in 1987.

For 1989, it would be more of the same. A fresh-looking new trim package was the Wrangler Islander—bold striping and fancy wheels, the same old formula that the public always responded to. Cherokees got a new, low-priced dress-up option called the Cherokee Sport, which gave buyers aluminum wheels, sporty stripes and the 4.0 engine.

The Cherokee Limited featured gold-tone exterior nameplates, leather upholstery and a host of luxury features that made it the most-desired sport utility on the planet, an urban status symbol with amazing prestige. The Comanche continued to offer its popular models, and Wagoneer Limited and Grand Wagoneer maintained their hold on the very top of the SUV market.

Cherokees and the Wagoneer Limited could be ordered with four-wheel anti-lock brakes (ABS) this year. It required purchasing the 4.0 engine

The 1989 Cherokee line included luxurious Limited and value-priced Sport models.

(which nearly everyone ordered anyway) and Jeep's wonderful Selec Trac all-wheel-drive system. The ABS worked in both two-wheel and four-wheel-drive, a Jeep exclusive. Systems from other manufacturers worked only in two-wheel-drive.

Sales fell a bit in 1989. Since 1989 was the final year of the decade, we should examine how Jeep performed in the ten-year span in comparison to two close competitors: GMC, and Jeep's closest import rival, Nissan. At the beginning of the decade the sales rankings in the U.S. were: GMC 141,029; Nissan (Datsun) 111,246; Jeep 77,852. Ten years later, in 1989, the numbers were: GMC 353,788; Nissan 163,188; Jeep 249,170. Thus, although mighty GMC was still leading Jeep by a considerable number, Jeep had narrowed the lead percentage-wise. In 1980, GMC's sales were nearly double that of Jeep's, but by 1989, they were just 42% higher than Jeeps. Additionally, Jeep had passed Nissan sales by a giant margin, a noteworthy feat since a common belief was that American manufacturers couldn't outshine Japanese companies.

Nor was Jeep standing still—in February of 1989, Chrysler and Renault signed a letter of intent to form the Association of Renault and Chrysler for Automotive Development, or ARCAD. The main purpose of ARCAD was to design, develop and co-produce a new line of small four-wheel-drive vehicles which would compete head to head with the tiny Suzuki and Daihatsu four-wheelers—and any other such vehicles that might enter the markets in America or Europe. The new Jeep concept became known as the JJ (for Junior Jeep?).

In many ways it had been a trying decade, beginning as it did with a devastating market fall, and ending with Jeep as a part of a different company. The decade of the 1990s was hopefully going to be more rewarding and less traumatic. It certainly looked encouraging.

There was little new to see in the 1990 Jeep line, but it was an exciting year for them regardless. In many ways 1990 was a year of marketing, as Jeep put an emphasis on non-product selling points, like its new 7/70 warranty coverage (something that would have been simply unthinkable in the 1970s!), as well as option group discount packages that encouraged buyers to load-up on optional equipment by offering them a discount on certain option groups. The 1990 Jeep sales brochure (called The Jeep Book) is one of the most beautiful catalogs Jeep ever put out, filled with pictures of Jeep vehicles in gorgeous outdoor settings.

Sales were off for the year, as the overall market, including the light-duty truck market that Jeep occupied, decreased a bit. U.S. retail sales came in at 196,863. Ford Motor Company had introduced its all-new 1991 Explorer in March of 1990. Explorer's impressive size and good looks made it

Jeep line for 1989 was the most complete in the four-wheel drive market.

The 1990 Jeep line was little changed from the prior year.

competition enough, but the fact that it offered a four-door model meant it would threaten Jeep's position in the market. The problem was many faceted—Ford had a loyal base of customers who in the past had crossed over to Jeep, simply because Cherokee was the only domestic four-door sport-utility vehicle available. With Explorer, these loyalists could now stay within the Ford family. Another worry was simply that buyers love to own the latest thing, and the Explorer was now IT—the Cherokee had been on the market for seven years without a substantial appearance change. Most worrisome of all, was a threat that hearkened back even to pre-World War II times—Ford's vast network of factories meant it would have the upperhand in sales, since it could out-produce Jeep. It

was that simple. When push came to shove, Ford could shove harder. How Jeep responded to this newest threat would determine its place in market for many years to come. The executives at Chrysler had much to discuss amongst themselves and they got to work.

It's not that Jeep was caught completely unaware. There was a new Cherokee on the drawing boards already. In fact, the vehicle had been under development almost from the time that AMC designers had signed off on the production tooling for the 1984 Cherokees. American Motors had brought the vehicle to a production-ready state, and it could have been introduced in 1990 or 1991, if anyone had authorized it. Yet by that time Chrysler was in control, and Chrysler decided to put through a re-

198

design of its core product, the mini-van, and place the new Jeep on hold in the meantime. Now, the program was back on track.

In early August 1990, the industry trade paper *Automotive News* published a spy photo of a new Jeep sport utility wagon planned for 1992, dubbed the ZJ. The paper claimed the new Jeep had originally been planned to replace the Cherokee, but would instead be an addition to the line. The overall market was soft in 1991, and Jeep had to slug it out with its competitors, both import and domestic, for every sale it made. The 1991 Jeep product line received many enhancements—exciting new models and trim packages, and a tougher approach to marketing.

The budget-priced Wrangler 'S' model, now $9910, was aimed at Geo Tracker and Suzuki Sidekick, which were $10,885 and $10,999 respectively, for their lowest priced four-wheel-drive models. In fairness, each did offer lower priced two-wheel-drive versions, which Wrangler, of course, did not. Yet if someone was in the market for a low-priced four-wheel-drive vehicle, there really wasn't any financial reason not to buy a Jeep. Other Wranglers

returning this year were the Islander, Base, and Sahara. A hot new model was created by installing the 4.0 liter engine, rated at an incredible180-hp, and adding bold graphics, special body parts and unique 5-hole aluminum wheels. Dubbed the Renegade, it recalled the glory days of the early 1970s when Renegades were the hottest small Jeeps. Even better, the 4.0 was now available on all Wranglers except the 'S', finally putting the rugged, if unremarkable, 258-cid six out to pasture.

There was no Wagoneer offered in 1991. Wagoneer sales had fallen below the point where it was economic to continue them. In 1990, less than 4,000 were retailed in the U.S. Having separate marketing and advertising programs couldn't be justified at that volume, so the Wagoneer was dropped from the line.

Comanche SporTruck was priced at $8767, a reasonable price, but at the upper-end of the budget truck market. From there, Comanche prices went up the ladder to $15,278 for the Eliminator four-wheel-drive. Comanche was in trouble—its sales had tumbled the prior year and were heading down further. Because compact pickups have a narrow profit mar-

The 1991 Jeep line included the hot-looking Renegade, tough Comanche Eliminator, luxurious Cherokee Limited, and stately Grand Wagoneer.

Jeep Wrangler line for 1992 included this base model.

gin to begin with, they rely on volume to produce adequate profits. With Comanche volume shrinking, its future was in doubt.

Cherokee Sport, Limited, Laredo and base models were joined by the new Cherokee Briarwood. Available only as a four-door, four-wheel-drive with wood-grain body side trim, the Briarwood was in the line to provide shoppers with a substitute for the discontinued Wagoneer. All models benefited by the availability of an upgraded 4.0 six, now rated at 190-horsepower and 225 lb.-ft. of torque—making the already potent Cherokee even more awesome.

The Grand Wagoneer, elegant queen of the sport-utility market, returned for another model year with only a few new colors to mark the new season. Grand Wagoneer's styling was getting long in the tooth—well, after 29 years in production, it should, but it had a very large profit margin. In 1990 it had outsold the cheaper Wagoneer, so it was still being produced. Besides, Chrysler executives loved to drive them. Suggested price on the GW was $29,241.

However, the year ended on a down note. The market overall was smaller and the light-truck market had shrunk even further. The Ford Explorer was joined in the market by a new four-door version of the Chevrolet S10 Blazer. Jeep's sales fell to 177,775 for the year, the worst showing since 1984. Wrangler and Comanche sales declined, and Cherokee sales were stuck in gear, not increasing because so many buyers were being lured by the hot-selling Explorer and four-door Blazer. Chrysler had some ideas to help increase Jeep sales, including a national campaign to sell specially equipped Cherokees as police vehicles. Production began in December 1991. Chrysler also announced that it would be terminating Renault's contract to sell Jeeps in Spain, Portugal, and Italy. Chrysler, which didn't have a manufacturing presence in Europe, was taking over distribution of its products there. Jeep sales in Europe were running in the area of 20,000 per year and Chrysler clearly felt it could do better if it had direct control over sales. The ARCAD joint venture to produce a small Jeep for world markets died too. The program had gotten so complex that it looked like it couldn't be profitable. Chrysler and Fiat discussed a similar joint venture, but that too came to naught.

The 1992 Cherokee Laredo was a popular seller.

The 1992 Jeep Comanche pickup was still the best-looking compact truck on the market.

The 1992 Jeep line looked a bit skimpy. It had been trimmed down in 1991, with the cancellation of the Wagoneer, and for 1992, was now without the big Grand Wagoneer—as things turned out, its 29th season had been its last. Jeep was getting itself slimmed down in anticipation of its all-new ZJ sport utilities, which were nearly ready for production. The bold Renegade model returned to the Wrangler line for 1992. With its plastic body side cladding, exaggerated wheel flares, monochromatic paint scheme and aluminum wheels it was the Porsche 911 of sport utility vehicles.

Cherokee Limiteds, featuring monochromatic paint, gold trim and fancy lace spoke wheels, were the ultimate in designer 4x4s, the must-have sport utility, the machine the whole country seemed gaga over. Additionally, the handsome, though slow-selling Comanches returned to round out the Jeep offerings.

The new Jeep ZJ model, which reporters had predicted would be announced with the 1992 models, didn't appear for the regular fall 1991 announcement, but given the scale of the project, that shouldn't have surprised anyone. They were scheduled to appear in the Spring of 1992, but would debut as early 1993 models. It was certain to be one of the most crucial new products in Jeep history. Because the market was growing by leaps and bounds, the new SUVs would either carry Jeep up to the top of the mountain, or cause it to lag further behind, perhaps never to catch-up. However, this new vehicle, a joint effort of American Motors and Chrysler designers, would show the world the depth and breadth of talent that both companies enjoyed. And in the process, a new legend would be born.

Chapter Eight

CLIMBING TO A NEW HEIGHT

1993-1999

Early prototype of new Jeep undergoes crash-testing.

As 1992 began, Ford and General Motors were enjoying large slices of the SUV market, courtesy of their highly competitive vehicles. Ford's Explorer was the segment leader, outselling Jeep Cherokee two-to-one. Some believed Jeep was so far behind that it would be a long time before it would again be a competitive threat.

But thoughts of that nature served only to ignore the traditions of history and the forces of the market. There is a great truth buried in the dry documents of the past, and that is that Jeep has never been a follower. Its heritage is one of leadership, choosing to take the first step in a new direction, not to be an imitator, but instead resolving to be the one that others copied, that others envied, that others tried to beat; and although the company was much changed now from even just a few years ear-

Overhead tilt conveyor was one of many innovations in Jeep's new Jefferson North plant.

lier, at its core there still beat the heart of a hero, the very essence of the Jeep heritage.

Work on the new ZJ had been going on for years, its foundation laid by AMC designers, its introduction delayed so that the new Chrysler minivans could be introduced and by now, the new Jeep was overdue. Chrysler turned the problem of needing to delay the new vehicle into an opportunity, by giving the design some extra months of development, much innovative hardware, new features, and a commitment to make the new Jeep a winner. The company also faced the very big problem of being out-produced by its domestic competitors, and this it answered in a unique and highly significant way.

Originally, the new ZJ was supposed to replace the Cherokee XJ. But AMC changed its thinking, deciding to make the ZJ an upscale addition to the line (and according to one source, it would have been built in Kenosha, Wisconsin). Now, as Chrysler executives studied the market, they came to a similar conclusion. The best solution to the threat from competition was to fight back on two fronts. The new ZJ line would take the high road, aimed at the luxury and near-luxury markets, while the old-style XJ Cherokee would be repackaged to serve the lower price market. The reason this could be accomplished with the existing Cherokee was because after so many years of production, much of its tooling costs had already been amortized. Now, by rearranging its model line-up, standard features and optional equipment, it could be priced and aimed to attract new buyers to the market. The Cherokee would continue to be built in the main Jeep plant in Toledo. However, rather than produce the new Jeep in Kenosha, a new plant would be built.

Several problems surfaced. The original plan called for using the Cherokee name on the new Jeeps, but if the old Cherokee was to remain in the line-up a new name would have to be found for the new vehicles. The Wagoneer name was an easy first choice, except it still had that same old connotation of a mature wagon for older people—not the image the new Jeep needed. A whole raft of alternative names were tested and abandoned. Finally, someone with more than average sense suggested calling the new Jeep the "Grand Cherokee," which would give it the sporty Cherokee label while easily placing it a full step 'above' a regular Cherokee. That settled the naming problem.

The other problem was where to build the new plant. Financial types had an easy answer for that too: build it in a southern or western state. It should be one that would grant enticing financial incentives to Chrysler, one with a young work force available, one with traditionally lower wages—in short, the sort of area the Japanese were locating their new plants in. It made great sense.

For some reason, Chrysler chose not to do so. It would instead build it in what had become the least likely place in America to build a new auto-making facility—Detroit, Michigan. The Motor City had become the sort of environment that industrial concerns avoided. It was crowded, had a highly organized labor force (which was old and getting older, a worry to cost-conscious firms who dreaded the high cost of medical insurance that meant), it had little open space, and it no longer had a reputation for quality workmanship. Perhaps it was Chrysler's way of repaying its work force for the sacrifices they had made on the company's behalf in the 1970s. Perhaps it was some limited incentives Chrysler was able to obtain, or maybe it was just that Lee Iaccoca saw something that no one else could see, but in the end, whatever the real reason was made no difference. The new Jeep plant was going to be built in Detroit. In all likelihood it would be the last new automobile manufacturing plant built in an American inner city area.

The new factory, called the Jefferson North Plant for the street it was on, was a marvel, the product of the latest thinking in plant layout, and equipped with state-of-the-art machinery. Special fixtures had been developed to ease the strain of assembly line work, in recognition of Jefferson North's mature work force. The company was anxious to publicize its unique choice of plant sites, stating in the Jeep sales catalog, "By reclaiming an existing urban industrial land site for the plant, development of virgin 'green space' was avoided." The factory had its own on-site water treatment plant capable of treating up to 500,000 gallons of

Francois Castaing was Vice-President of Vehicle Engineering when the Grand Cherokee debuted, and had worked on the project while he was with AMC.

water daily. Liquid sludge left over from painting operations was transformed into a dry, non-hazardous powder for use in other commercial products, not dumped into a nearby river. Paint fumes were filtered to reduce volatile organic compounds. Around 30,000 tons of cardboard and wooden pallet waste annually were eliminated by the use of returnable parts containers, rather than one-time shipping containers common in the industry. Jefferson North was more than just a new plant—it set a new standard for the entire industry.

Everything was ready for the April 19, 1992, announcement date. The Grand Cherokee thus was the first 1993 Jeep, and was initially offered in three series; base, Laredo and Limited. The two upper-scale models included fancy bodyside cladding for a more aggressive appearance. The body design was clearly Cherokee inspired, but was longer, wider, sturdier and more substantial looking. Only one engine was offered, the class-leading 4.0 FI six, rated at 190-hp and 225 lb.-ft. of torque. As Chrysler noted, "Grand Cherokee's acceleration, whether from a stop or at passing speeds, is simply the best-in-class. And Grand Cherokee's ability to climb a steep grade exceeds anything in its class."

The Grand Cherokee was in a class by itself.

All models came standard with a four-speed automatic transmission. All models were four-wheel-drive, with the base and Laredo receiving Jeep's part-time shift-on-the-fly system as standard. Limited's came standard with an all-new premium four-wheel-drive system, Quadra-Trac, which shared the name and ease of use of the old Quadra-Trac, but not the mechanical guts. The new Quadra-Trac reacted automatically to changing road conditions without any need for the driver to shift. There was, however, a low range that could be selected for severe conditions. Quadra-Trac could be ordered on the two lesser series, and Selec Trac was optional on all models.

Like the plant that produced it, the Grand Cherokee was a new standard of excellence, a new rung on the ladder, a new height of accomplishment. The Grand Cherokee was the first and only sports utility equipped with a driver's side air bag—an important safety consideration, and a difficult thing to engineer in a machine designed for driving in rough, bouncy off-road conditions. Grand Cherokee also had the only four-wheel-drive system with high-range lock-up for highway speeds and a low-

range gear for severe off-road conditions. It was still the only SUV (except for the old Cherokee) to boast the superior UniFrame construction. In addition, it was the only SUV to offer three different four-wheel-drive systems. Grand Cherokee's were "green," too—by weight about 90% of the vehicle was made of recyclable materials. Besides that, the Grand Cherokees were the first Jeeps to include four-wheel ABS on all models, the first Jeeps with an available compact disc player, and the only ones with an automatic temperature control system. Another little plus—heated outside mirrors standard on the Limited, optional on the others.

Grand Cherokee also debuted a new suspension system, a multi-link, four-wheel coil spring set-up. Jeep engineers were still wary of switching to an independent front suspension, as many competitors had, because of the inherent weakness of such systems. There wasn't any question about it—off-road, a solid front axle was stronger. However, the drawback was the solid axle, leaf spring suspensions rode harder, and that would be a competitive disadvantage in the market. Jeep engineers came up with the premium four-coil system to be able to

The Good News Is Jeep. Grand Cherokee Is Now Available With A V8. There Is No Bad News.

Just when you thought you had heard all the good news that Jeep had to offer this year with the introduction of Grand Cherokee, we're making headlines again.

Presenting the 5.2 litre V8. With 220 horsepower, this available engine makes Grand Cherokee Limited the most powerful sport utility vehicle in its class.

Of course, Jeep Grand Cherokee's advantages go beyond horsepower. It also comes with a revolutionary all-the-time four-wheel drive system, four-wheel anti-lock brakes, and an exclusive standard driver's side air bag.

For more information, call 1-800-JEEP-EAGLE. And see why Grand Cherokee's new V8 is the most powerful news story to come out of the 4x4 world this year.

There's Only One Jeep®...
A Division of the Chrysler Corporation.

See limited warranties, restrictions, and details at dealer. Jeep is a registered trademark of Chrysler Corporation.   Buckle up for safety.

This advertisement says it all—the V-8 Grand Cherokee stood out in a crowded market.

offer the strength of solid axles with an amazingly smooth ride.

Dubbed Quadra Coil, the new suspension gave unexpected benefits in handling expertise. Jeep claimed skid pad numbers of .78G, which it said was, "...comparable to such world-class sedans as BMW 525i, Acura Legend, and Mercedes-Benz 300CE"—very impressive company. Some credit for the refined handling has to go to Emerson Fittipaldi, colorful and charismatic Formula One Champion and Indianapolis 500 winner. Fittipaldi worked as a consultant to Chrysler, helping engineers test and refine suspensions. With talent like

that, it was no wonder the Grand Cherokee handled so well.

Roomier than the old Cherokee, with wider doors making it easier to get into and out of, the Grand Cherokee was the greatest SUV ever made up to that time, an innovative, class-leading machine, and everyone knew it. Jeep introduced the Grand Cherokee in a thick, handsome sales brochure that bore a simple title, "The New Jeep."

The Grand Cherokee seemed like a sure winner, but there were many worried people viewing its launch. Chrysler executives were concerned about the strength of the Jeep dealer network, which was

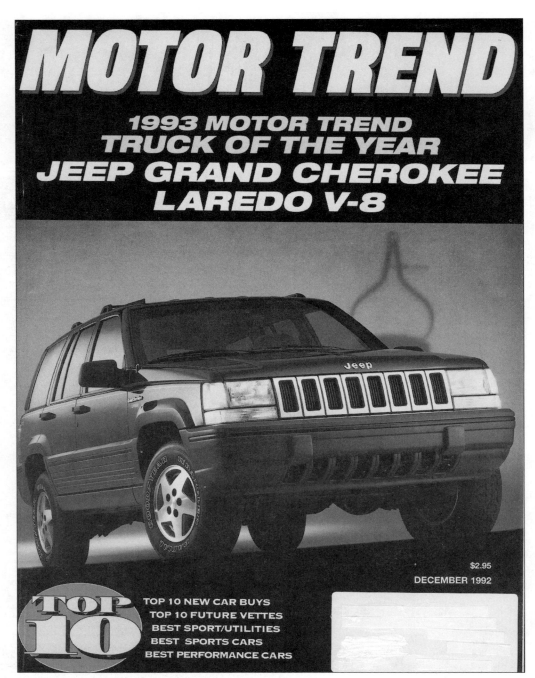

Motor Trend named Grand Cherokee its 1993 "Truck of the Year."

still composed primarily of former AMC/Jeep dealers. It was feared the dealer group might not be large enough or strong enough to sell all the Grand Cherokees the new plant could build. If they failed to do so, the company wouldn't make back their investment (and adequate profits) as quickly as was hoped. The plant capacity was 150,000 units on a one-shift straight-time (without overtime) basis—about 96 units per dealer per year. As Gary Gray, chairman of the Jeep-Eagle National Dealers Council, put it to a reporter from the *Automotive News,* "Have we got a big job to do? You bet. Can we do it? We think we have a shot at it."Chrysler made no bones about what would happen if the Jeep dealers couldn't sell out the plant—Dodge dealers would get a Dodge-badged version of the Grand Cherokee to sell in their stores. The Dodge network could certainly sell all they could get—and anybody could see that if they ended up selling more than Jeep dealers did, they could get a greater and greater share of production, become the dominate voice in design and production of future models, and sooner or later a Jeep wouldn't

The 1994 Wrangler Sahara was an attractive, popular vehicle.

seem much like a Jeep anymore. Obviously, a great deal was at stake. In response, Jeep dealers had only two requests: 1) Price the new Jeep roughly equal to the market-leading Explorer and 2) Give us a chance to show what we can do.

Jeep dealers were as good as their word, and total Jeep sales climbed sharply for the calendar year, to 268,724, versus 177,775 in 1991, setting a new record. Wrangler and Cherokee sales both rose slightly, to 49,724 and 128,960 respectively, while Comanche sales sputtered down to just 3,181. Grand Cherokee sales for the abbreviated year were a very commendable 86,859.

Not all the news in 1992 was about the Grand Cherokee. Malaysia was preparing a plant to assemble right-hand-drive (RHD) Cherokees for the local market. Production was to begin in mid-1993, pegged at about 1,000 units per year. Chrysler was showing an interest in revitalizing Jeep's overseas distribution.

The 1993 Jeep line showed a number of changes. The Wrangler line was expanded to include a stripped Wrangler, as well as a Wrangler Base that, although only slightly better equipped, offered a

greater range of optional equipment than the bottom line model. Also available were a Sport model (with fancier wheels, power steering, outline white letter (OWL) tires, graphics, bodyside steps etc.), the popular Sahara, and the line topping Renegade. Cherokee Base and Sport models were joined by a high-line Cherokee Country model. Sad to say, the Comanche was dropped, a victim of the tough competition in the compact pickup market. Since the Scrambler, J-series and Comanches had all fizzled in the market, Jeep now had no pickup truck in its lineup. To add irony to the situation, Jeep's Toledo plant was given the job of assembling Dodge Dakota pickups to help meet heavy demand for that product.

There were a host of changes to the Grand Cherokee when the rest of the 1993 Jeeps were introduced that Fall. Though it was still a 1993 model (naturally), it now was joined by a stable mate that brought back a great old name. The Grand Wagoneer was simply an upmarket version of the Grand Cherokee, but came with several important differences. First and foremost, Grand Wagoneers came standard with a 5.2 liter (318-cid), 220 hp V-8 engine, something no competitive make offered in its

Cherokee Sport two-door for 1994 was sporty but not as popular as four-door models.

class. Grand Wagoneers also came with a standard wood-grain bodyside treatment that recalled the classic look of the old Grand Wagoneer.

The Grand Cherokee base and Laredo now came with a five-speed transmission as standard, while the Limited came only with the slick four-speed automatic that was optional for the lesser two models. The same sequential multi-point fuel injection 5.2 liter V-8 that came standard with the Grand Wagoneer could be ordered on any Cherokee with Quadra-Trac, and turn it into a road rocket. Acceleration times of 0-60 in 9.37 seconds were claimed (an astounding figure for an SUV at that time), as well as best-in-class towing capacity—a maximum of 6500 lbs. It might be said that if the Wrangler Renegade was the Porsche 911 of the four-wheel-drive market then the Grand Cherokee was the BMW 540i. Late in the season a two-wheel-drive model was added, available in base and Laredo trim, but only with the six-cylinder engine. The two-wheel drive Cherokee had proved popular in southern states, where the lack of snow and ice conditions made four-wheel-drive less necessary, so it was a cinch the two-wheel-drive Grand Cherokee would find a ready audience.

The Grand Cherokee continued to wow the press—*Automobile* magazine said, "The Explorer, in one fell swoop, has become yesterday's news." *Motor Trend*, in its December 1992 issue said "The versatility and finesse of the Grand Cherokee combined with the power of a V-8 equal a new class standard." The magazine named the Grand Cherokee the "1993 *Motor Trend* Truck of the Year." It was one of many awards the new Jeep would win.

However, the most important prize the new Jeep could win was sales, and in 1993, it did so in a big way. A total of 217,232 Grand Cherokees were retailed in calendar 1993—a phenomenal showing and a preview of the sort of sales and production levels Jeep was now capable of. The entire line did well, with Wrangler sales jumping up to 65,648 and regular Cherokees selling 125,443 units, giving a grand total of 408,323 Jeeps retailed in the U.S.A.—yet another record! Jeep even outsold GMC for the year. Ford Explorer, by virtue of its greater production capacity, still managed to outsell the Grand Cherokee, but that was okay. As Chrysler officials explained, Jeep didn't need to outsell the Ford—it only needed to sell out its plant, and it did, despite scheduling a great deal of

These rarely-seen vehicles are the base SE models of the 1994 Grand Cherokee line. Note that they lack the lower body cladding that the more expensive models have. Despite good pricing, the base Grand Cherokees were far outsold by the Laredo and Limited models.

overtime to help meet demand. Any plans to share Jeep products with Dodge were dropped.

A look at the 1994 Jeep sales catalog may have prompted a feeling of *deja vu*—the Wrangler photos were identical to the ones used in the 1993 brochures. However, there was change in the line-up. The stripped Wrangler was once again called the 'S', the old base model renamed the SE, the Sport and Sahara returned, and the Renegade was dropped from the line-up. The popular Cherokee line returned with improvements in roof and door strength, use of non-cfc refrigerant in the A/C unit, and the base model was renamed SE. Also new was a RHD Rural Postal version, for rural postal delivery route drivers, available in two-wheel-drive or four-wheel-drive, and in two- or four-door models. The Grand Wagoneer was dropped from the line. Evidently the wood-grain decals were considered

too old-fashioned for the hip 'Y' people who were the primary buyers of compact SUVs. In any event, other than in appearance, the Grand Wagoneer offered little difference from a well-equipped Grand Cherokee.

The 1994 Grand Cherokee line was further strengthened. Four-wheel disc brakes were introduced on the Limited model, front and rear side guard door beams added to all models, and a power sunroof option became available. Like the rest of the Jeep line, the Grand Cherokee's base model was renamed the SE.

Chrysler decided it was time to force the market in Japan. Under pressure from Honda, which distributed Jeeps in Japan, it cut Cherokee prices drastically. Its 1993 sales had leaped after an earlier price cut, and it was felt another round of price slashing might increase market share even more. It did—more than 10,000 RHD Jeep Cherokees were sold in Japan for the 1994 fiscal year (helping Chrysler set a record for sales of American-built vehicles in Japan). The RHD Cherokee was also launched in Australia that year, and Chrysler also announced a partnership with Volvo to assemble RHD Cherokees in Volvo's small plant in Thailand. Jeep sales were climbing in Mexico too, a result of President Clinton's recent (and very controversial) NAFTA free-trade agreement.

However, the biggest news in Jeep's international markets occurred with the start-up of Grand Cherokee production at a plant in Graz, Austria. The new plant would not only better serve Europe, it would relieve some of the strain on U.S. distribution, since fewer Grand Cherokees would have to be directed to overseas markets. Jeep's U.S. dealers were hollering for more production.

Meanwhile, back in the U.S., Jeep was having another record-breaking year. Sales continued to climb as production ramped upwards to meet the hottest Jeep demand ever. Wrangler sales exceeded the 1993 numbers, with 74,952 sold at retail in calendar 1994. Cherokee sales slipped a bit to 122,981—still a solidly profitable number. Grand Cherokees climbed again, this time selling 238,512 units—and more could have been sold if they could have been built. The Jefferson North plant was running two shifts with heavy overtime, and in May 1994, it announced the addition of a third shift, boosting production to 315,000 units for the 1995 model year. The total number of Jeeps retailed in America for 1994 was 436,445 units—another

Cherokee Country for 1995 had fancy wheels, body cladding, and elegant interior trim.

A new level of luxury was achieved with the 1995 Grand Cherokee Orvis edition.

The Orvis edition interior trim was simply breathtaking!

The 1995 Grand Cherokee Limited was a plush, comfortable vehicle, yet still was capable of outstanding off-road performance.

record and proof that Jeep dealers could sell any number of vehicles the factory could manage to build. Although it's not recorded, Renault executives must have been kicking themselves for selling what was now one of the hottest automotive brands in the world.

Since 1994 marks the mid-point of the decade, its time once again to review Jeep's competitive position in the market. Even though a resurgent GMC managed to outsell it by a tiny margin, Jeep's sales of 436,445 compared well with GMC's strong showing of 444,425. Nissan, which at the beginning of the decade had been only 21,000 units behind Jeep, sold 237,102 light trucks in 1994—or nearly 200,000 less than Jeep.

"The earth has music for those who listen." Those words, from an unknown source, made up the opening sentence of the 1995 Jeep sales catalog. For 1995, Jeep continued to refine its offerings. Wrangler 'S', SE, Sport and Sahara models were joined by a new up-level trim package called the Rio Grande, available on the 'S'. Evidently someone in the marketing group realized that buyers attracted by a low price might want something a bit flashier than the 'S', without going to the expense of the Sport or Sahara models. The Rio Grande was good-looking, too. Included was the base four-cylinder/five-speed powertrain, power steering, bigger tires, styled steel spoke wheels, rear bumperettes, AM/FM cassette stereo with Dolby and a "sound bar" (speakers mounted on the rollbar), full carpeting, special Pueblo Cloth upholstery, and a "Rio Grande" decal on the rear quarter panels. In addition, several new exterior colors debuted.

The 1995 Cherokee line got a driver's side airbag, a first for the small Cherokee. Reclining front seats and dual horns were added to the standard equipment list, and four new exterior colors made their debut. A four-cylinder engine/three-speed automatic transmission power team was to become available mid-year.

Grand Cherokee got the most improvements that year. Chrysler's clever Integrated Child Safety Seat was now available, as was a flip-up liftgate window. Torque on the V-8 engine was increased to an even 300 lb.-ft. Biggest news was a new trim option called the Orvis edition, named for the long-established Vermont sporting equipment company. The Grand Cherokee Orvis Edition included sumptuous leather and vinyl-trimmed seats in Champagne with Dark Green leather inserts and Roan Red accents. It also had Green and Champagne door-trim with the Orvis medallion, Moss Green exterior color with Maize and Roan Red accents (and Orvis decals), Quadra-Trac, Up Country suspension, lattice wheels with Moss Green accents, eight-speaker stereo and more—a plush and exclusive package that attracted many shoppers. Grand Cherokee SE and Laredo now also got four-wheel disc brakes, previously only offered on the Limited. An overhead mini-console with compass, trip computer and outdoor temperature readings was newly available, and the Limited now also offered a two-wheel-drive model. Unfortunate news for driving enthusiasts was that Grand Cherokee no longer offered a five-speed manual transmission—the four-speed automatic overdrive was the only gearbox available.

Chrysler's new emphasis on overseas markets was the impetus behind several big announcements in 1995. In what was the end of a very frustrating situation, Chrysler finally won the right to sell Jeeps in Brazil. Chrysler had announced in 1992 that Jeeps would be sold once again in Brazil, only to discover that Autolatina, a joint venture between Ford and VW, claimed ownership of the rights to the Jeep name in Brazil. Ford had purchased the old Willys-Overland Brazil company in the mid-1960s, along with the rights to the Jeep name in Brazil. Over time the W-O plants had switched over to mainly Ford products, and later Autolatina's, but the company felt it still was the only one that could use the Jeep name in Brazil. It was finally settled in Chrysler's favor in 1994, and in 1995, the company announced it was setting up a wholly-owned subsidiary to import and market Jeeps.

It was revealed that a new plant would be built in Argentina to produce Grand Cherokee models for Argentina, Brazil, Paraguay, and Uruguay. Chrysler also announced it was taking over Jeep sales in Japan, investing $100 million to develop its own distribution system. Although Honda had done a first-rate job selling Jeeps, it was time Chrysler took responsibility for its own products. In China, Beijing Jeep reported its best year yet. A two-wheel-drive Cherokee, introduced in 1994, was proving especially popular. Jeep also re-entered the South African market, with its range of RHD models giving it a better chance for success than past attempts. The overseas operations were a huge success. By year's end, Chrysler boasted that

Grand Cherokee for 1996 continued to impress road-testers.

Top down view of the Rio Grande. Note the spoke wheels and 'Rio Grande' decal on rear quarter panel.

Cherokee Sport for 1996 was a value-packed vehicle.

The 1997 Wrangler boasted superior engineering.

The all-new 1997 Wrangler lineup included the popular Sahara model.

nearly 40% of all Jeep Cherokees built in Toledo were shipped to markets outside the U.S.

Grand Cherokee came won a great deal of acclaim in 1995. Grand Cherokee (and also Wrangler) made *Consumer Review's* Top Ten Trucks list, *Family Circle* called Grand Cherokee its Family Activity Vehicle of the Year, and *Four Wheeler* named it Four Wheeler of the Year. Petersen's *4-Wheel & Off-Road* also found favor in the Grand Cherokee, naming it 4x4 of the Year, *Trailer Boats* rated it Tow Vehicle of the Year, and the *Texas Auto Writers Association* called it Best Full-Size Sport Utility Vehicle.

The company was not planning on taking a break. Plans were announced to build a new $1 billion plant to produce state-of-the-art fully electronic transmissions for the next generation of Jeep vehicles, as well as $750 million for a plant to produce all-new V-8 engines for the 1999 model year. In 1995, Jeep sales volume in the U.S. was 426,628—down slightly from the previous year.

For 1996, the Grand Cherokee line was pruned a bit. Gone were the Orvis Edition and SE models, (though later press information indicates the Orvis

was returned to the line mid-year). As regards the demise of the SE, a surprising lesson had been learned in the years since the Grand Cherokee was first announced and that was that relatively few buyers wanted the basic model—the majority opted to spend the extra money for either the Laredo or Limited series (and the Orvis as well), and inventory turnover of basic Grand Cherokees wasn't as frequent as the loaded models. Jeep buyer demographics proved to Chrysler officials that Jeep buyers were some of the wealthiest in the industry, and expected a certain level of comfort and convenience options in their vehicles. Needless to say, these same executives were happy to comply with the customer's wishes.

The 1996 Grand Cherokees received a whole raft of improvements and refinements. Big news was a redesign of the 4.0 engine. The engine received a stiffer block, new state-of-the-art aluminum pistons, and a revised camshaft profile. In addition, the valve cover was isolated and a new main bearing brace was added. The results were a smoother, quieter engine that produced its 225 lb.-ft. of torque at lower rpm (peaking at 3000 rpm ver-

Traditionalists were especially pleased to see the return of round headlamps on the redesigned 1997 Wrangler.

Rear styling of 1997 Cherokee looks a bit like a Volvo wagon, and featured an improved liftgate.

The 1997 Cherokee Sport proved extremely popular with young families.

Cherokee's new interior for 1997 was a big improvement over previous models, and was easier to engineer for left- or right-hand drive.

sus 4000 rpm the prior year) giving owners improved driving "feel." Grand Cherokee's V-8 remained the most powerful in its class. Transmissions were revised too, with V-8 models getting a new wide-ratio transmission, while six-cylinder models got improved torque converters. Command-Trac four-wheel-drive was dropped, with an upgraded Selec-Trac full-time four-wheel-drive system now standard equipment, and on-demand Quadra-Trac optional. All Grand Cherokees also got an all-new interior, greatly upgraded from the already lavish interior of previous models. The Limited series got some new toys—speed-sensitive variable-assist power steering, memory seat, mirror and radio settings, and optional heated front seats.

There was a new enhancement to Quadra-Trac this year, which allowed it to automatically vary power distribution between the front and rear axles to take greater advantage of traction. All Grand Cherokees now had dual air bags and heated power mirrors, upgraded front suspension, and new seat fabrics. An interesting new option was an AM Stereo/FM Stereo Radio with integral cassette and CD players.

Grand Cherokee also got its first appearance change this year, in the form of a new grille, fascias, body side cladding and new nameplates. However, the factory was so reluctant to make a radical appearance change (fearing it might hurt sales) that they really needn't have bothered—it took a sharp eye to notice the changes. The regular

219

Jeep Cherokee for 1997 still offered two-door models, as demonstrated by this handsome, sporty SE.

Thunder and Lightning—the awesome 1998 Jeep Grand Cherokee 5.9 Limited. The 5.9 combined luxury features with blistering speed.

The 1998 Jeep Cherokee Classic was a plush new model.

Cherokee line received only moderate revision. The revised 4.0 six was available, and the standard four also received some alterations for quieter running and greater smoothness.

The 1996 model year was highly irregular—because there was no 1996 Wrangler! Jeep had an all-new Wrangler coming in the spring, which it would label an early 1997 model. It made little sense to invest good money in producing, certifying and advertising a 1996 model for what would be only a half year of sales, so Jeep simply continued to build the 1995 models right to the end of 1995, and then began converting its production lines to build the new 1997.

Work on the new Wrangler had gone on quietly, with few spy photos appearing and little comment from Jeep designers, so when the new Wrangler came out it was a surprise, and a very agreeable one at that. It debuted in April 1996, as an early 1997 model. Traditionalists were instantly gratified by the Wrangler's return to round head lamps, not seen on a Jeep since the CJ-7. While the style was slightly "retro" (like every Wrangler and CJ), engineering and production reached new levels of excellence.

The single biggest engineering change was the introduction of Quadra-Coil suspension on the Wrangler line. Previous Wranglers (and CJ's) had utilized a leaf spring suspension, but the new Wrangler had coil springs for all four wheels, providing a greatly improved on-road ride. A major plus was greatly enhanced off-road capability, made possible by the additional seven inches of articulation, as well as the improved ground clearance and approach and departure angles that Quadra-Coil provided.

Nearly 80% of the parts that made up a Wrangler were new-for-1997. Hood hinges and fasteners remained exposed, but were now flush with the surrounding sheet metal for a cleaner appearance. Hood latches, a Jeep styling cue, still remained but were neater looking and easier to use. The grille retained its seven slots, but the hood now sloped a bit for improved aerodynamics.

The base of the windshield was pulled forward four inches, again for better aerodynamics and also to allow room under the cowl for an improved heating, ventilation and air conditioning (HVAC) unit. Wheelhouses were enlarged to accommodate bigger tires. Wrangler's interior was all-new and vastly improved. Big news was the introduction of dual airbags, continuing Chrysler's emphasis on safety engineering. The instrument panel was also new and for the first time featured an integrated HVAC system.

Black-on-white gauges were inspired by early Willys' designs, but everything else reflected the latest in design, including a center stack that housed the radio, HVAC controls, ash tray and accessory switches. Three new audio systems were available including a combination AM/FM/Cassette/CD. All-new seats provided better comfort, with six inches more width for the rear seat. Yet, Wranglers' interior still could be washed out with a garden hose. Both tops were all-new, with the soft-top operation made much easier, while the hardtop got quick release header latches, and was 15 lbs. lighter. The Wrangler line consisted of three trim levels, SE, Sport and Sahara.

Fit and finish were much improved over previous Wranglers and, combined with the other improvements (Wrangler got the improved 2.5 and 4.0 engines, of course), and a base price of $13,495, Wrangler offered a value story that was hard to beat. Jeep platform manager Craig Winn was pleased. He said, "This is a package that the entire Jeep team is very proud of. We improved Wrangler's capability and function; added safety features; improved the on-road ride and handling; we developed a new Wrangler that is still a Wrangler. And all for a relatively low $260 million." As Chrysler put it, "While making the biggest evolutionary changes in the history of its storied bloodline, the '97 Wrangler remains true to its Jeep heritage...."

In August, President Bill Clinton visited the Toledo plant to take part in a celebration commemorating the production of the Two Millionth Cherokee and posed with the vehicle. And in September, Chrysler announced it had established a distribution company in South Korea and also opened a Southeast Asian regional headquarters in Singapore to oversee business for 15 Southeast Asia markets, including Thailand, Malaysia, Indonesia, the Philippines, and Singapore.

Sales in 1996 went through the roof—up nearly 20% to a total of 509,183 in the U.S.—a new record. When one recalls the unkind assessment made by *Dun's Review* in 1969, or the depressing fall-off in sales in the early 1980s and the struggle to rebuild the product line after that, it might seem a miracle that Jeep could now retail over half a million highly desirable (and tremendously profitable) vehicles in a single calendar year. All three lines increased, with the new Wrangler climbing to 81,444 units, the regular Cherokee coming in at a very strong 148,544 units, and Grand Cherokee selling 279,195 units.

Jeep was on a roll, and it would continue to upgrade its product line. When the balance of the 1997 models were announced, a greatly revamped Cherokee debuted. The Cherokee had been in production since late 1983 (when it debuted as a 1984 model), and despite the passage of time it didn't need a lot of changes, so what appeared on the 1997 models was more in the way of correcting old problem areas, and upgrading the vehicle to current customer expectations. One of these expectations was that sport utility vehicles should have passenger-car interior comfort, so the new Cherokee received an all-new interior. Most visible was the new modular instrument panel with a center 'stack' that contained all HVAC, accessory and radio controls (and which, like Wrangler's center stack, made it easier to produce both left- and right-hand-drive models). A passenger side air bag was added, plus new gauge clusters, steering column and wheel, plus a new heating, ventilating and cooling system. Door trim panels were new, as were both power and manual window regulators; there was also a new overhead console with a five function trip computer added to the compass and temperature functions offered on earlier versions. A new floor console included integrated cupholders, storage compartment, and new shift levers.

The Cherokee's exterior came in for change as well, its first since introduction. Revised grille, bumpers and end caps changed the frontal appearance somewhat, while the rear end featured a new stamped steel liftgate to replace the prior fiberglass unit. Front door glass was now ventless, to improve appearance and reduce wind noise. Redesigned wheel flares and new mirrors were featured as well. Interior noise was reduced by new door seals, as well as by a new sound/insulation package. Cus-

Buyers were calling for even more luxury so the 1998 Cherokee line included this Limited model.

Jeep paused in 1998 to recall some of the accolades it had won since 1984.

tomer quality expectations had increased sharply since 1984, so the Toledo plant received new or reconditioned stamping dies for all of Cherokee's major body panels. New electronic test equipment and new robotic spray equipment were also utilized to greatly increase quality levels.

In overall appearance Cherokee's styling looked nearly identical to previous models, but now had a hint of Grand Cherokee (as well as a slight resemblance to the Volvo station wagon). In technical features, however, the Cherokee was a greatly improved machine. It had to be—Cherokee was a worldwide volume-seller. In addition to Toledo, Cherokees were assembled in Thailand, Indonesia, Malaysia, Venezuela, Egypt, Pakistan, and China. As Richard Winter, General Manager, International Product Planning explained, "Jeep is the most significant element of Chrysler Corporation's international operations." The revised Cherokee went into production late in 1996, so it was several months into 1997 before dealers had an adequate supply on hand, and that would hurt sales somewhat.

Grand Cherokee for 1997 had a number of new features to talk about—surprising after so many changes and refinements the prior season. Two-wheel-drive models were now available with the 5.2 liter V-8 engine, a full-body anti-chip primer paint entered production in October 1996, floor carpet fit and appearance were upgraded, three new exterior colors were added, and the entry-level cassette radio was refined. At announcement time, Grand Cherokees were available in Laredo, Limited and Orvis editions, and were later joined by an upscale TSI model. The Grand Cherokee TSI came with all the features found on the Laredo 'Y' option package (full overhead console, deep tinted glass, OWL tires, heated mirrors and more), and added Quadra-Trac, sporty 16 inch aluminum wheels with Goodyear Eagle LS all-weather performance tires, front fascia-mounted fog lamps, body-color grille, leather seats with 10-way power adjusters, remote radio controls (on the back of the steering wheel), and unique bodyside cladding. Slotted in between the Laredo and Limited models, the TSI was a sporty alternative.

1997 export versions of the Grand Cherokee were available in left- and right-hand-drive models, and with an available 2.5 turbo-diesel engine. Chrysler reported record sales overseas for 1997, with Cherokee accounting for 24.2% of international sales, and Grand Cherokee taking another 16.8 %. Venezuela and China—where Jeep sales had been pioneered by American Motors—were Chrysler's top two overseas markets.

The entire Jeep line was well-received, with the new Cherokee being named *Four Wheeler* magazine's 1997 Four Wheeler of the Year, while *4-Wheel & Off-Road* named the new Wrangler "4X4 of the Year ." Sales for the year were down a bit from 1996s record-busting pace, coming in at 472,872, but it was still the second best showing in Jeep history—and more than 21,000 units higher than GMC.

To start 1998 off with a bang, Jeep announced a new Grand Cherokee model, the 5.9 Limited, which it proudly boasted was the world's fastest sport utility vehicle. The new model came equipped with Chrysler's 5.9 liter V-8 engine, a powerhouse capable of generating 245 horsepower and an unbelievable 345 lb.-ft. of torque. Here was horsepower to spare, enabling 0-60 acceleration times of 7.3 seconds—a new level of performance that other builders of SUVs could only dream of. Priced at $38,700, the 5.9 Limited became the new top-of-the-line. Besides being the fastest Grand Cherokee it was also the most luxurious and included premium leather seats with heating controls and 10-way power adjusters, a 60/40 folding rear seat with a wide fold-down armrest, a rear sound bar housing four speakers and a spare tire cover that included storage pockets. It was easy to spot a 5.9 Limited, because it came with functional hood louvers, a wire-mesh grille, large chrome-plated exhaust tip and Ultra Star cast-aluminum wheels.

The balance of the Grand Cherokee line-up included the Laredo, TSI and Limited models- the Orvis Edition was dropped. New Wrangler HP VSB tires were standard equipment, improved airbags that deployed with less force and improvements to the steering system were Grand Cherokee highlights for the new year.

Two new models were added to the regular Cherokee line for 1998, the Cherokee Classic and the Cherokee Limited. The Classic was positioned between the Sport and the top-line Limited, giving many of the appearance and luxury features of the Limited at a lower cost. Included on the Classic were monotone paint, body color fender flares and air dam, full gauge package including tachometer, floor mats, dual power mirrors, 4.0 liter six with

The All-New 1999 Jeep Grand Cherokee.

Here's your look under the sheet.

For 1999, the Grand Cherokee is all-new, with engineering that will once again set the standard for years to come.

four-speed automatic transmission, and Ecco cast-aluminum wheels. To that list, Limiteds added standard air conditioning, cargo cover, overhead console, deep tint glass, power windows and locks, remote keyless entry, leather seating, and its own unique aluminum wheels.

Both of these new models were needed. In the years since the introduction of the Grand Cherokee, the old Cherokee had been pitched mainly as a more Spartan alternative, but buyers were demanding more and more luxury at every level of the SUV market, and few vehicles could deliver on that count like Jeep. The Sport continued as perhaps the best value in the four-wheel-drive market, and the SE was still available for shoppers on a budget. In the Cherokee line, there truly was something for everybody.

1998 Wranglers got detail improvements, gaining, like the rest of the Jeep line, new airbags that deployed with less force. Also new was improved off-road performance made possible by the availability of a Dana 44 rear axle with a 3.73 ratio. Wranglers also received steering system improvements.

In what was becoming an excitingly repetitious event, a Jeep vehicle was once again named *4 Wheel & Off-Road* magazine's "4X4 Of The Year." This time the award went to the unmistakably impressive Grand Cherokee 5.9 Limited. In the six years from 1993-1998, a Jeep won the award four times. As a proud Chrysler noted in its advertisements, "In fact, no other brand of 4X4s in the world has won more awards than Jeep." In February, it was announced that the Grand Cherokee TSI models were being dropped—likely in anticipation of the all-new 1999 Grand Cherokee being readied for a fall 1998 introduction.

Chrysler CEO Bob Eaton displayed a flair for the dramatic when he held up a small bag in front of a room full of journalists, telling them that the sack contained the only parts that were being carried over from the existing Grand Cherokee to an all-new Grand Cherokee that would debut for 1999. The bag, he explained, held 127 parts, most of which were fasteners. It was known that an all-new 4.7 liter V-8 would be offered, as well as an improved 4.0 liter six, and a new five-speed automatic transmission. International markets would

Sixty years after an army major predicted "I believe this vehicle will make history," the eternal Jeep is still proving just how right he was.

see a new 3.1 liter five-cylinder turbo-diesel option. Also scheduled to debut on the new Grand Cherokee was Quadra-Drive, an exciting new four-wheel-drive system, with a patented transfer case that would, like the Grand Cherokee itself, mark yet a new level in Jeep technology.

That has been the legacy of Jeep, from the wartime MB to the civilian CJ-2, and from the first steel-bodied station wagon to the Willys' pickup, the CJ-5, and the classic Wagoneer. It's a baton that's been handed off in succession from the Jeepster to the Renegade I, the CJ-7, and to today's Grand Cherokee. In the passing of time, this noble tradition has taken on the trappings of mythology itself; and so has become a legend.

The story of Jeep is the story of America's greatest industry, its pitfalls, its opportunities, its tremendous capacity to go through trial and fire, and yet exit out the other side stronger, smarter, and greater. Its stature as a legend is secure—it has fought the battles, won the wars, and has the scars to prove it. Its future seems secure too, in the custody of the great Chrysler Corporation, which has polished, shined, and preserved that which is the very essence of Jeep, and stands ready to guard its heritage. May it always be so.

Chapter Nine

THE JEEP OF THE FUTURE

Photographed in the Willys test labs, not much is known about this wide-bodied experimental Jeep, though styling resembles the CJ-5.

It's often the custom in books of automotive history to include a few words about the next generation of vehicles. These are the ones that will be debuting in the years after the book is in print— in other words, the "cars of the future." This approach has its dangers—suppose the author has guessed wrong about what's to come? He'll be proven wrong soon enough, and it will stay there, in print, to haunt him at least for as long as he is still able to read the printed page.

Such an approach doesn't serve the cause of automotive history. We historians are dedicated to researching, preserving and protecting history, not to the creation of it—especially not to the creation of speculative, possibly spurious history-that-might-be.

In 1951, Willys built this experimental Jeep CJ-4 which did not go into regular production. This vehicle still exists.

227

Designer Brooks Stevens, under contract with Willys, created this stylish concept wagon called the Harlequin, which had a luxury-trimmed interior and custom exterior trim.

In the 1950s, Alcoa tried to interest Willys in building a coupe version of the Jeepster, which would have used several aluminum body panels. This vehicle still exists.

There is, I believe, a better approach to the subject and that is to take a look at what the "JEEP OF THE FUTURE" has looked like in past years, instead of trying to guess what it might look like in the years to come. Besides, looking at how people in years past viewed the future tells a great deal about what society was like back then. Hopeful people dream hopeful futures; disaffected or indifferent people do not.

So enjoy the visions that appear on the next few pages; they are in all likelihood the largest gathering of concept Jeeps ever put into one book.

Brooks Stevens designed this proposal for a revived Jeepster for the Brazilian market sometime around 1959. It used the re-styled front end of Willys-Brazil Rural wagon, but had a unique body aft of the cowl.

Note the continental-type spare wheel and extended rear bumper. Brazilian Jeepster wasn't built because Willys-Overland Brazil lacked sufficient plant capacity to add it to its product mix.

Here's Brooks Stevens at the wheel of his creation. Note that in this photo the Jeepster name has been replaced by script that reads "Saci," evidently used for some auto shows.

Another Stevens proposal for a future Jeep model was this Jeep Sportif sport roadster.

This Jeep 'Dispatcher 100' evidently was planned to be a compact two-wheel drive pickup, and would have been unique in the market. Designer Brooks Stevens is at the wheel.

Brooks Stevens designed a series of small van and van-pickup vehicles as proposals for future models. This interesting small pickup didn't make it to production, though a van with similar styling was built for a time in Spain.

This proposal for a replacement for the Willys wagon bears a resemblance to a later Wagoneer.

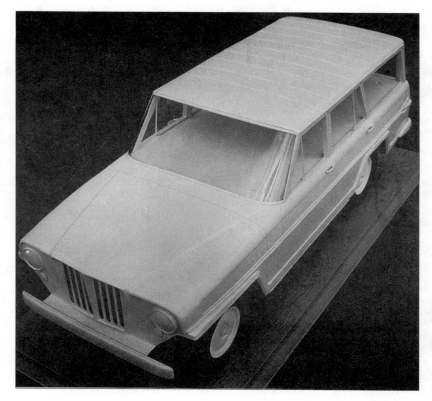

Front view shows how Stevens attempted to blend front styling theme of the Jeep CJ into a boxy wagon body.

Exciting Jeep XJ001 prototype, circa 1970, proposed an on- and off-road sports car for Jeep.

Jeep XJ001 prototype was equipped with a V-8, and had a fiberglass body. Unfortunately, the only prototype built was destroyed in an accident.

Modern cockpit of XJ001 was revolutionary when it debuted.

Fiberglass mock-up of a proposed small Jeep pickup, called the Cowboy, as seen inside AMC design studio.

Two Jeep Cowboy running prototypes were built for testing in late 1971; one still exists.

The 1977 Concept Jeep II predicted a small CJ, with a four-cylinder engine. Despite good styling, the vehicle was not approved for production.

This prototype evidently was first planned as a Renegade. Note the 304-cid V-8 engine emblem and Renegade wheels. It debuted in 1973 as the limited production Super Jeep CJ-5.

Rare sketch of a future Jeep, circa 1977, which still looks modern today.

Called the Jeepster II, this 1979 design by AMC Vice-President of Styling Dick Teague would still be a good approach in today's market. Note that the grille is similar to the later Wrangler.

In 1989, Jeep showed this Concept I, which evolved into the Grand Cherokee.

This 1990 proposal for a Cherokee convertible looked like a modern rendition of the Willys Jeepster.

This drawing shows one model of the JJ Jeep, part of ARCAD, the proposed joint venture of Renault and Chrysler to build a Jeep for world markets.

237

The JJ small Jeep project first involved having Renault as a joint partner. After talks with Renault failed, discussions were opened with Italian automaker Fiat. These talks also failed to come up with a workable program. Chrysler President Bob Lutz later told a reporter for Ward's Auto World that the reason the project failed was "What started out as a narrow, tightly focused program became--in the old Detroit tradition--too big, too all-encompassing. The vehicle got more and more expensive and heavier and heavier."

In 1993, Jeep introduced the small Jeep Ecco concept.

Early 1997 brought one of the most exciting Jeeps-of-the-Future ever—the Dakar four-door concept. According to several sources, this vehicle will go into production someday.

Also appearing in 1997 was this Jeep Icon concept vehicle, which introduced several styling themes that may show up on future Jeep models.

The 1998 Jeep Jeepster concept predicts a sportier Jeep. This has almost a hot rod look to it.

Chapter Ten

COLLECTIBLE JEEPS

One of the most collectible of all Jeeps is the famous old Willys Jeepster, the last phaeton from a major U.S. producer. This is a 1950 model.

Any Jeep enthusiast, worthy of the name, will surely tell you that all Jeeps are collectible. That is certainly true, just as every set of salt and pepper shakers is collectible, even if they will never have much monetary value. However some Jeeps, (as is the case with some salt and pepper shakers), are more collectible than others. On the pages that follow we illustrate some of the Jeeps we believe are the most desirable and collectible among the millions of Jeeps that have been built. Furthermore, we'll tell you why they're so hot!

The 1950-'51 Willys Jeepster featured more rounded front end styling than earlier versions.

The 1967-1971 Jeepster and Jeepster Commando series looked somewhat similar to Willys models, but were entirely different. The combination of four-wheel drive, automatic transmission, modern (optional) V-6 engine and convertible top make this an outstanding collector car. Shown is the top-of-the-line Jeepster convertible.

The 1970 Jeep Renegade I looks rather quaint today, but was considered audacious when new.

For 1971, Jeep unveiled the Renegade II, an improved, sportier Renegade.

The 1971 Jeep Renegade II has beautiful aluminum wheels, bigger tires, and padded roll bar.

It's not known how many of these 1971 Hurst Jeepster specials were built, but best guess is less than 100. This may be the most collectible Jeep of all.

The 1971 Jeepster SC-1 was an interesting trim package, with a sporty stripe and nice wheel covers. Not really a sought-after model, its combination of fun and functionalism marks it as a good low-cost collectible.

SUPER JEEP

Not a bird. Not a plane. But a new thrill under the sun—4-wheel drive fun-mobiling.

At first glance, that same familiar profile, but underneath that super-stripe stands a baby brute with the guts to go where others fear to tread.

Super Jeep® is *all* guts from the brawny suspension to the heavy-duty axle—an open-end design that can turn in just 32.9 ft. And while you're checking out the special color treatment on the front and rear seats, the roll bar's saying "go!" and the 258 six answers "r-r-i-i-ght!"

Oversize L78 x 15 Polyglas® white wall tires are included along with those black rubber lip extensions on the fenders. Plus chrome front bumper and a safety rail for your more easily flustered passengers. She's available in all kinds of color combinations and lots of extra goodies.

So don't just sit there, hit the trail in a gen-u-ine Super Jeep.

Jeep

Toughest 4-letter word on wheels.

Anyone interested in really off-beat collectibles might set their sights on a 1973 CJ-5 Super Jeep. No one seems to know how many were built, or even if any still survive, but road-testers of the day thought highly of the Super Jeep.

INTRODUCING A LIMITED EDITION: THE SILVER ANNIVERSARY CJ-5

WE WROTE THE BOOK ON 4-WHEEL DRIVE OVER 40 YEARS AGO. 25 YEARS AGO WE ADDED A NEW CHAPTER, THE CJ-5.

25 and goin' strong! That's our rugged CJ-5. And to celebrate we've created a limited edition that'll knock you out! Just listen to these one-of-a-kind features: slick Quick Silver Metallic finish; racy silver-toned Renegade accent striping; black soft top, black vinyl buckets and bold silver accents. And if that isn't enough, a dashboard plaque commemorating the occasion. So, what're you waitin' for?! An anniversary like this only comes around once every 25 years!!! The Silver Anniversary CJ-5... at your Jeep dealer, now!

Jeep

WE WROTE THE BOOK ON 4-WHEEL DRIVE

The 1979 Silver Anniversary CJ-5 featured a unique silver color, special seat trim, chrome wheels and a commemorative badge on the instrument panel.

Only 2,500 of these 1982 Jeep Jamborees were produced and each has a numbered commemorative plaque mounted on the instrument panel. The only color available was a special Topaz Gold.